# Additional Praise for *Getting Started in Global Investing*

"With record-breaking performance in U.S. markets, the conventional wisdom is that this is the place to be. *Getting Started in Global Investing* puts this performance in perspective . . . separates myth from reality . . . and makes the case for a broader approach for investing. A must read for all investors!"

—Robert S. Roath
former CFO, RJR Nabisco Chairman,
L.E.K. Consulting Advisory Board

"As a manager of global asset allocation portfolios, I view a meaningful exposure to non-U.S. equity markets as a critical component of a well-structured portfolio. . . . 'The Island Principle' will give investors reason to pause before throwing a disproportionate share of their assets at a large cap U.S. equity market."

—Stephen A. Gorman, CFA
author, *The International Equity Commitment*;
Senior Vice President, Director of Quantitative
Research & Portfolio Design, Putnam Investments

"An excellent primer for the long-term investor who seeks an alternative to single-market risks. Chapters 5 and 6 alone are worth the price of Mr. Kreitler's book."

—Wilbur M. Yegge, PhD
Managing Director, W. M. Yegge & Company

# The Getting Started In Series

Getting Started in Online Day Trading by Kassandra Bentley

Getting Started in Asset Allocation by Bill Bresnan and Eric Gelb

Getting Started in Online Investing by David L. Brown and Kassandra Bentley

Getting Started in Stocks by Alvin D. Hall

Getting Started in Mutual Funds by Alvin D. Hall

Getting Started in 401(k) Investing by Paul Katzeff

Getting Started in Security Analysis by Peter J. Klein

Getting Started in Global Investing by Robert P. Kreitler

Getting Started in Futures by Todd Lofton

Getting Started in Financial Information by Daniel Moreau and Tracey Longo

Getting Started in Technical Analysis by Jack D. Schwager

Getting Started in Hedge Funds by Daniel A. Strachman

Getting Started in Options by Michael C. Thomsett

Getting Started in Real Estate Investing by Michael C. Thomsett and
    Jean Freestone Thomsett

Getting Started in Annuities by Gordon K. Williamson

Getting Started in Bonds by Sharon Saltzgiver Wright

# *Getting Started in*
# Global Investing

## Robert P. Kreitler

### John Wiley & Sons, Inc.

New York • Chichester • Weinheim • Brisbane • Singapore • Toronto

ISBN 0-471-38524-7

Printed in the United States of America

10  9  8  7  6  5  4  3  2  1

*To my mother, Edith Wightman Kreitler*

# Contents

Foreword                                                      ix

Preface                                                       xi

Acknowledgments                                              xv

Introduction                                                xvii

**Chapter 1**
A Fresh Perspective                                          1

**Chapter 2**
All at Sea about Risk                                        17

**Chapter 3**
A Compass to Steer By                                        47

**Chapter 4**
Mapping Goals                                                69

**Chapter 5**
Casting Off                                                  85

**Chapter 6**
Choosing Individual Managers                                129

**Chapter 7**
Assembling the Crew and Staying on Course                   163

**Appendix** 195

**Glossary** 223

**Bibliography** 237

**Index** 239

# Foreword

Global investing is appropriate for all of us. Bob Kreitler and I have shared that perspective as long as we have known each other. Several years ago, Gary Brinson and I co-authored *Global Investing: The Professional's Guide to the World's Capital Markets* to encourage investment professionals to think globally. *Getting Started in Global Investing* outlines global strategy for individual investors. I am delighted that Bob is bringing this much larger audience into the global arena.

*Getting Started in Global Investing* introduces The Island Principle. This approach simply asks investors to think of themselves as residents of a small island instead of as citizens of the United States. Then they can look at all investments around the world objectively, instead of with a strong bias toward markets located in their own country. Truly global investors have more investment opportunities. This means they can create not only more diversified portfolios with potentially lower risk, but also those with a potential for higher return.

The Island Principle tries to motivate us to change our investment ways. We need this encouragement because, despite the logic favoring a global perspective, very few investors practice truly global investing. To be sure, many of us invest in some international securities, but Bob wants us to embrace global investing fully. Investors who do may likely have over half their portfolios in international markets. Only an investor living on an island, who is not focused on a particular market, would seem to be that bold. Bob seeks to change our whole perspective on global investing so that we give other markets fair consideration. Even for me, personally, becoming an island investor would mean increasing my exposure to international investments.

*Getting Started in Global Investing* takes up the great challenge of convincing us all to change our ways. It keeps The Island Principle theme intact through its chapter headings. We are at sea about risk but The Island Principle can help us steer and chart a course. We cast off and assemble a crew. While the headings keep us focused on the basic theme, Bob provides the theory, the empirical data, and the analysis to support the logic of a global course of action. Much of the backup support was developed using software and data Bob obtained from my firm, Ibbotson Associates. I am pleased that he makes such persuasive use of the raw data we provide. I am not surprised, however, that the data supports global investing. The evidence has always been there. Bob stepped up to the challenge of communicating and making this information understandable to the individual investor.

*Getting Started in Global Investing* is not just content to convince us as to the best course of action. This very practical book also helps us distinguish among global, international, regional, and country funds, then guides our choice of specific global investment funds and managers. It tells us where to look for data on global funds and how to interpret it. It gives us advice on how many funds to select, how to select them, and how to use appropriate benchmarks to evaluate the results of our choices. The book not only helps investors develop their initial global portfolios, but also offers guidelines for revising them over time.

By not only giving us theory but also providing the navigational tools to put our portfolios on a global course, Bob makes it easy for all of us to get started in global investing.

Roger G. Ibbotson
*Chairman, Ibbotson Associates*
*Professor in Practice, Yale School of Management*

# Preface

I f an investor lived on an island in the middle of one of our oceans, how would that location affect the way he or she constructed an investment portfolio?

With a whole world full of stocks, this island investor would probably not limit him or herself to buying only companies headquartered on the island, but would buy stocks from many countries. He or she would have a globally diversified portfolio.

Why, then, do most U.S. investors have portfolios that are exclusively or almost exclusively invested in U.S. stocks? Most U.S. investors limit their holdings in stocks outside the United States to about 15%. Those holding up to 25% non-U.S. stocks consider themselves bold. Yet neither is truly globally diversified.

I had the opportunity to discuss this paradox with a small group of professionals when I conducted a workshop at an investment seminar in Palm Beach several years ago. If two-thirds of the world's investment opportunities were outside the United States (a number that keeps changing), why were we recommending that our clients have only 15% to 25% of their investments in stocks outside the United States? If economists had won prizes for demonstrating how diversification reduces portfolio risk, why were investors so concentrated in the United States and so timid about buying stocks from other countries?

My colleagues offered the usual cautious mutterings about the risks of investing outside the United States and the difficulty of buying and selling stocks around the world. No one could offer any reasonable rationale, however, for ignoring global investment opportunities.

Barely a half hour later, all of the attendees at the seminar listened to speaker Mark Holowesko discuss global investing. Holowesko is the senior investment manager for the Templeton Funds (now Franklin-Templeton), which include some of the oldest global and international mutual funds available. Following his talk, Holowesko responded to a question from the floor about what percentage of his personal portfolio was invested in U.S. stocks versus other holdings. His answer, as I recall it, was roughly 25% U.S. and 75% non-U.S.

The Templeton Funds were, at that time, headquartered in the Bahamas.

Holowesko lived on an island.

Why, I thought, should his portfolio look so different from that of a U.S. investor living only 100 miles away?

On another occasion, I was excited about expanding investment opportunites in the Pacific Rim and was discussing a Pacific Rim fund with its portfolio manager by telephone. I was impressed with his explanation of the fund's philosophy and how he picked stocks from various Pacific Rim countries (as a regional fund, these were the only countries this fund could invest in) and was ending our dialogue assured that he was a solid manager who deserved my confidence in him.

Almost in passing at the end of our conversation, I asked why the global funds that he also helped manage (and which can invest anywhere in the world) were underweighted in the Pacific Rim and overweighted in Europe. His response was that the worldwide research conducted by the funds' analysts indicated that the stock bargains were in Europe, not the Pacific Rim.

As I hung up, I realized that I had been assuming I knew what part of the world held the best investment opportunities and, by selecting the countries or regions I wanted to invest in, I was second-guessing the experts.

This raised further questions in my mind. Even if investors agreed that they should have significant holdings of non-U.S. stocks in their portfolios, who should decide what countries or regions had the best investments? This is an asset allocation question, and researchers studying professional money managers have concluded that asset allocation controls a major part of a portfolio manager's performance. If deciding what countries to invest in is such an important question, should I be the one making this decision? Should only one person ever make this all-important decision on his or her own?

The global investment theory and application that I call The Island Principle evolved over a period of several years as I attempted to answer all of these questions. In explaining my rationale, I chose to use a metaphorical island to help investors move away from their bias as U.S. citizens, to open their eyes to the investment opportunities around the world. Approached logically and with thought, global investing is not the risky proposition many investors believe it to be. Rather, it provides new ways to diversify that can help them reduce portfolio risk. Then they can enjoy another benefit: Lowering risk gives investors the freedom to make new choices that can increase their portfolio returns.

The Island Principle does not just explain why investors should globally diversify their portfolios; it also offers them a simple way to do this by accessing expert global portfolio managers through the investment vehicle of mutual funds. I invite everyone to join me on my figurative island to gain a fresh perspective on investing.

# *Acknowledgments*

Writing this book explaining how to invest globally based on The Island Principle could not have been done without the help of my wife and editor, Bonnie Kreitler. Her two years of extraordinary effort to organize ideas, write lucid text, and put up with the idiosyncrasies of her husband have made this book possible. Many others have provided invaluable assistance including Roger Ibbotson, Ted Green, Robert Roath, Elizabeth Stevens, Nicole Deese, and Stephen Gorman. My father, Robert David Kreitler, and brother, Charles W. Kreitler, reviewed multiple drafts as the book came into being. They provided valuable advice and encouragement. The assistance of my associates made it possible to continue to run a business while I was engrossed in writing the book. Kim DiRaffaele, Josephine Costanzo, and Michael Grennan all provided critical support in making the book possible.

# Introduction

For many investors, the hardest part about investing globally is moving away from the familiarity of Wall Street and toward uncharted "foreign" markets where investing is said to entail extra risk. This book is designed to open investors' eyes to investment possibilities around the world, to allay their fears about the supposed risks of investing outside the United States, and to describe a simple global investing strategy available to any individual investor regardless of the size of his or her portfolio.

This global investing strategy is called The Island Principle because it asks investors to move mentally to an imaginary island and abandon their very normal bias toward Wall Street. Shifting to an island perspective dramatically changes the investor's view of the investment prospects around the world.

The Island Principle asks investors to diversify into multiple geographic markets. To do this investors must start viewing the world as many separate market choices, not just two investment pools—the United States and everywhere else. This simple change in viewpoint increases their investment opportunities exponentially. It allows them to apply the unique ability of diversification to markets. By investing in multiple markets, they can both reduce risk and improve returns in their portfolios. Developing a global investment perspective and shifting away from a focus on the U.S. market is key to implementing The Island Principle.

The Island Principle also asks investors to diversify the critical decisions about choosing which markets around the world they should invest in. They do this by using several global investment experts, typically the managers of global mutual funds. These experts are the island investor's crew, hired to do the research and analysis on both U.S. and non-U.S. markets and the individual stocks available in each one that investors themselves would find difficult or impossible to do on their own. Once they have assembled their crew, island investors allow them to do their work without interference. The investor's job becomes one of steering the portfolio's course and monitoring its progress toward his or her investment goals.

# NAVIGATING THE ISLAND PRINCIPLE

*Getting Started in Global Investing* offers both novice and seasoned investors a new perspective on investment theory and strategy. Chapters 1 through 5 provide investors with the basic investment rationale behind The Island Principle. They provide a clear explanation of many investment basics as they relate to global investing and show how The Island Principle is an extension of what has come to be called Modern Portfolio Theory. Chapters 6 and 7 outline clear steps any serious investor can easily take to create a global portfolio with surprisingly little effort.

## Chapter 1: A Fresh Perspective

Investors whose portfolios are invested heavily in U.S. stocks need to get away to an island perspective in order to reassess what they think they know about building a portfolio. The habit of lumping all markets outside the United States into a single "foreign" category severely limits an investor's options to two markets—U.S. and non-U.S. In reality there are 50 different markets around the world, and 21 of them (including the United States) are considered developed markets. Astute investors recognize that 21 individual markets provide them with new opportunities for portfolio diversification.

From the island vantage point, investors can see that the United States has not always been the world's best-performing market over the long term. Going global can also be good for an investor's bottom line. Investors can also see that having 100% of their portfolios—even 90% or 75%—in a single market not only ignores their many global investment opportunities but is also unnecessarily risky.

## Chapter 2: All at Sea about Risk

Every investor confronts an age-old bugaboo—risk. Investors accept the fact that risk and return are inescapably coupled—that seeking higher returns means accepting more risk or, conversely, that keeping risk at low levels means accepting low returns. Many investors believe global investing is risky even though, approached the right way, it can actually reduce portfolio risk.

Regulatory bodies require that investors be warned about the risks of foreign investing whenever they purchase stocks in companies outside the United States or mutual funds that invest in non-U.S. stocks. These dire warnings about things like political instability, confusing accounting systems, currency fluctuations, and lax regulatory environments scare many investors away from non-U.S. stocks. The Island Principle points out how many of these risks also apply to U.S. investing and how global investing can actually reduce them.

Most investors are unaware of all of the very real risks that every investor faces. Investing only or evenly mostly in a single market is actually quite risky, while investing in multiple markets (countries) can reduce long-term risk. Global investing is not only less risky than many investors believe, but it can also be a wonderful tool to reduce the long-term risk in their portfolios.

## Chapter 3: A Compass to Steer By

Through time, investors have sought ways to manage investment risk. Some choose to simply ignore it (assuming their resolve holds). Others invest conservatively, understanding that this will limit their portfolios' performance. Some decrease their portfolios' allocation to stocks, again understanding that this will affect their returns.

Diversification is a tool investors can use to manage risk without reducing returns. The secret to making diversification work is to choose investments that have low correlations. That means that they move differently from one another: What affects one has little or no effect on the other, and vice versa. Most investors understand that they should diversify by owning multiple stocks, multiple industry sectors, and multiple asset classes such as stocks, bonds, real estate, or cash.

Diversification with low correlation is the cornerstone of Modern Portfolio Theory. The Island Principle extends this investment theory to multiple markets to give investors a new level of diversification to help them manage risk.

## Chapter 4: Mapping Goals

No single investment strategy works for every investor. Before applying the global investing strategy of The Island Principle, investors need to examine their personal motives and financial goals. The Island Principle can help many but not all investor types.

The Island Principle is a long-term investment strategy, so it offers little to those who see investing as a game or sport and relish frequent trading. It can, however, help other types of investors. The Island Principle's rationale can encourage investors whose current investment strategy is to match a particular index to reexamine their investment objectives. Risk-averse investors who want to preserve their capital or enjoy a fixed level of income can follow The Island Principle to become more comfortable with investments that have potentially higher returns. Investors seeking growing income in their portfolios, those pursuing total portfolio returns, and those seeking aggressive growth can all benefit from The Island Principle's ability to narrow the range of outcomes they face from following any strategy over a long term. By helping them reduce risk, The Island Principle increases their chances of reaching their financial objectives.

## Chapter 5: Casting Off

Island investors are in for the long term. They want to manage risk, seek higher returns, or do some of both within their portfolios. They are willing to own stocks outside the United States and to abandon their fixation with the Dow or the S&P 500 or any other index. They are concerned not only with their portfolios' current value but also with their future buying power. Very importantly, they are willing to share the decisions about where to invest with others rather than making these very important decisions on their own.

The Island Principle extends Modern Portfolio Theory to markets and treats countries as though they were an asset class. This new level of diversification helps investors deal more easily with investor psychology and helps them escape the inevitable risks that exist in any single market (including the United States). Diversifying currencies helps protect an investor's future buying power. Using multiple global managers to decide what countries to invest in reduces the risk that the island investor will buy stocks in the wrong markets.

Setting realistic goals for portfolio risk and returns is a crucial step in applying The Island Principle's strategy. That done, investors can search for several global money managers to help them decide what markets are most suitable to meet their goals. Individual investors, even those with small portfolios, can gain easy access to global experts through mutual funds. Global mutual funds also offer a simple way for investors to surmount the difficulties of trading in other markets and dealing with multiple currencies.

## Chapter 6: Choosing Individual Managers

With their sights fixed on their future financial goals, island investors understand that the decisions about which countries to invest in are crucial to achieving long-term success. They research and choose their portfolios' global managers with care.

"Global" is the operative word. Island investors want managers who are free to choose stocks from any market throughout the world, not those limited to a single market or even a single region. They look for experience and pay close attention to philosophy and style. They analyze the available hard data about a global mutual fund and its manager, interpret the information they find in the financial press, and then use their best judgment to select multiple managers who appear to meet their criteria.

## Chapter 7: Assembling the Crew and Staying on Course

Island investors want a balanced crew of managers. They want managers whose styles are different so that the stocks they choose for the investors' portfolios will behave differently. This adds yet another level of diversification that helps island investors manage risk.

Investors who are primarily invested in the U.S. market will probably develop their global portfolio in stages, gradually moving from 100% in the United States to a portfolio invested in markets throughout the world over a period of several years. Once their portfolios are in place, island investors will monitor the performance of each individual global manager as well as that of the portfolio as a whole to make sure that it is on track.

Again, the hardest part of developing a global portfolio is making that initial shift away from Wall Street and becoming comfortable with "foreign" markets. Investors who are ready to drop their preoccupation with the Dow or the S&P 500 and who want to put the power of new levels of diversification to work in their portfolios are ready to follow The Island Principle to secure their financial futures.

# *Getting Started in*
# Global
# Investing

*Chapter*

# 1

# A Fresh Perspective

Most U.S. investors view *Wall Street* as the center of the financial universe. They anxiously track *stock* prices in the newspapers and on the Internet. As their cars start on the home commute they tune their radio to catch the latest movement in the Dow or Standard & Poor's stock market *indexes*. But what if they lived in Paris or Tokyo or Santiago?

What if they lived on an island in the middle of an ocean?

Think for a moment how different their investment perspective might be if, instead of being United States citizens, these investors inhabited a tiny nation surrounded by water with few publicly held companies and no stock market of its own. How would this island location affect the way its inhabitants constructed investment *portfolios*?

It is unlikely they would buy stocks only in the few companies headquartered on their island, buy only U.S. stocks, or invest only in a single market anywhere. They would use their access to markets around the world to full advantage. They would develop globally diversified portfolios that were not heavily concentrated in a single market like the United States or Germany or Japan. From their island perspective, they would search around the globe and select stocks from many markets. They would use their worldwide *diversification* to both reduce portfo-

 **Wall Street**
colloquial term used to refer to the U.S. stock market and all the surrounding institutions; street in New York City where the New York Stock Exchange is located.

 **stock**
a negotiable security indicating ownership of a company.

1

**index**
a composite of individual stocks that is designed to represent the movement of a particular market or segment of a market.

**portfolio**
an investor's overall holdings of mutual funds, individual stocks, and bonds, viewed as a whole.

**diversification**
owning a variety of different types of investments to reduce risk in the portfolio.

**investment strategy**
a comprehensive plan for achieving one's investment goals and objectives.

lio risk and seek higher returns. I call their *investment strategy The Island Principle*™.

Most U.S. investors all but ignore markets outside their country. It is normal for investors to favor the market in their homeland. The familiar feels comfortable. They can follow events that may influence the market on the local news broadcasts or in the daily paper. Detailed information about individual companies and industries is readily available. This broad and easy information access is particularly important to investors who prefer making all of their own investment decisions.

---

*Investors favor familiar markets.*

---

In the United States, investors feel confident that regulations make their market a fair place for everyone who participates. The U.S. dollar is sound. They feel they have a lot of investment choices and the U.S. market has treated them well recently. They are not alone in their preference for investing close to home. Investors around the world show a strong bias in favor of their national markets.

From an island perspective, however, the decision about where to invest looks very different. With no market of their own, *island investors* search the world over for the best-performing stocks or markets. With their investment vision unobstructed by the blinders of national loyalty or the comfort of the familiar, they see opportunities for investing in countries or regions that are ignored by investors with strong national markets of their own.

Investors focused exclusively on Wall Street are ignoring the global sea change occurring in world markets. They are missing incredible opportunities in a world that has become a very dynamic place to invest. In recent history, the fall of communism and the spread of capitalism made enemies into trading partners. Businesses gain access to new markets at an increasing pace. Information travels at lightning speed as computers revolutionize commerce and stimulate growth. The Internet knows no borders and spurs a new spirit of entrepreneurship. Goods and services trade among countries at an accelerating rate. Many of the companies benefiting from this global expansion are located outside the United States.

## A FRESH PERSPECTIVE ON THE WORLD

Investors who change their perspectives and start thinking globally open themselves to enormous investment potential. Imagine telling a *portfolio manager* to make the best possible stock picks then handing over a list that restricts the choices to a small portion of the total stocks available. That's exactly what investors do when they limit their investments to U.S. companies.

Some U.S. investors are already daring to venture away from Wall Street. However, many of them have a distorted perspective about just what *foreign investing* is that still limits their ability to take full advantage of their global opportunities.

First, many U.S. investors view *foreign* as a single, conglomerate market that they compare against the U.S. market. The problem with defining all non-U.S. investing as "foreign" is that this view lumps all of the other markets around the world into a single market. When investment advisers talk about *international investing*, they also mean *non-U.S. investing*. Mentally, these investors put all of their investment opportunities into just one of two boxes (Figure 1.1).

Actually, there are over 50 separate foreign markets around the world. With the spread of capitalism in the past 10 years there are now over 50 countries with stock markets, and the number is still growing. So the *global* investment picture actually looks more like Figure 1.2. *True global investing* treats the United States and all other markets throughout the world equally.

Investors who see the United States as one market and everything else as a second market restrict their opportunities around the world to just two investment pools. Getting away to the perspective of our island helps

**The Island Principle™**
a long-term global investment strategy using diversification into multiple markets around the world chosen by multiple global mutual fund managers in order to reduce portfolio risk, increase portfolio returns, or do both simultaneously.

**island investor**
an investor who follows the concepts of The Island Principle.

**portfolio manager**
the individual who decides which stocks to own in a mutual fund.

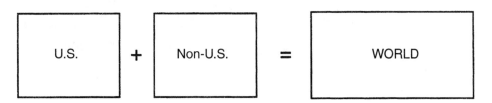

**FIGURE 1.1**  Most U.S. investors think of the world as only two markets. *Source:* Kreitler Associates.

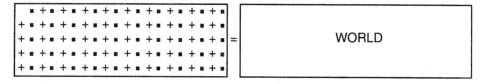

**FIGURE 1.2**  The investment world actually consists of over 50 separate markets. *Source:* Kreitler Associates.

 **foreign investing**

investing in non-U.S. stocks; used interchangeably with the term "international investing" within the financial community; sometimes mistakenly equated with global investing.

us realize that the so-called foreign market is not a single market but literally dozens of individual markets.

*Foreign investing includes many markets. It is not a single, non-U.S. market.*

Second, many U.S. investors are so focused on their home market that they are unaware that there are many sound markets around the world they can choose among. In June 1997, the *Wall Street Journal* classified the then existing markets around the world into five groups based on characteristics including *performance*, value, *risk*, market regulation, *market efficiency*, economic health, *capitalization*, and liquidity (Table 1.1). The *Journal* grouped 11 other markets with the United States in its "developed" category and grouped another 9 countries as "other developed." These two groups together provide island investors with 21 established, *developed markets* around the world offering a wide range of investment opportunities to choose among. Most were started in the 1800s (in 1817,

| TABLE 1.1 Markets around the World | | | | |
|---|---|---|---|---|
| *Developed Markets* | *Other Developed Markets* | *Mature Emerging Markets* | *Newly Emerging Markets* | *Frontier Markets* |
| Australia | Austria | Argentina | China | Egypt |
| Canada | Belgium | Brazil | Colombia | Jordan |
| Denmark | Finland | Chile | Czech Republic | Morocco |
| France | Hong Kong | Greece | Hungary | Nigeria |
| Germany | Italy | Korea | India | Pakistan |
| Ireland | Japan | Malaysia | Indonesia | Peru |
| Netherlands | Norway | Mexico | Israel | Russia |
| New Zealand | Singapore | Philippines | Poland | Turkey |
| Sweden | Spain | Portugal | Sri Lanka | Zimbabwe |
| Switzerland | | South Africa | Taiwan | |
| United Kingdom | | Thailand | Venezuela | |
| United States | | | | |

*Note:* Markets around the world are grouped here according to factors including performance, value, risk, market regulation and efficiency, economic health, capitalization, and liquidity. *Source:* The *Wall Street Journal,* June 26, 1997.

New York brokers formed the *New York Stock Exchange Board*, which evolved into the *New York Stock Exchange)* but several have been operating since the 1600s and 1700s (Table 1.2).

    Lumping all of these developed markets around the world into that single so-called foreign investment pool ignores the very important fact that many of these markets are similar to the United States in terms of things like political stability, accounting practices, market regulation, and data access. Investors who overlook them miss tremendous opportunities to reduce risk, increase portfolio returns, or do both.

 **foreign** term used within the financial community to indicate investment opportunites around the world excluding the United States; everywhere except the United States.

*The United States is only one among 21 developed markets around the globe.*

**international investing**

investing in countries throughout the world excluding the United States; used interchangeably with the term "foreign investing" within the financial community; sometimes mistakenly equated with global investing.

**non-U.S. investing**

investing in securities of companies that are based outside the United States; used with the same meaning as foreign or international investing within the investment community.

| **TABLE 1.2  Developed Markets Worldwide** | |
| Year Established | Market |
| --- | --- |
| 1611 | Netherlands |
| 1771 | Austria |
| 1775 | Germany |
| 1776 | Sweden |
| 1799 | Ireland |
| 1801 | Belgium |
| 1802 | United Kingdom |
| 1808 | Denmark |
| 1808 | Italy |
| 1817 | Canada |
| 1817 | United States |
| 1819 | Norway |
| 1831 | Spain |
| 1850 | Switzerland |
| 1861 | France |
| 1871 | Australia |
| 1872 | New Zealand |
| 1878 | Japan |
| 1891 | Hong Kong |
| 1912 | Finland |
| 1930 | Singapore |

*Note:* Many of the world's developed markets are as old as or older than Wall Street. All but two have over a century of regulatory experience and performance history. *Source:* Ennis, Knupp & Associates.

Rather than looking at the world in terms of the raw number of markets, most investment analysts prefer to look at markets in terms of stock *market capitalization,* or the amount of the world's total investment assets that market represents. They take the market price of each stock, multiply it by the number of shares, and then add them all up to get total capitalization. Popular market indexes such as the *Standard & Poor's 500 Index (S&P 500)*, *Morgan Stanley Capital International Europe, Australia, and Far East Index (EAFE®)*, or the *Morgan Stanley Capital International World Index* (commonly referred to as the *World Index*) weight the stocks they include based on capitalization.

The current value of the U.S. stock market is approximately 40% of the total value of all world markets combined. From the standpoint of market capitalization, investors who limit their portfolios to U.S. stocks are missing 60% of the opportunities around the world! Put another way, on the basis of capitalization alone, an investor choosing global stocks has two and a half times as many opportunities to find good investments as someone investing in the United States alone.

*On the basis of capitalization, global investors have two and a half times as many investment opportunities as those who limit their investing to U.S. stocks.*

From an island perspective, however, capitalization is not a rational criterion for deciding how much of a portfolio should be in a particular market or stock. Deciding how much to invest in a company (or market) because of its size or capitalization is justified only if size is related to risk or return. Investors may favor larger companies or larger markets if they believe they will have higher growth or lower *volatility*, but they favor them because of those expected benefits, not because of their larger size. Their size is an indirect factor.

The same principle applies to investing in multiple markets. Fancy *portfolio theory* models used to determine how much of a global portfolio to allocate to individual markets ignore the size of each of these markets (their capitalization). Instead, they use factors like *expected returns*, standard deviations, and correlation coefficients.

 **global**
term used within the financial community to identify investment opportunities in markets throughout the world including the United States (the term "foreign" excludes the United States).

 **true global investing**
treating all of the world's available markets as potential opportunities without restricting choices by geographic location.

 **Wall Street Journal**
financial paper published by Dow Jones Publishing Company throughout the United States that emphasizes investment-related news.

**performance**
how the price of
a stock or market
has done over a
period of time;
typically mea-
sured as a rate of
return.

**risk**
a term used with
many different
meanings related
to unpredictabil-
ity; the chance
that an investor
will not achieve
the expected
outcome.

*Market capitalization is not a relevant factor
when determining how much to invest in a particular stock or market.*

More significantly, the perspective of a world with 21
developed markets provides investors with more possibilities to diversify their portfolios in order to reduce risk.
Using just the developed markets, they have 20 times
more options for diversification than an investor with a
portfolio 100% invested in the U.S. market.

*Island investors who perceive each of the world's
developed markets as a separate investment opportunity have 20 times more opportunity for diversification than investors who see Wall Street as
their only investment choice.*

## MANY HAPPY GLOBAL RETURNS

When U.S. investors adopt an island perspective, they
may find themselves surprised at the opportunities to increase investment returns that they have. Although many
U.S. investors are pleased with their recent returns during
the long-running bull market in the 1980s and 1990s, the
United States has rarely offered the best returns compared
to the world's other developed markets.

What many investors all too easily forget in the euphoria of a strong bull market providing above-average returns is that those extraordinary returns do not continue
indefinitely. What is normal is that markets have periods
of very good performance followed by periods of average
returns or even below-average returns. A longer view of
the U.S. market shows this. Since 1970, the U.S. market's
performance has been quite average, or even below average, when compared either to other single markets or to
world indexes.

*Despite its bullish performance in the late 1980s and the 1990s, the U.S. market has never been the best-performing developed market in the world since 1970 on an annual basis.*

Most U.S. investors are surprised to learn that since 1970 (when reliable worldwide records become available), the United States has never been the best-performing developed market in the world. Figure 1.3 compares how the United States (as measured by the S&P 500) has annually performed since 1970 versus the best-performing country of the developed markets. (Note that, throughout the book, comparisons between the U.S. and other markets are made in U.S. dollars. See the Appendix for country performance numbers in terms of both dollars and local currencies.)

In recent years, the United States has been a very good place to invest and foreign markets have looked particularly weak. From 1995 through 1998, the S&P 500 averaged a spectacular 30% annual rate of return. Those four years set a U.S. record. Meanwhile, from 1995 through 1998, investors tracking the Morgan Stanley Capital International Europe, Australia, and Far East Index saw only a 10% annual return. The EAFE index, which specifically excludes the United States and Canada, is a weighted average of all of the developed markets in Europe, Australia, and Asia often used as the standard index for measuring non-U.S. stock performance.

This comparison can lead investors astray, however, unless they understand that because the EAFE index is based on market capitalization, it is heavily weighted toward the Japanese market. The poor performance of the Japanese market during the same period when the U.S. market was booming dragged the EAFE index down and gave the impression that all foreign investments did badly.

Psychologically, investors overweight recent or short-term market trends and discount long-term trends. This is a normal but dangerous practice. U.S. in-

 **market efficiency**
a measure of how well market prices reflect information. In an efficient market, all investors gain access to information simultaneously and act on it instantaneously, so new information is reflected in immediate price movements.
In an inefficient market, investors gain information access at different times so prices move more slowly. The first investors to gain access to information have a competitive advantage.

 **capitalization**
the total value of a company, a market, or an index.

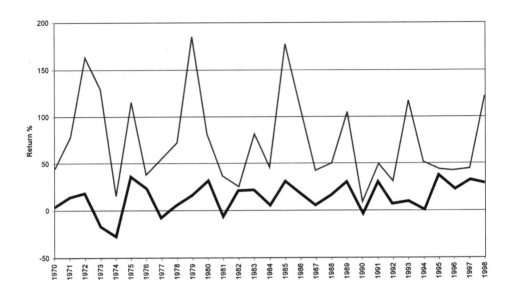

**FIGURE 1.3** The S&P 500 Index (black line) versus the best of the 21 developed markets around the world (percent return in U.S. dollars). *Source:* Morgan Stanley Capital International.

 **developed markets**
those 21 markets around the world with a proven history of relatively strict regulator climates.

**New York Stock Exchange Board**
the organization that predated the New York Stock Exchange.

vestors are justifiably delighted with Wall Street's incredible performance from 1995 through 1998. The 20% plus annual returns by U.S. blue chip stocks from 1988 to 1998 have also lulled many investors into thinking high returns are the norm. Assuming that market performance over the next 10 years will show the same extraordinary returns is a very risky investment bet, however.

Once again, taking a longer perspective changes the view. Checking Wall Street, Ibbotson Associates reports that U.S. large company stocks had an annual compounded rate of return of 11.2% from 1926 through 1998. Looking around the world we find that, on a yearly basis since 1970, the U.S. market has often failed to match the *average* of the non-U.S. markets as measured by either the Morgan Stanley Capital International Europe, Australia, and Far East Index (EAFE®) or the unweighted average of the developed markets.

An unweighted average of all the developed markets from 1995 to 1998 when the U.S. market was booming shows a very acceptable 18% average return. Meanwhile, the EAFE index was only 10%. Since the EAFE index is the international benchmark most investors watch, it is not surprising that they felt non-U.S. markets were underperforming.

Figure 1.4 shows the difference between the performance of the U.S. (represented by the S&P 500 index) and the average of the 21 developed countries using an arithmetical average rather than the capitalization-weighted EAFE index. A positive number indicates the United States outperformed the average of the developed markets. A negative number indicates the United States underperformed it. For example, in 1970, the United States performed 5% better than average of the developed countries. From 1970 to 1998, there were 15 years when the United States was better than the average and 14 years when it did worse, sometimes substantially so.

---

*The developed markets have done better than the U.S. market alone approximately half the time since 1970. Or, put another way, the U.S. market has underperformed this world average about half the time.*

---

Another way to look at the performance is in 10-year rolling periods. From an investment standpoint, a single year is a very short time horizon even though it might seem like infinity to an Internet day trader. Ten years is long enough to be a meaningful investment time horizon. During the 10 years from 1989 to 1998 the U.S. market produced a spectacular 19.2% average return. It will probably surprise most U.S. investors to learn that during this 10-year period the United States was not the best-performing of the developed markets, but was only third behind Switzerland and the Netherlands.

From 1970 through 1998 there are 20 10-year rolling periods as shown in Figure 1.5 (1970–1979 is one; 1971–1980 is number two, etc., up to 1989–1998, which is the 20th). Ten-year periods of time are more meaningful than a single year. The chart shows that, except for the

**New York Stock Exchange**
a major stock exchange based in New York City; one of several marketplaces for the trading of U.S. stocks.

**market capitalization**
the value of all stocks in a particular market, determined by taking each stock's market price times the number of shares and adding them all together.

**Standard & Poor's 500 Index**
a broad market index that includes stocks of 500 of the largest companies in the United States; commonly referred to as the S&P 500.

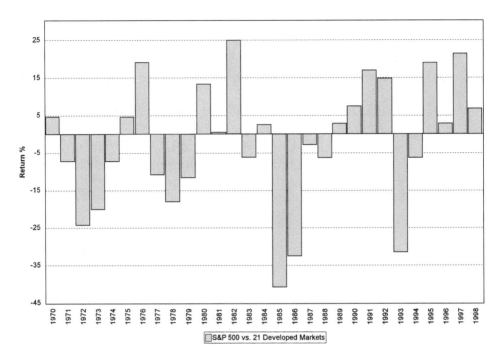

**FIGURE 1.4** The S&P 500 Index versus the average of 21 developed markets (percent return in U.S. dollars). *Source:* Morgan Stanley Capital International.

**S&P 500** abbreviation for the Standard & Poor's 500 Index.

last three rolling periods, the United States was consistently *below* average (again, the benchmark used here is the average of the developed countries, not the EAFE index). Typically, markets excel and then their performance falls back. Eight developed countries claimed the top 10-year rolling average at least once. The United States has never made it to this top spot.

Markets move in cycles but have a habit of eventually reverting to the mean. Ten years ago many investors assumed the powerful Japanese bull market would continue indefinitely. They watched with dismay as the Japanese with inflated balance sheets gobbled up real estate in New York and other cities. Then the inevitable happened. What went up went down then stayed down for over 10 years. Experienced investors acknowledge the cyclical nature of markets but even they find it difficult to know when to get out to avoid disaster.

# WHY MULTINATIONAL ISN'T GLOBAL

Many U.S. investors consider themselves globally diversified if their portfolio includes a few U.S.-based multinational or global companies like Coca-Cola or Procter & Gamble. Investing in the stocks of U.S. multinational corporations in the hope of gaining international exposure in a portfolio works only partially. There is a very strong correlation between a stock's performance and the market in which the stock is traded. The actions of local investors affect the behavior of all stocks in a market, including those of multinational companies. Thus investors owning these stocks enjoy only part of the benefits of global diversification.

Additionally, these multinational companies represent a very small fraction of the world's investment opportunities. The investor using them for global exposure is still missing out on the huge number of other excellent investment opportunities around the world. And they

> **Morgan Stanley Capital International Europe, Australia, and Far East Index** a stock index that includes all of the 19 developed markets in Europe, Australia, and Asia but excludes the United States and Canada; abbreviated EAFE.

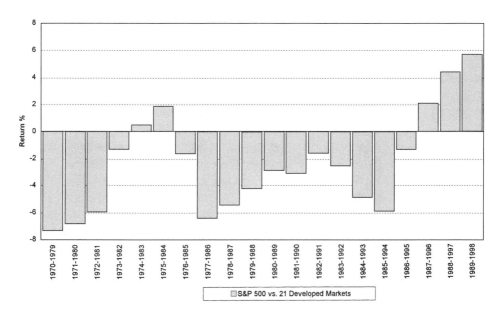

**FIGURE 1.5** The S&P 500 Index versus the average of the 21 developed markets (10-year annualized returns). *Source:* Morgan Stanley Capital International.

**EAFE®**
an abbreviation for the Morgan Stanley Capital International Europe, Australia, and Far East Index.

**Morgan Stanley Capital International World Index**
a stock index that includes all the world's 21 developed markets (including the United States and Canada) as well as many of the world's developing markets; referred to as the World Index.

**World Index**
shorthand for Morgan Stanley Capital International World Index.

deny themselves the opportunity to reduce risk through geographic market diversification.

---

*Correlation between a stock and the market it trades in reduces the diversification benefits of owning a U.S. multinational stock.*

---

## GOING GLOBAL

The average U.S. investor's portfolio contains a very low percentage of companies headquartered outside the country. Many U.S. investors who consider themselves globally diversified have only 10% to 20% of their portfolios in non-U.S. stocks, typically through mutual funds. Individual investors who consider themselves more aggressive may have 15% to 25% non-U.S. stock holdings.

From the perspective of an island investor, however, these levels of global holdings actually appear rather small. Even though some investors have stopped looking to Wall Street alone for all of their returns, they are still dramatically underweighting other markets available around the world.

The incredible advances in computer technology and the speed with which information is shared have had a downside for U.S. investors. The U.S. market has become an extremely efficient market. In an efficient market, everyone has access to and acts on the same information simultaneously. Stock prices reflect this universal information access. Profiting by moving quickly before others possess the same market intelligence is almost impossible to do. That means the U.S. market determines how a U.S. investor's portfolio performs. An individual investor cannot do better than the U.S. market without taking on more risk than that of the market. To do better means going global.

---

*It is very difficult for investors to outperform the market when that market is very efficient without taking on more risk than the market.*

---

The Island Principle asks investors to move away from their preoccupation with Wall Street and the daily gyrations of the U.S. market. It suggests that they incorporate two new levels of diversification into their portfolios. The first is to diversify into markets around the world much as they already diversify their holdings among different stocks and industry sectors. This diversification strategy, coupled with the management diversification discussed in Chapter 6, enables them to both reduce risk and seek better returns. For the purposes of this book's discussion, The Island Principle has been applied only to the stock portion of an investor's portfolio even though most portfolios include other asset classes such as bonds or cash.

With risk under control, investors are psychologically better prepared to stick with their investment strategies when markets go crazy. Even more importantly, The Island Principle's diversification increases the odds of achieving financial goals and avoiding the long-term risks every investor faces. Investors can increase potential portfolio returns by increasing the amount of their portfolios allocated to stock or they can choose some more risky stocks—with their potential for higher returns—without necessarily increasing their portfolio volatility.

The first step in the process of redesigning their portfolios to take advantage of The Island Principle's risk and return benefits is that investors must move away from their familiar, comfortable home market and develop a fresh perspective on global markets.

 **volatility**
the up-and-down movement of the price of an investment or a market, often equated with risk and used interchangeably with that term.

 **portfolio theory**
the body of economic theory used by investment analysts to develop investment portfolios.

 **expected return**
the amount an investor hopes to earn on the capital used to purchase a particular investment, usually expressed as a percentage of that capital.

_Chapter_

# 2

# All at Sea about Risk

Investors tend to focus on returns. However, risk is return's counterpart. As they seek returns in order to reach their financial objectives, island investors must navigate the hazards of risk. It is critical that investors understand risk as well as possible before they commit their _capital_. The Island Principle's primary goal is to help investors manage the investment risks they face in order to increase the likelihood they will reach their investment objectives.

Paradoxically, many investors fear that so-called foreign investing is risky even though investing in non-U.S. stocks is actually an important tool they can use to manage risk. Semantics is partly to blame for this investor phobia. The regulatory warnings delivered whenever investors purchase a non-U.S. stock or mutual fund only add to their problem.

Most individual investors have only a vague understanding of the actual risks they face. They tend to equate risk with _market volatility_—those daily or weekly or monthly value fluctuations in a given market—and seldom look much farther than this short-term indicator.

Island investors define risk more broadly as the possibility that investors will not achieve their expected results. They understand that risk is normal, so they anticipate it and use a global investment strategy that

**capital**
a person's investable assets.

**market volatility**
the normal up-and-down movement of stock prices. Stock prices are continuously changing as investors receive new information and change their desire to own stocks.

helps them manage risk when it does occur. Island investors are aware that short-term volatility is only one of many risks they face and that the long-term risks they face are far more serious.

## FOREIGN PHOBIA

The word "foreign" carries a lot of negative psychological baggage for some investors that biases them against investing outside the United States. Foreign means strange, alien, exotic, and unknown—and, therefore, uncomfortable, threatening, or risky.

In the investment world, the term "foreign" is often abused and misused to the confusion of investors. Investment pundits use the words "foreign," "international," and "global" interchangeably when they are really talking about very different things. Emotionally loaded terminology and sloppy usage contribute to the reluctance many investors have about investing outside the United States.

*The term "foreign" carries negative connotations for many investors.*

**developing markets**
those markets around the world that are growing and progressing but that do not yet have a proven regulatory climate.

Adding to the confusion, some people think of *developing markets* or *emerging markets* whenever they hear about foreign investing. The terms "developing markets" and "emerging markets" are relatively new as investment jargon goes. They refer to the markets that are rapidly evolving and that became popular as many countries have responded to the spread of capitalism by creating their own stock markets.

**emerging markets**
developing markets.

*Many investors mistakenly equate non-U.S. investing with riskier developing or emerging markets.*

Investors who confuse "foreign" with "developing" or "emerging" can easily fall into thinking that all non-U.S. investing is extremely risky. Emerging markets have great potential but they tend to be very risky. Many investors still remember lessons learned the hard way when *Pacific Rim* markets collapsed in 1997 and 1998.

Some people use terms like "international investing," "non-U.S. investing," or "*offshore investing*" when referring to investing anywhere in the world except the United States. These terms do get away from the emotional connotations the word "foreign" can carry, but they fall into another trap by categorizing investment opportunities as though the world consisted of only two markets—us and them.

Instead of thinking "foreign," island investors think "global." Global markets include all markets around the world—including the United States. Thinking globally avoids the trap of mentally dividing the world into just two markets when there are actually many markets. The Island Principle involves global investing in multiple markets around the world. For island investors, investments away from Wall Street are not foreign or strange; they are quite ordinary.

Investors who want to minimize their investment risk can invest globally in the world's 21 developed markets. More adventuresome investors may want to consider investing some of their assets in the developing or emerging markets. There are excellent opportunities in these markets for both appreciation as well as additional diversification as long as investors understand that they take on higher risks along with the potential for higher gains.

## THOSE RISKY FOREIGN MARKETS

Any investor apprehension about foreign investing is only compounded by the litany of warnings that the *National Association of Securities Dealers (NASD)* requires be enumerated in the *prospectus* of any mutual fund that invests in companies outside the United States. The NASD also requires that brokers specifically point these risks out

 **Pacific Rim** that area of the world including the countries of Hong Kong, South Korea, Singapore, Taiwan, China, Malaysia, Indonesia, the Philippines, New Zealand, and Australia. Because of its size and influence, Japan is frequently treated as a region separate from the Pacific Rim.

 **offshore investing** a term sometimes used to describe investing in non-U.S. stocks but more frequently used to mean investing in a way to avoid U.S. government regulations—a practice not described in this book.

**National Association of Securities Dealers (NASD)** an organization established by securities dealers to regulate the actions of their member firms and brokers as they buy and sell stocks, bonds, mutual funds, and other securities for their customers.

when recommending any mutual fund that invests outside the United States. The exact wording may vary from one adviser to another but the warning against non-U.S. investing must call an investor's attention to the "special risks" of "foreign investing" (that slippery term again) including obtaining data, *currency fluctuations*, differing *accounting standards* and regulatory environments, and possible political and economic instability. Some of these are real risks. Others could more correctly be classified as challenges.

What many investors do not understand, however, is that many of these "special risks" apply to *all* investing regardless of what market an investor is in. An investment in U.S. stocks is subject to most of the same risks as an investment in non-U.S. stocks. Buying any stock is a risk. This is why investors demand higher returns from stocks than they do from certificates of deposit or from bonds.

> *Most of the "special risks" of foreign investing that brokers warn their clients about also apply to investments in U.S. stocks. Investing in all stocks is risky.*

The irony is that the diversification provided by true global investing actually reduces overall portfolio risk. Using The Island Principle as an investment strategy can help investors reduce the risks inherent in any market that the NASD warns them about.

> *Global investing reduces risk rather than increasing it.*

Let's consider these so-called special risks of non-U.S. investing that the NASD has identified and take a look at how *global investing* actually helps investors hedge these risks and reduce them rather than increasing them.

## Risk 1: Political Instability May Undermine Investment Value

While the United States may look stable to U.S. investors, political scientists do not always rate the United States as the world's most stable country. They are aware that things like impeachment, new laws, or wars can quickly change a nation's stability. For example, at a 1997 seminar on developments in global portfolio management sponsored by the Association for Investment Management and Research and the International Society of Financial Analysts, University of Chicago professor of international political economy Marvin Zonis used 10 measures of political stability to rank the world's top 10 nations in terms of political stability. He ranked Switzerland, Japan, France, and the Netherlands above the United States, followed by Italy, Germany, Australia, Finland, and Spain. While others may quibble with Zonis's ranking or his criteria, the fact remains that many observers agree with him that the United States does not necessarily rank as the world's most politically stable country. Another way to look at this is that investing in non-U.S. markets does not necessarily involve taking on additional *political risk*. This runs contrary to the belief of many U.S. investors.

---

*The U.S. is not the most stable political environment in the world as many investors believe.*

---

Depending on their age when they start investing, investors should have a time horizon of 25 to 50 years or even more. Government policies in any country including the United States will change a great deal over this span of time, affecting both stock prices and buying power. Sometimes these changes are so gradual that investors do not see how they are going to affect their portfolios until it happens. Other times, the changes come so fast there is not time to restructure the portfolio before the changes affect it. Diversification into multiple markets reduces the

**prospectus**
a legal document describing the goals, investment criteria, management criteria, costs, and past performance of a mutual fund, which must be offered to anyone seeking to invest in that fund. Historically these have been filled with legalese and have been difficult to read; regulators are encouraging mutual fund companies to make them more consumer friendly.

**currency fluctuation**
a change in the value of the currency of one country versus that of another. Like stock prices, most currency prices are changing all the time.

**accounting standards**
the way companies are required to report their finances. The standards may vary from one country to another.

**global investing**
investing anywhere throughout the world without specifically excluding any particular geographic market.

**political risk**
risk investors face because governments may change their laws, regulations, and other policies.

risk that changes in the political climate in any single market will significantly reduce the value of an investor's portfolio. It does not increase the risk. Diversification means that a single government's action does not control an investor's financial future.

### Risk 2: Accounting Systems in Other Countries Can Be Different and Confusing

Investors are warned that because the financial accounting systems in other countries may be different from that used in the United States, they may be handicapped in their attempts to interpret whatever type of financial data is available.

It is true that accounting systems and rules on disclosure of corporate information in many countries are quite different from those used in the United States and are, therefore, confusing when investors try to use the data and compare it to U.S. data. On one hand, this can be interpreted as a liability because it discourages many investors from putting money into these markets and depresses their stock values. On the other hand, it can be viewed as an opportunity because these markets are not as efficient as the U.S market. Investors who do the extra research and gain an understanding of the local accounting practices can gain additional profits because they can buy undervalued companies that others shun.

---

*Additional profits are available to those willing to do the research to find undervalued non-U.S. companies.*

---

Standard accounting systems are being adopted throughout the world as global investors demand better accounting from companies that want to raise international capital. As companies adopt these standard practices, investors will be willing to pay more for them and their prices should rise. Those who own stock in the companies before the standard accounting provisions are adopted will benefit from this transition as prices rise.

Researching overseas companies can be a daunting task. Investors following The Island Principle use high-quality, proven professional money managers who have the resources to do the extra research that enables them to profit from the differences in accounting systems in other countries by purchasing undervalued companies.

### Risk 3: Currency Fluctuations in Other Countries Increase the Risk of Investing There

Some investors fret that *local currencies* are subject to un-predictable fluctuations. They correctly point out that changes in currency values often can be as important as stock price movements in determining their short-term returns as measured in U.S. dollars.

**local currency** the currency in which a stock is traded in its home market.

As an example, a Japanese stock may increase by 10% in Tokyo. But if the Japanese *yen* declines 12% in value versus the U.S. dollar over the same period, the U.S. in-vestor suffers a net loss of 2%. The decrease in the value of the yen against the U.S. dollar more than offsets the stock gain. However, if the yen had appreciated 7% in value ver-sus the dollar, a stock that increased 10% would actually be worth 17% more in terms of its dollar value (Table 2.1).

**yen** currency used in Japan.

| TABLE 2.1   Effect of Currency Value Fluctuations on a 10% Increase in Stock Value | | |
|---|---|---|
| | If Yen Declines versus Dollar | If Yen Increases versus Dollar |
| Change in the value of yen versus dollar | −12% | +7% |
| Net change in value to U.S. investor | −2% | +17% |

*Note:* This example showing how currency value fluctuations can affect a U.S. investor holding non-U.S. (in this case, Japan-ese) stock assumes a 10% increase in Japanese stock value in lo-cal currency (yen). *Source:* Kreitler Associates.

**currency risk**

the additional risk added to a portfolio because a portion of it is denominated in non-U.S. currencies and is, therefore, subject to the effects of currency fluctuations.

**exchange rate**

the price at which two currencies are traded for one another. In an open market this rate is continually changing.

**short term**

a length of time that deals from an hour to a day to as much as a year, or perhaps longer.

Protecting buying power, not reducing currency fluctuations, is the investor's primary long-term challenge. Clearly currency fluctuations increase short-term unpredictability and risk of investing. Again, however, investors who think these *currency risks* exist only outside of the United States are not looking at the broad picture. The power of the U.S. dollar to buy goods and services around the world is subject to change just as the buying power of the yen, the pound, or the euro may change. The buying power of a portfolio invested only in U.S. stocks can be eroded by domestic inflation or by depreciation of the U.S. dollar versus other currencies.

*Exchange rates*, the value at which one currency can be converted into another, fluctuate over time. As currency values in different markets change relative to one other, their fluctuation affects not only the values of stocks and portfolios denominated in those currencies but also the investor's buying power in the world's markets. These fluctuations can be sharp over the *short term* and cause increased portfolio volatility. However, changes over the *long term* are more important for investors striving to reach a financial goal.

For example, Table 2.2 shows that from 1970 through 1998 the U.S. dollar gained about 44% of its value versus the pound but lost 68% versus the yen and 54% versus the deutsche mark (now converted to the euro). This means that Japanese and German goods became more expensive to buy while goods from England became cheaper. Citizens of a country whose currency depreciates against other currencies must pay more for imports, and this can badly erode their living standard.

A U.S. citizen has no way of knowing what today's dollar will be worth in the future. Yet the future buying power of his or her portfolio is dependent upon this future dollar value. Actions by the U.S. government could destroy the investor's ability to achieve his or her objectives, particularly if the entire portfolio was invested in the United States and, therefore, valued totally in dollars.

Currency diversification through ownership of assets denominated in several different currencies is an excellent hedge against the potential forces at work

| TABLE 2.2 Change in the Value of the U.S. Dollar versus Major Currencies, 1970 to 1998 | | |
|---|---|---|
| | *Percent Change 1970 to 1998* | *Percent Change on an Annualized Basis* |
| Franc | +0.71 | +0.02 |
| Deutsche mark | −54.78 | −2.70 |
| Yen | −68.29 | −3.88 |
| Pound | +44.67 | +1.28 |

*Source:* Kreitler Associates.

 **long term**
a period of more than several years. Typically, an investor should not own stocks unless he or she intends to be in the market for five years or more; therefore, the long term would be five, ten, or more years.

within each individual country that could erode the value of its currency and affect the buying power of an investor's portfolio. Investors diversified in multiple currencies increase the odds that they can protect their portfolios' long-term buying power. While owning *unhedged* non-U.S. stocks may increase a portfolio's short-term volatility, it should decrease long-term *buying power risk*.

 **unhedged**
not hedged against currency fluctuations.

*Over the long term, owning foreign stocks in local currencies actually reduces buying power risk rather than increasing it.*

 **buying power risk**
the uncertainty that individuals face because they do not know the purchasing power of their dollars in the future.

### Risk 4: The Regulatory Systems in Other Countries Are Not As Good As That in the United States

Some investors worry about investing outside the United States because they feel the systems in other countries for clearing stocks, receiving funds, or even assuring that they really own the stocks they bought are inferior to the *regulatory system* in the United States.

These may be valid concerns for investors venturing into developing or emerging markets around the world.

**regulatory system**
the rules and regulations that cover the buying and selling of securities.

However, the financial regulatory climate in most of the developed markets is typically as strict as that in the United States.

---

*Most of the world's developed markets have a century or more of regulatory history.*

---

An investor following The Island Principle should have most of his or her money in the world's 21 developed markets, so regulatory concerns should not be a major issue. At most, an island investor would have relatively small holdings (up to perhaps 5% to 10% of total portfolio value) in developing markets. Investors should factor an unreliable regulatory system into the price of these stocks.

### Risk 5: It Is Difficult to Obtain and Interpret Data from Other Markets

Some investors feel distances and the differences in languages, reporting customs, and different regulatory environments make it too difficult to obtain and interpret information that investors need in order to determine which companies to own. The United States is a leader in assuring that investors have access to a great deal of information and that all investors have equal access to this information. *Insider trading*—buying and selling stock based on company information not available to the general public—is prohibited. Many non-U.S. markets lack this strict control. Companies in other markets often report their data very differently from U.S. companies, or make less data available than U.S. companies do. In financial jargon, their transactions have less *transparency* than those of U.S. companies, which must make information available to all investors. Publicly traded companies operate in a fishbowl—everyone can see everything they do. While foreign companies are now under pressure from global investors to move to the U.S. standards of auditing and disclosure, investors may not have access to all of the data they are accustomed to getting from U.S. companies.

**insider trading**
using information from company sources that is not available to the general public when buying or selling stocks; generally an illegal activity in highly regulated markets.

*In markets where information is difficult to get or interpret, those who do get the information can profit from their knowledge.*

Gaining an advantage because of better information is difficult to do in the United States because the market is very efficient. Market efficiency means that all investors receive information about the market at the same time. For example, 10 years ago if Company A announced bad news that would affect its stock prices, shareholder relations mailed information to shareholders and released information to the press. Financial analysts had their own news sources. It might take days or weeks for the information to filter through many information channels to reach individual investors and, by then, the stock's price already reflected the information.

Today, satellite hookups allow investors and the media alike to electronically sit in on Company A's corporate press briefings. Announcements hit the Internet and cable television stock programs almost instantaneously. It is not unusual for share prices to move almost immediately. Stock price moves of 20% or 30% in a single day are common as all investors react at one time rather than over a period of several days or weeks.

In a very efficient market, an investor typically cannot beat the market because everyone receives the same information simultaneously. While the U.S. market may not be a totally efficient market, it is far more efficient than most other markets. Investors in less efficient markets outside the United States can gain an information advantage that allows them to profit from this information.

Just as with financial accounting systems, investors can see data reporting and accessibility issues as liabilities or as assets. When data is difficult to find or distributed unevenly to investors, those who do find it and who learn to use it are at an advantage. This risk of non-U.S. investing becomes an advantage for those willing to do the extra research to learn about those other markets. They are able to earn extra profits, profits over and above

**transparency**
the ability for investors to see information about a company's finances and plans. U.S. security rules require a great deal of disclosure for companies whose stocks are publicly traded. Investors in other geographic markets frequently do not have access to this level of information, although investors are beginning to require it of companies seeking financing from global sources.

the returns that would be expected in an efficient market. Island investors use professional money managers who understand how to obtain and use data from inefficient markets and use that information to seek these extra profits.

## NO IMMUNITY FROM RISK

Global investing does carry risks, but all investing carries risks. What many investors fail to understand is that investing in the United States carries many of same risks as investing outside the United States.

Buying stocks is risky. An investment axiom holds that investments offering higher potential returns come with higher levels of risk. Investors buy stocks with the expectation that they will earn a premium over what the money could earn in guaranteed investments like Treasury bills or certificates of deposit or a savings account. The risk, of course, is that they may not only fail to realize this earnings premium but also that they may lose part or all of the amount they invested. This is why investors demand higher returns from stocks than they do from Treasury bills or savings accounts.

An investment in U.S. stocks is subject to most of the same risks as an investment in foreign stocks. Any market can hit periods of stormy weather and heavy seas and the United States is no exception.

---

*Investors seeking increased returns take on increased risk regardless of the market or markets they are in.*

---

## VOLATILITY AND INVESTOR PSYCHOLOGY

Emotions play a larger role in investing than many investors will openly admit. They like to think their investment decisions are based solely on careful analysis of available information and logical investment strategy. The truth is that investing has a very important psychological side as well. Investors are basically risk averse. They may intellectualize about their risk tolerance and talk about balancing risk and return. When they are staring risk in the face, however, their actions often speak louder than their words.

To understand the risks investors face, it is easiest to categorize them as *short-term risks* or long-term risks. They are very different. Investors tend to overreact to short-term risks while overlooking many long-term risks.

Short-term risks tend to be more visible, more immediate than long-term risks. Investors commonly think of volatility—the daily, weekly, monthly, or quarterly ups and downs of the market—whenever risk is mentioned. Day-to-day market volatility is a short-term risk that frankly makes them nervous. Figure 2.1 shows the monthly price changes of large company stocks plotted chronologically from 1926 to 1998. Viewed on a short-term basis, volatility looks erratic and unpredictable. Market volatility makes investors worry that their basic investment strategy may be wrong. Or that their judgment is not as good as they thought it was. Due to their *risk aversion*, they lose confidence and often abandon otherwise good strategies.

If investors took a longer view of the market's short-term gyrations, however, they would see that the market's continual movements actually fall into a normal pattern. Figure 2.2, called a histogram, plots the number of times from 1926 to 1998 that large company stocks had a particular rate of return. Plotted this way, annual fluctuations fall into a typical bell-shaped curve or *normal distribution*.

Most investors, however, have a hard time thinking of market drops as normal. They cannot help reacting to short-term volatility because it makes investing seem unpredictable. While investors realize they cannot know precisely what will happen in the future, they like to think that the general direction it will take is somewhat predictable. They develop certain expectations about how future events will unfold and as long as the

 **short-term risk**
the volatility normally seen in the market on an hourly or a daily basis, or even as long as a year or more.

 **risk aversion**
the tendency for investors to avoid risk of loss of capital.

 **normal distribution**
a statistical term that shows how data tends to fall within a bell-shaped curve.

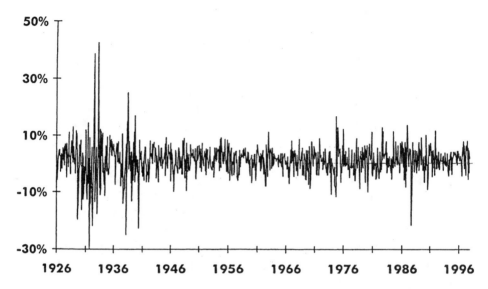

**FIGURE 2.1** The monthly changes (short-term market volatility) in U.S. large company returns from 1926 through 1996 shown here indicate the continual fluctuations in market value that investors must be prepared to face.
*Source:* Calculated by Kreitler Associates using information and data presented in Ibbotson Investment Analysis Software ©1999 Ibbotson Associates, Inc. All rights reserved. Used with permission.

**predictable risk**

a term used in this book to mean an event that is within the range of outcomes that an investor expects.

future unfolds within these expectations, they are comfortable.

Investors are willing to accept this *predictable risk* because they have anticipated it. They expected it and they are not surprised by it. Predictable risk is actually a *range of expected outcomes*, and this range will be different for every investor. An individual investor is comfortable and can stick with his or her long-term strategy as long as events unfold within this expected range.

*Unpredictable risk* occurs when events that occur fall outside of the range the investor predicted. If the unexpected event is positive (a stock split or merger boosts the value of the investment), the investor feels good about investing. When the unpredicted event has a negative effect (for example, earnings come in much lower than forecast), people lose confidence.

Psychologically, investors are especially averse to market drops that are greater than they expected. It makes

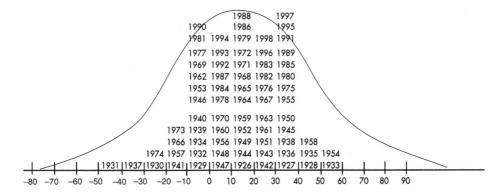

**FIGURE 2.2** When the annual rates of return of large company stocks from 1926 to 1998 are plotted on a graph, a normal bell curve distribution emerges that would lead U.S. large company investors to believe that in a given year they will typically face a wide range of returns. *Source:* Calculated by Kreitler Associates using information and data presented in Ibbotson Investment Analysis Software © 1999 Ibbotson Associates, Inc. All rights reserved. Used with permission.

them worry that all is not right. If they own stocks, they are likely to sell them. They abandon their long-term investment strategies no matter how good they are.

---

*Investors abandon their strategies when they face unpredictable risk.*

---

This unconscious need to be able to predict the future makes many investors uncomfortable with global investing. In a familiar home market they believe it is much easier for them to understand and predict the risk they face. When their investment universe expands to include more markets, they feel the likelihood of unpredictable risk increases.

The Island Principle helps investors deal with this unpredictability. A portfolio based on The Island Principle anticipates the unexpected. When something unpredicted does occur, the island investor's portfolio is already positioned to deal with it without major changes. The Island

**range of expected outcomes**
a term used in this book for the range of likely outcomes that an investor expects to achieve; not just a single point.

**unpredictable risk**
a term used in this book to refer to an event that is outside the range of outcomes that an investor expects.

Principle adds new levels of diversification to investors' portfolios that enable them both to dampen portfolio volatility and to control the long-term risks of investing. With risk under control and their investing outcome more predictable, investors are better able to keep their long-term investment strategies in place when the unexpected happens and their view of the future is threatened.

Investors instinctively understand that since they cannot predict future events and trends with pinpoint accuracy, they can never be certain that their investment strategy is the best one. There is always a nagging doubt that their strategy may be wrong. That is what makes it so hard not to jump ship and abandon their strategy when markets become more volatile than expected. Obviously, choosing a good strategy in the first place—one that can help them deal with market volatility or even ignore it—can be very important to investment success.

## FIVE VERY REAL RISKS

Short-term risk, that daily up-and-down market gyration or volatility, captures the lion's share of attention from investors and the financial press. Investors focused on market volatility and their ability to predict short-term market swings can easily ignore other, far more important risks or uncertainties that they face. Many investors think that as long as they can handle short-term risk (in the form of market volatility), they will be able to achieve their investment goals. They are convinced that a buy-and-hold strategy is all they need. They believe that as long as they do not react emotionally to short-term risk and abandon their investment strategy prematurely before it has a chance to work, they can reach their financial goals.

There are, however, a number of very real, long-term risks that stand between them and investment success. These risks make reaching their investment objectives uncertain. When investors initially choose a strategy, they make conscious or unconscious assumptions about the way future events and trends will occur. Their assumptions, however, may prove wrong. There are several real risks that many investors do not factor into their long-term financial strategy, including:

1. The *normal range of outcomes* they potentially face in the future is wider than most investors realize.

2. Projecting current trends into the future can result in badly erroneous forecasts.

3. Investing in a single market makes it impossible to escape the risk of that market (what economists refer to as *systematic risk*).

4. The future buying power of their portfolios may be eroded by the actions of a single government.

5. They may be choosing the wrong markets.

Investors who ignore these risks when they set their investment strategy are less likely to achieve their financial goals. Any strategy that neglects these long-term risks sets an investor up for possible failure. If they invest for 20 or 30 years only to find they have not achieved the investment objectives they set out to reach, they may not have time to make a correction. Following The Island Principle can help investors avoid being blindsided by these long-term uncertainties.

### Long-Term Risk 1: Normal Range of Outcomes Risk—Just Assuming Normal Market Volatility, the Long Term Is Not As Predictable As Many Investors Believe

Most investors have heard the saying, "It is the time in the market, not market timing, that counts." So "buy and hold" becomes part of their investment strategy. Staying in the market for the long term allows investors to benefit from the magic of compounding. If they leave $100,000 in the market and their investment grows at 10% annually, it will be worth $672,750 in 20 years.

Most investors feel their biggest challenge is to ignore market volatility so they can leave their investment in place. While short-term market ups and downs may

 **normal range of outcomes**
a term used in this book to mean the range of events that an investor expects to happen, recognizing that there is uncertainty in the future and the expected outcome is a range of expected events, not a single point.

 **systematic risk**
the risk that is inherent in the market (or the system). Systematic risk cannot be eliminated through additional diversification in that market (by buying additional stocks).

make them nervous, they are lulled into thinking that if they can just ignore them, the long term is less problematic. They believe that while the market behaves in unpredictable ways over the short term, market behavior over longer periods is predictable. Investors who focus on normal market volatility, however, may be surprised to find that long-term risk is actually greater than short-term risk. This is contrary to what they believe but it becomes obvious when we take a fresh look at volatility and its long-term implications.

Figures 2.1 through 2.5 show how the same short-term market data can be plotted in various ways to predict market behavior. The figures show that using different analytical methods to interpret the very same data can lead to very different conclusions regarding the importance of short-term and long-term volatility.

Figure 2.1 shows the monthly price changes of large company stocks plotted out chronologically from 1926 to 1998. This is the short-term volatility that gets so much investor attention. Figure 2.2 plots annual rates of return. It takes the number of times from 1926 to 1998 that large company stocks had a particular annual rate of return and plots the distribution of those returns. Then it uses a mathematical distribution formula to smooth out the returns. This shows that, over time, annual rates of return show a typical bell curve or normal distribution pattern.

Figure 2.3 uses the same normal distribution formula used to create Figure 2.2 to plot the expected range of annual returns over given time periods of 1, 7, 12, and 20 years. This produces the *trumpet chart* that investors often use to support the point that the short term is riskier than the long term so "buy and hold" is a good strategy.

Figure 2.3 shows that 90% of the time in a single year an investor could expect to have returns between −15% and +50%. Over a 20-year period, however, the investor could expect between 3% and 20% returns 90% of the time. This trumpet chart appears to validate the argument that the day-to-day market fluctuation that causes investors so much angst becomes less important to their investment decisions over time.

**trumpet chart**
a chart that looks like a trumpet or horn, which shows that the range of expected returns narrows over time.

Compound Annual Return

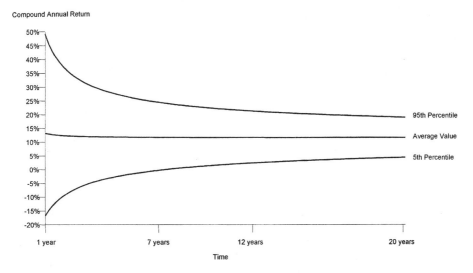

FIGURE 2.3 When the short-term volatility of large company stocks (measured in terms of annual rate of return) is plotted over time, a trumpet-shaped graph emerges that leads investors to believe that the longer they are in the market, the narrower the range of volatility they face becomes. "Buy and hold" looks like their best strategy. *Source:* Calculated by Kreitler Associates using information and data presented in Ibbotson Investment Analysis Software ©1999 Ibbotson Associates, Inc. All rights reserved. Used with permission.

The trumpet chart leads investors to believe that while there may be a great deal of uncertainty in the near term, over the long term the outcome of their investment strategy is much more certain. However, investors need to take a much closer look at the amount of risk within that narrower range of 3% to 20% return that they still face after 20 or 25 years. This *normal range of outcomes risk* is larger than many investors realize.

When the range of 3% to 20% returns is used to calculate the portfolio's expected value after 20 or 25 years, the investor's uncertainty about future portfolio value becomes greater as time goes on, not smaller, because of the impact of compounding over time. Figure 2.4 shows not only how the value of a portfolio is expected to grow, but also how the range of expected outcomes gets wider over time. The difference in expected portfolio value between a 3% and a 20% return may not be very great after one year. After 20

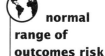

**normal range of outcomes risk** a term used in this book to mean the amount of risk investors face given normal market volatility and expected long-term rates of return.

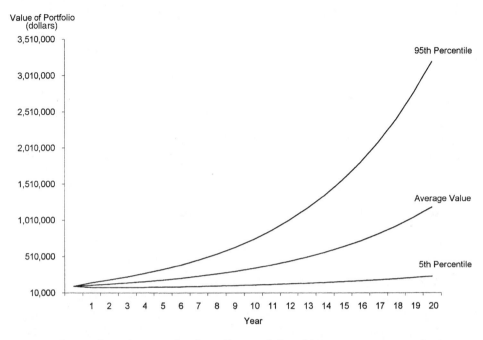

**FIGURE 2.4** When the actual value of a portfolio of large company stocks is plotted instead of annual rates of return, a different picture of long-term emerges. The range of actual values that the portfolio might attain over time becomes wider, not narrower. *Source:* Calculated by Kreitler Associates using information and data presented in Ibbotson Investment Analysis Software ©1999 Ibbotson Associates, Inc. All rights reserved. Used with permission.

years of compounding, however, the difference it makes in the value of an investor's portfolio can be substantial.

The range of possible long-term outcomes in portfolio values that investors face is much wider than the short-term trumpet chart leads them to believe. In fact, the range of long-term uncertainty is wider than the range of short-term uncertainty. The chart shows that 90% of the time, a $10,000 portfolio will grow to between $100,000 and $3.5 million. This is a huge range.

The problem with both Figures 2.3 and 2.4 is that while the first emphasizes short-term risk and the second emphasizes long-term risk it is hard to see whether short-term risk or long-term risk is larger. Figure 2.5 goes one step further by using a *semilog scale* to show both short-term and long-term risk in a way that they can be compared and understood.

This scale makes the vertical changes in actual numbers proportionate to one another. In other words, a 50% variation in the first year appears the same size on the scale as a 50% variation in the fifth, tenth, or any other subsequent year even though the actual numbers may have a much different spread. When the numbers are plotted this way in Figure 2.5, it becomes obvious that uncertainty or risk actually increases over time rather than decreasing as many investors believe.

 **semilog scale**
a graphing scale that makes all of the numbers proportional to one another; one axis uses a logarithmic scale, while the other uses a normal scale.

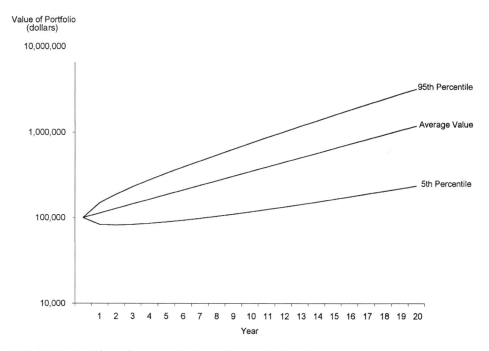

**FIGURE 2.5** When the actual value of a portfolio of large company stocks is plotted using a semilog scale, which makes the actual numbers proportional to one another, it becomes more obvious that the range of actual portfolio values that investors face becomes wider, not narrower, over time. "Buy and hold" is not the foolproof strategy for countering risk or short-term market volatility that many investors believe. *Source:* Calculated by Kreitler Associates using information and data presented in Ibbotson Investment Analysis Software ©1999 Ibbotson Associates, Inc. All rights reserved. Used with permission.

*Normal market volatility leads to increasing uncertainty or risk over time, not decreasing risk as many investors believe.*

The uncertainty about his or her portfolio's long-term value threatens an investor's whole investment program. Beating their investment goals is never a problem. But failing to achieve them or falling far short of them can be very painful. Understanding just how large this risk can be is important information every investor needs before choosing an investment strategy.

### Long-Term Risk 2: Forecasting Risk— Projecting Current Trends into the Future Can Result in Erroneous Forecasts

Many investors use historical data to predict future market behavior. The assumption that trends will continue or patterns will repeat themselves is very prevalent. It underlies most of today's investment projections, including the presumption that future market behavior will follow the trends reflected in a typical *bell curve* or normal distribution curve. Investors want to believe that they face a predictable range of future outcomes.

Investors need to realize, however, that there is a real risk that past trends may not continue into the future, that the future may be outside the expected range of outcomes by a considerable amount. This is *forecasting risk.*

In terms of their predictability, the financial world and stock markets behave more like the weather. Weather forecasting predicts future weather patterns using past data but does it in a relational way rather than a linear one. Forecasters understand that very small differences in the data they use can make a very large difference in their predictions. This is what makes both weather forecasting and stock market predictions so difficult.

When we look at weather data, it is frequently the exceptions to the normal trend lines that have the most impact on our lives—tornadoes, hurricanes, relentless

**bell curve**
symmetrical curve of a normal distribution.

**forecasting risk**
the risk that the future will not be a simple linear projection of historical trends and events.

**market crash**
a sudden drop in the market in a relatively short period of time, typically in excess of 30%.

rainstorms that bring on flooding. Similarly, exceptions to stock market trends like the 1929 worldwide *market crash*, inflation in the 1970s, the Japanese stock *market bubble* in the 1980s, or the 1997 Pacific Rim crash destroyed many investors' portfolios. The long term did these investors little good if they were wiped out.

Markets exist in the real world and in the real world there are many unpredictable things that happen. Events do not always unfold in a linear progression. Large, unexpected events can have a major impact on the lifetime performances of investors' portfolios. For example, few individuals predicted the worldwide impact of the rise of fascism, the spread of communism, or communism's ultimate failure. The fortunes of different countries may rise or fall. All these political events have had major long-term effects on millions of investors' portfolios.

---

*Unexpected events of great magnitude can destroy an investor's portfolio.*

---

There is a tendency for many U.S. investors to feel nothing can go wrong in their market. They look at the recent decade and project it into the future. While the recent past generally has been very good to investors, the U.S. market has known bad times. Deflation in the 1930s wiped out many investors' financial resources as did hyperinflation in the 1970s.

The Japanese market bubble that collapsed in 1989 is a more recent example of what can happen to investors who project past trends linearly into the future. In the 1980s, Japan was overtaking the United States in financial power. It was the envy of the world. Eager investors, assuming things could only get better, poured their money into Japanese stocks. They could neither see that an investment bubble was building nor choose the right time to get out before the market crashed. Figure 2.6 shows that nearly 10 years after the bubble burst in 1989, the Japanese market had still not recovered.

Assuming that the future is simply an extension of the past can be very dangerous for an investor's financial well-

 **market bubble**
a situation where stock prices increase way beyond rational valuations because of investor enthusiasm. Then, when investor enthusiasm peaks and wanes, stock prices collapse and the market crashes. Because it is difficult to determine when investor enthusiasm will falter, the timing of a bubble's crash is impossible to predict reliably.

**Value of Investment**
(dollars)

**FIGURE 2.6**  The Japanese market built into a bubble that burst in 1989 and after 10 years still has not recovered. *Source:* Morgan Stanley Capital International.

 **single-market risk**
the risk inherent in being in a single market, a risk which an investor cannot escape as long as he or she invests only in that market.

being. Depending on when they begin building their portfolios, investors may be exposed to the market for a very long time. An investor starting a portfolio at age 22 may be investing for up to 70 years. When investors review world history, it is easy to see that a great deal can change in 70 years. A sound investment strategy should recognize this.

### *Long-Term Risk 3: Single-Market Risk— Investors in a Single Market Cannot Escape the Risk of That Market*

A decision to hold stocks in only one market like the United States and avoid stocks in other markets creates *single-market risk*. If a portfolio is invested in a single country's market, the swings in that country's politics and economics will control the future returns of that portfolio. Within a particular market, it is very difficult to be immune from the risks of the market itself.

Economists classify the risks facing investors as systematic risk and *nonsystematic risk*. Nonsystematic risks are those unique to an individual company. They are internal factors driving a company's success or failure. A patent on a unique new product or process, opening of new overseas markets, or poor management that forces a company into bankruptcy are examples of nonsystematic risk. Investors protect themselves from nonsystematic risk by diversifying and owning more than one company.

Systematic risk is the risk inherent in the market itself (*market risk*). For instance, changing policies of the *Federal Reserve Board*, taxes, inflation, and foreign relations all affect the entire stock market. Systematic risks are external to individual companies and, taken together, they influence the direction of the market or system. Systematic risk creates broad market moves like the 1987 crash that affect all stocks. When all of an investor's portfolio is in the same market, the investor takes on all the systematic risk of that market.

---

*Investors cannot reduce market or systematic risk if they only invest in a single market.*

---

Investors can reduce the risk of their portfolios below the systematic risk of the market by diversifying into multiple asset classes such as bonds and cash. These asset classes typically have lower returns than stocks, however. So the problem with this risk management solution is that it lowers the portfolio's expected rate of return.

## Long-Term Risk 4: Buying Power Risk— The Future Buying Power of a Portfolio May Be Eroded by the Actions of a Single Government

There is the risk that in the future, a portfolio will pay an investor back in depreciated dollars. Most U.S. investors

**nonsystematic risk**
risk that is unique to individual stocks that can be eliminated by buying multiple stocks.

**market risk**
the risk inherent in a market that affects all of the stocks in it.

**Federal Reserve Board**
the board that oversees the operations of the Federal Reserve System; important for its role in setting the interest rates at which banks can borrow from the Federal Reserve System.

**dollar valuation**
the value of a stock or mutual fund or market measured in U.S. dollars instead of foreign currencies.

measure everything in U.S. dollars. Taken from this viewpoint, foreign currencies do add risk. However, an investor who is interested in protecting long-term purchasing power, and not just the *dollar valuation* of the portfolio, will recognize that having all assets denominated in one currency is actually more risky.

The question whether to hedge a portfolio against currency fluctuations is hotly debated by investment experts. They agree that the issue is important but they disagree on the best way to handle it. Most investment advisers concentrate on maximizing a portfolio's U.S. dollar returns. The Island Principle is predicated on the belief that protecting an investor's long-term buying power is more important than maximizing U.S. dollar returns.

The purpose of investing is to create wealth. At retirement, for example, an investor wants his or her portfolio to provide a particular lifestyle. Even though the investor may achieve their goal to grow their portfolio's value from, say, $200,000 to $1 million in 15 years, he or she will not achieve the objective of comfortable retirement if that $1 million no longer has the buying power they need.

Most investors are familiar with the way inflation erodes buying power. In 1998, it took $4.83 to buy what $1 bought 30 years earlier. One benefit of stock investing is that historically the returns from stock prices have exceeded inflation. So stock investors have achieved a positive rate of return.

In most cases, stocks have kept ahead of inflation. However, stocks are not a true inflation hedge because stocks and inflation are not closely correlated. In his 1993 book *Global Investing: The Professional's Guide to the World's Capital Markets*, economist Roger G. Ibbotson observed that most world markets have historically reacted negatively to inflation. Frequently stocks do poorly during periods of high inflation and do better in periods of low inflation. Investors in a single market cannot assume that stocks will protect them from inflation.

---

*Stocks are not a true inflation hedge.*

---

The investor's buying power risk is not just the risk of U.S. inflation. Consumers are affected by global events. They now buy goods and services from all over the world. When the U.S. dollar drops in value versus other currencies (regardless of whether the drop is caused by a U.S. policy or by a foreign country), foreign goods and services become more expensive. Investors need to protect themselves against this depreciation risk. Even if investors own non-U.S. stocks, they have no protection against a drop in the value of the dollar if these non-U.S. stock positions are hedged and effectively held in U.S. dollars. A portfolio with stocks denominated in many different currencies hedges this risk and increases the long-term odds that investors will achieve their investment objectives.

*A portfolio value in U.S. dollars will lose global purchasing power if the dollar declines in value. A portfolio valued in multiple currencies protects against this loss of purchasing power.*

Buying electronics is an example. If the U.S. dollar drops in value against the Japanese yen, a U.S. consumer buying a surround sound system from a Japanese manufacturer will have to pay more for exactly the same system. As we continue to move toward a global economy, U.S. consumers will buy more and more products made in foreign countries. Their future living standards are more affected by any erosion of the value of the U.S. dollar. This is a major risk.

Investors with portfolios heavily denominated in foreign currencies will face frustrating periods when a strong dollar hurts their returns. Weak foreign currencies pull down the value of non-U.S. stocks when they are converted to U.S. dollars. Global investors can face periods lasting from a few months to several years when deteriorating exchange rates test their patience. Over long periods of time, currency fluctuation is a self-correcting problem. A company in a country with a weak currency

**market selection risk**
the risk of choosing the wrong market or markets to invest in.

**global fund**
a mutual fund with holdings throughout the world including the United States; a world fund.

**market allocation**
distribution of assets to various geographic markets.

**allocation**
the process of dividing a portfolio's total assets among several different subsets such as mutual funds, geographic markets, stock sectors, or other subsets selected by the investor.

gains a price advantage when selling into global markets and, over time, its price should rise to reflect this advantage.

### Long-Term Risk 5: Market Selection Risk— The Portfolio May Be Invested in the Wrong Markets

Choosing which markets around the world to invest in is the individual investor's challenge. Investing globally requires gathering and analyzing a great deal of technical information about the market even before one can begin looking at individual stocks within it. Even the most knowledgeable professionals can make bad calls and choose the wrong markets (*market selection risk*).

High-quality global money managers have large staffs of researchers and analysts with decades of experience tracking and evaluating other markets around the world. They have access to resources and information that individual investors cannot easily tap, even in these days of freewheeling information access over the Internet.

Researching and tracking trends on even the world's 21 developed markets, however, is a job the typical individual investor does not have the time—or expertise—to tackle. Most individual investors interested in global investing attempt to close this knowledge gap by using professional money managers, typically the managers of global mutual funds.

No matter how expert a *global fund* manager is, allowing one person (including the investor himself or herself) to determine a portfolio's geographic *market allocation* still carries a high risk. The risk is that the investor as sole decision maker will not select the right markets or, worse, will choose the wrong markets. No matter how good the investor is, he or she will make mistakes. Sophisticated investors understand that buying only one stock, investing in only one market sector, or putting all of one's money into a single asset class is risky. Similarly, using a single person to determine geographic *allocation* is a risky investment strategy.

*Allowing a single decision maker to choose the portfolio's geographic allocation carries a risk similar to owning a single stock or investing in a single market.*

The Island Principle builds on many of the techniques investors already use to control the long-term risks they face. It invites investors to adopt a new perspective and extend the risk management techniques most are already using to reduce risk further.

# A Compass to Steer By

As investors set sail toward their investment goals, they need a well-mapped strategy and a reliable compass. They must steer the right course between risk—that market volatility investors are so sensitive about—and the returns they need to reach their goals. Risk and return tend to blow investors in opposite directions. Going for high returns usually means accepting a great deal of risk. Conversely, limiting risk in a portfolio usually means settling for below-average returns. Investors have traditionally dealt with risk or volatility by:

- ✔ Focusing on the long term and trying to ignore short-term market volatility.
- ✔ Investing in conservative stocks and avoiding aggressive or highly leveraged stocks.
- ✔ Adjusting the amount they hold in stocks versus less volatile asset classes.
- ✔ Using diversification to spread risk among multiple investments.

Island investors not only employ many of the same risk management techniques as other investors but also use true global investing to add new levels of diversification as a compass that helps them steer through the perils of both short-term market volatility and long-term investment risk. Greater control over these fundamental risks allows them to pursue higher returns, which, in turn, makes it more likely that they will achieve their financial goals. Before explaining how The Island Principle manages risk, it is worth reviewing how investors traditionally try to control risk in their portfolios.

## IGNORING VOLATILITY

Some investors try to handle the risks inherent in owning stocks by ignoring short-term volatility. Instead of allowing short-term price swings to influence them, their risk management strategy is to stay focused on the long term.

Investors can and should have a long-term outlook. The length of time some people will be investing is considerable. If you start an investment program like a *401(k) program* or *individual retirement account (IRA)* at age 25 and maintain it until age 95, you will invest for 70 years. A single, one-time contribution of $1,000 growing at 8% annually becomes an impressive $2.2 million after 70 years. That is the magic of compounding.

One problem with this strategy is that most investors do not really have enough courage to completely ignore short-term volatility. Notwithstanding their claims that they can handle it, when investors are faced with volatility and the threat of losses, their emotions often take over. They lose confidence in their own decision-making ability, they worry that the market and the risk they are facing have become too unpredictable, and they abandon their investment strategies. Even if their long-term strategy was sound, they then fail to achieve their goals.

A large drop in the market makes many investors anxious. They based their investment strategies on certain expectations about the market's future behavior. If the market is now behaving out of character, these investors become uncertain. They may feel they are facing an unpredictable future and decide they want out of the market. A relatively small proportion of today's investors have experience with down markets.

**401(k) program**
a popular retirement program sponsored by many companies in which income taxes are deferred.

**individual retirement account (IRA)**
a popular retirement program authorized by the federal tax code. There are two types: regular IRAs and Roth IRAs.

Controlling volatility and creating steady returns are important for keeping these anxious investors in for the long term. The Island Principle can help them because it is based on the assumptions that markets are unpredictable to begin with, that the unexpected will happen, and that volatility in any single market is less relevant if investors have stocks in multiple markets. The net results are more stable portfolios and investors more able to stick with their long-term strategies.

*Managing risk enables island investors to ignore volatility and stick to their investment strategies.*

## INVESTING IN CONSERVATIVE STOCKS

Based on the type of stocks investors buy or the style of the portfolio manager they choose, investors can make their portfolios more or less risky or volatile than the market itself. Some portfolios are inherently more volatile than the market, some less, depending on the characteristics of the stocks in them. An investor seeking higher returns may build a portfolio of more aggressive, volatile stocks or choose an aggressive portfolio manager. More risk-averse investors will choose more conservative stocks or a more conservative manager.

When investors track performance over long periods of time, they find that risk and return do go together. Stocks with the potential for higher returns tend to have higher risk or volatility. Less volatile stocks tend to have lower returns. An investor choosing a stock portfolio with half the volatility of the market would expect to have returns reduced correspondingly.

*Investors who want less volatile stocks accept lower long-term returns. Investors who want higher returns accept more volatility.*

Investors who want less volatility in their portfolios so they can confidently remain in the market face a real dilemma. Because this strategy lowers portfolio returns, there is a very real chance that they will not achieve their investment objectives.

## ADJUSTING THE AMOUNT IN STOCKS

One of the best ways to reduce the volatility of a portfolio is to limit the amount invested in stocks versus other, less volatile asset classes. Consciously or subconsciously, most investors already use this risk management technique. A portfolio 50% invested in stocks and 50% in cash or cash equivalents such as CDs, money market accounts, or Treasury bills has roughly half the volatility of a portfolio that is 100% in stocks. Historically, the real return on cash has been small or even negative after taking inflation and taxes into account. So along with its lower volatility, one would expect that this 50/50 portfolio would provide only about half the returns of a portfolio fully invested in stocks.

If investors are willing to take on more risk and volatility in the hope of improving their portfolios' long-term performance, they can increase the amount they invest in stocks. Very aggressive investors hold no cash and even borrow to increase the size of their holdings. For example, an investor with $100,000 might borrow an additional $100,000 to invest so he or she now has holdings worth $200,000. The investor now has twice the volatility on the original capital. This leveraging means the investor's profits or losses should be double those of the investor with $100,000 fully invested in stocks, less the cost of borrowing the additional money.

When an investor begins changing *both* the mix of stocks and cash and the mix of conservative versus aggressive stocks, there are an unlimited number of combinations for balancing portfolio risk and performance. Many combinations will result in the same level of risk. For example, an investor with 50% in cash and 50% in aggressive stocks that have double the volatility of the market basically faces the same amount of risk as the investor who is 100% invested in stocks with the volatility of the market.

Whether an investor should keep half of the portfolio in cash or borrow to double the stock holdings in the portfolio are questions at different ends of the risk management spectrum. Many investors consider borrowing to invest very risky. Others consider having large amounts of idle cash a waste of capital.

---

*Traditional techniques used to reduce risk also reduce returns.*

---

Changing the mix of stocks and cash or the mix of aggressive versus conservative stocks in a portfolio are both valid ways to manage risk. But using traditional techniques to reduce risk almost always means accepting lower potential returns. Taking on more risk offers the potential for higher returns. The additional risk also means investors face greater uncertainty about the expected value of their portfolios in 20 or 30 years. This future value is critical if investors are to meet their financial objectives.

## DIVERSIFICATION

Obviously, the biggest problem with commonly accepted risk reduction techniques—loading a portfolio with conservative stocks or shifting investment funds from stocks to less volatile assets like cash or Treasury bills—is that the investor is going to lower expected portfolio returns as well as lowering risk. The solution to this dilemma lies in diversification. Diversification is a very special tool for controlling risk because it permits investors to reduce risk *without* reducing potential returns. It is the most powerful risk management technique investors have at their disposal. Diversification offers investors the opportunity for simultaneously:

✔ Making portfolio returns equal to the average of the investments.

✔ Making portfolio risk lower than the average of the investments.

Figure 3.1 illustrates how investment diversification affects portfolio returns. Either Investment A or Investment B, taken alone, increases from $10,000 to $20,000 over six years. Both are volatile and neither follows a smooth path or even moves the same direction as the other all the time. The line in the middle represents a $10,000 portfolio with equal amounts of Investments A and B. This portfolio also grows to $20,000 over the long term but has much less volatility than a portfolio of A or B alone.

Most individual investors already use some level of diversification to manage risk. They understand that they should own more than one stock, own stocks in more

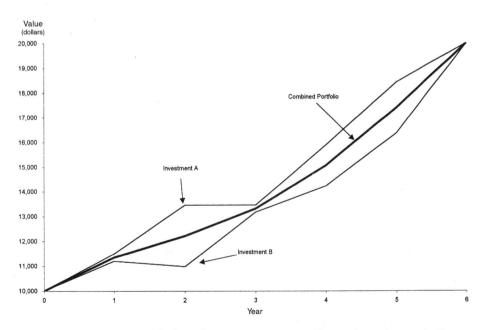

**FIGURE 3.1**   It is possible for two investments together to have less volatility over time than either investment considered alone. *Source:* Kreitler Associates.

than one sector, and own more than one kind of asset in order to have a diversified portfolio. However, diversification is a little more sophisticated than simply putting your investment nest eggs into multiple baskets. Those multiple baskets must have the right relationship to one another or, to use economic terminology, the right correlation to one another in order for diversification to work its risk reduction magic.

## CORRELATION: THE KEY TO DIVERSIFICATION

*Correlation* describes the way that two investments, whether they be stocks, markets, or asset classes, tend to move relative to one another. *Low correlation* means that investments, whether stocks or markets or asset classes, tend to move differently from one another. The movement of one tends to be independent of the movement of the other. High correlation means they tend to move similarly. Knowing the movement of one, an investor can generally predict the direction the other will move.

Economists use a complex mathematical formula to calculate correlation coefficients that measure how much the price movement of one investment affects the movement of another:

✔ A correlation coefficient of 1.0 means two investments are perfectly correlated. They move together in the same direction.

✔ A correlation coefficient of 0.5 means half the movement of one investment is reflected in the movement of the other.

✔ A correlation coefficient of zero means there is no correlation between the two assets. They move independently of each other.

✔ A negative correlation coefficient of −1.0 means that prices of the two investments move in opposite directions.

**correlation**
a description of how the prices of two investments, indexes, or markets move in relationship to the other.

 **low correlation**
a relationship where the movement of one investment does not appear to be greatly affected by the change in price of another investment.

If two investments are perfectly correlated (meaning they have a correlation coefficient of 1.0), putting both of them together in a portfolio gives the investor a return that is the average of the returns of the two investments, but it does not reduce risk in the portfolio. The investor does have multiple "baskets" but without gaining the benefits of diversification. When diversification involves the deliberate choice of investments with low or negative correlation, it permits an investor to lower the risk of the portfolio without lowering returns.

*Low correlation between two or more investments is essential in order for diversification to reduce risk in a portfolio.*

Diversification into markets with low correlation is key to The Island Principle's global investment strategy. It creates multiple options for investors to balance risk and return within their portfolios, enabling them to:

✔ Reduce risk while maintaining the same level of returns.

✔ Increase returns without increasing risks.

✔ Both reduce risk and increase returns.

When investors talk about market volatility or risk, they are usually referring to the market's up-and-down movements in raw numbers. For example, broadcasters will announce at the end of the day that the market was up or down so many points compared to its closing on the previous day. Investment professionals, on the other hand, assign a slightly more sophisticated meaning to risk. They measure risk as standard deviation, a statistical measure of the up-and-down price movements of a stock or a market around its *mean* value. Standard deviation is sometimes expressed as a raw number, sometimes as a percent. In other words, a standard deviation of 0.25 may also be called 25% standard deviation or 25% risk.

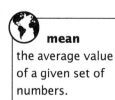
**mean**
the average value of a given set of numbers.

For many investors, standard deviation is an abstract term. Comparing the standard deviation of a portfolio against the standard deviation of a known benchmark helps to give this risk measurement a relationship they can grasp more easily. For example, the risk or standard deviation of the Standard & Poor's 500 Index was 17.6 from 1970 to 1998. A portfolio with a standard deviation of 13.2 would have approximately 25% less risk than the S&P 500 Index. Table 3.1 shows the standard deviation of several major market indexes.

Investment analysts use a combination of expected returns, standard deviations, and correlation coefficients to compare one portfolio mix to another to determine which is more likely to enable investors to reach their objectives. A simple example using just two investments with the same expected return and the same risk or standard deviation is useful to help understand how diversification into multiple investments with low correlation can reduce risk without affecting returns (Table 3.2). Investment A has an expected return of 12% per year and carries

---

**TABLE 3.1 Standard Deviations of U.S. Bonds and Major Market Indexes, 1970 to 1998**

| Index or Market | Standard Deviation |
|---|---|
| Long-term U.S. government bonds | 11.71% |
| S&P 500 Index | 17.60% |
| EAFE | 19.32% |
| World Index | 16.19% |
| Japan | 20.83% |
| United Kingdom | 25.75% |
| Germany | 20.29% |
| France | 24.31% |

*Note:* This is a measure of the volatility of each market on a monthly basis. The higher the number, the greater the volatility. Of these indexes, the Morgan Stanley Capital International World Index has been the least volatile. The United Kingdom has been the most volatile. *Source:* Morgan Stanley Capital International.

**TABLE 3.2  Diversification Using Low Correlation Can Reduce Overall Portfolio Risk**

| Correlation Coefficient between A and B | Portfolio Return | Standard Deviation (Risk) of the Portfolio |
|---|---|---|
| 1.0 | 12% | 15% |
| 0.6 | 12% | 13.42% |
| 0 | 12% | 10.61% |
| −1.0 | 12% | 0% |

*Note:* Assuming that investments A and B both have a risk (as measured by standard deviation) of 15%, that the investor expects a 12% return from each of them, and that the portfolio consists of equal amounts of A and B, note how portfolio risk decreases as the correlation between A and B decreases. *Source:* Kreitler Associates.

a risk of 15% as measured by its standard deviation. Investment B also has an expected return of 12% and also has a risk factor of 15% as measured by standard deviation. The sample portfolio has equal amounts of A and B.

Since the performance of a portfolio is the weighted average of the individual investments within it, our example portfolio has an expected return of 12%. Calculating the portfolio's risk level (as measured by its volatility or up-and-down movement) is more complicated than calculating its expected return. Portfolio volatility is based not only on the risk factor of each investment in the portfolio but also on how these investments move relative to one another or, in other words, how they are correlated.

If Investments A and B have a correlation coefficient of 1.0, meaning they move together, the risk of the portfolio is the average of the two investments or 15%. If Investments A and B have a correlation coefficient of 0.6, which means that only 60% of the movement of one can be explained by the movement of the other, portfolio risk drops to 13.42%. If Investments A and B had a correlation coefficient of −1.0, meaning they tended to move in opposite directions, portfolio risk would drop to 0. This is what

professional traders using hedging strategies strive for when they want to provide a particular level of returns with little or no risk.

The statistical number crunching required to calculate portfolio risk is highly complex but Table 3.2 shows the effect of correlation on portfolio risk. It shows that the risk of the overall portfolio can be lower than that of the lowest-risk investment in the portfolio depending on the correlation of those investments. Diversification using investments with low correlation is almost magical in its ability to reduce risk without reducing returns. It works whether the investor is dealing with individual stocks, asset classes, or multiple geographic markets.

*Diversification into investments with low correlation is a way to reduce risk without reducing returns.*

## UNDERSTANDING DIVERSIFICATION

Few investors completely use the full potential of diversification to help them manage risk or how to diversify without adversely affecting returns. They typically choose multiple stocks from multiple sectors and assume they have done an adequate job. More sophisticated investors also spread their investments among various asset classes such as stocks, bonds, and cash to reduce risk. As they strive to manage portfolio risk, investors typically use increasing levels of diversification.

### Owning Multiple Stocks

Investors and investment advisers universally agree that putting all of your investment dollars into a single company—or even just a few companies—would be an incredibly risky thing to do. Investors should own multiple stocks.

Economists present ample evidence that investors

are not adequately compensated for the risk they take on if they own a single stock. The U.S. market prices all stocks relatively efficiently. This eliminates bargains. Investors using diversified portfolios, and thus not worried about the risk of a single stock, bid a stock's price up and eliminate the return premium a one-stock investor needs to be compensated for the additional risk. The market simply does not permit investors to be adequately rewarded for the risk they take when owning a single stock.

Owning only a single stock maximizes the investor's exposure to nonsystematic risk, the risk unique to an individual company. It is the risk that a new product will not come out on time as promised to its distributors, that there will be financial surprises like a component's cost doubling overnight, or that the company's president will die suddenly without an heir apparent to take up the reins.

It is easy to see graphically in Figure 3.2 how owning multiple stocks can reduce this nonsystematic risk. The nonsystematic risk of a portfolio containing a single stock is shown by line A–B. A single stock carries the most risk. The portfolio's overall risk decreases as more stocks are added. By the time investors own 30 or so stocks (line C–D), they have eliminated nonsystematic risk and adequately protected themselves against an unexpected happening that will adversely affect one of those stocks.

*Owning multiple stocks reduces nonsystematic risk.*

### Owning Multiple Sectors

As investors add more stocks to their portfolios to reduce risk, they need to pay attention to the correlation of those stocks to one another in order to reduce risk. Stocks that

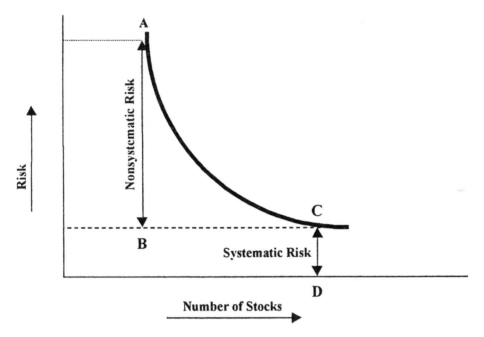

**FIGURE 3.2** Owning multiple stocks helps investors reduce nonsystematic risk (the risk unique to each stock or sector) but it does not enable them to escape the systematic risk of the market itself. *Source:* Kreitler Associates.

are similar (that is, they have a correlation of 1.0) do not provide diversification against risk. To do that, investors need stocks with low correlation. Typically investors seek that low correlation by choosing stocks from different industry sectors.

Market analysts group companies into sectors based on common characteristics. Technology, utilities, transportation, and consumer goods are all examples of industry sectors. Because of their common characteristics, the prices of companies within a given sector frequently move the same way in response to outside events and influences. So their price movements are *highly correlated.*

New federal regulations on emission standards will affect all automakers. All electric utilities are affected by

**highly correlated**
a relationship where two investments move closely together or exactly alike.

the deregulation of electricity. Holding multiple companies within a sector may protect investors against the unexpected event that is unique to that company (the company's new product just bombed and wiped out all of last year's profits) but it cannot protect them against an event that affects all companies in that sector (a new federal regulation will increase the entire industry's costs dramatically).

In order for stock diversification to help investors reduce nonsystematic risk, they must own stocks in different sectors that they not only feel will do well in the future but which also have low correlation with each other. For example, electric utility stocks and computer stocks would be expected to have a low correlation because one is an energy stock and the other is a technology stock. Coal mining companies and oil companies, however, would be expected to have a higher correlation because they are both energy stocks.

*Owning stocks in multiple sectors reduces nonsystematic risk.*

The goal of a diversified portfolio is to own stocks that will move differently. Grouping your stock holdings by sector in a summary similar to that provided by many mutual funds in their *annual reports* is an excellent way to keep track of both sectors and stocks. Figuring out how closely various sectors are correlated is often a judgment call.

**annual report**
a report provided by a mutual fund company summarizing its activities for the prior fiscal year; frequently an excellent source of data about the mutual fund.

### Owning Multiple Asset Classes

Owning multiple stocks or sectors with low correlation helps investors eliminate the nonsystematic risks they face in investing. When adding more stocks to the portfolio no longer reduces risk, the risk remaining is systematic risk (line C–D in Figure 3.2), the risk inherent in the market. This is the risk that a government policy may change and affect all stock prices. Owning more stocks in that same market cannot reduce this systematic risk below a certain level because when an event influences an entire market, it influences every stock in that market. Investors who put all of their stock holdings in a single market cannot escape the systematic risk of that market.

Owning multiple asset classes helps investors solve this dilemma. Stocks, bonds, real estate, and cash are separate asset classes. Again, the theory is similar to that for stocks. Because various asset classes have different correlations, they will move differently. For example, a change in interest rates tends to affect real estate and Treasury bills differently. Stocks and bonds tend to move differently.

*Owning multiple asset classes is a way to overcome systematic risk.*

Economic researchers have given diversification among asset classes, or *asset allocation*, special attention. Nobel prizewinners *Harry Markowitz*, James Tobin, and William Sharpe have contributed at various times to a body of investment ideas that has come to be known as *Modern Portfolio Theory*. Markowitz first published his ideas in his 1952 doctoral thesis, but it took more than two decades before Modern Portfolio Theory began to have a major influence on institutional investors. Now individual investors as well are gradually beginning to benefit from its ideas.

Modern Portfolio Theory holds that a given market is relatively efficient. Everyone has the same information, so picking individual stocks adds little to portfolio performance. This runs counter to the belief of individual investors who go to great effort researching and picking individual stocks. Instead, Modern Portfolio Theory says that the main determinant of your portfolio's performance is the mix of assets in it.

 **asset allocation** distribution of investment funds among asset types such as stocks, bonds, or cash, among stocks themselves, among sectors, among markets, or among any other subsector chosen by the investor.

 **Markowitz, Harry** Nobel prizewinning economist who did work in 1952 to define and calculate the efficient frontier.

**Modern Portfolio Theory**
a group of investment theories that have been developed by economists starting in the 1950s with a ground-breaking dissertation by Harry Markowitz.

*Asset allocation, not stock selection or market timing, is the main determinant of portfolio performance.*

Research studies published in *Financial Analysts Journal* by Gary Brinson, Randolph Hood, Brian Singer, and Gilbert Beebower in 1986 and by Brinson, Singer, and Beebower in 1991 confirmed this. These studies covered the investment returns of professional money managers from 1974 to 1985 and showed that, over time, 90% of a portfolio's *movement* was due to the money manager's asset allocation. The remaining 10% could be attributed to the manager's investment expertise (ability to pick stocks and time transactions).

A recent study by Roger G. Ibbotson and Paul Kaplan revisited this issue and looked at it from a different perspective. First, Ibbotson and Kaplan looked at asset allocation and confirmed the results of the Brinson et al. study that allocation is responsible for 90% of a portfolio's *movement*. Then, however, they looked at investment expertise and compared *manager versus manager* (or portfolio movement across managers, to use their terminology). When one manager was compared to others, they found that only 40% of the portfolio's movement was due to asset allocation while the manager's investment expertise explained the remaining 60%.

Interestingly, when Ibbotson and Kaplan looked at portfolio *returns* as distinct from portfolio movement, they found that 100% of a portfolio's long-term rate of return could be attributed to asset allocation. This underscores even more dramatically the importance of asset allocation.

Earlier we discussed how diversification can reduce risk without lowering performance as other risk management techniques commonly do. Just as investors can put several stocks with low correlation coefficients into their portfolios to reduce risk, they can mix several asset classes with correlation coefficients less than 1.0 to reduce portfolio risk.

*Diversifying into asset classes with low correlation can reduce risk.*

Using correlation coefficients, standard deviations, expected returns, and some mathematical formulas developed by Markowitz, analysts versed in Modern Portfolio Theory determine an optimum mix of asset classes. This optimum mix is not a single point, but a whole series of points along a curve. For each level of risk there is a unique mix of assets that provides an optimum return for a specified risk. Markowitz dubbed this optimum curve the *efficient frontier*.

Each investor could be at a different point on this curve, based on his or her risk tolerance. If a portfolio's asset mix is not on the efficient frontier, investors can change the asset mix to move it there. By changing to this optimum mix, they can reduce risk, increase returns, or do both. They will increase the efficiency of their portfolio.

The curved line in Figure 3.3 shows an efficient frontier for two asset classes—stocks and bonds for the period 1970 to 1998. Risk is measured on the horizontal axis. Return is measured on the vertical axis. Each point on the efficient frontier is a different optimum mix of stocks and bonds. The appropriate point on the efficient frontier will be different for each investor depending on the returns they are after and their tolerance for risk.

 **efficient frontier** a computer-modeled curve charting the optimum return for two or more investments for any given level of risk.

*Investors can adjust the levels of risk and return in their portfolios by moving to different points along the efficient frontier.*

An investor whose asset allocation between stocks and bonds is not on this efficient frontier can improve his or her position simply by adjusting the allocation so the asset mix is on the efficient frontier. For instance, an

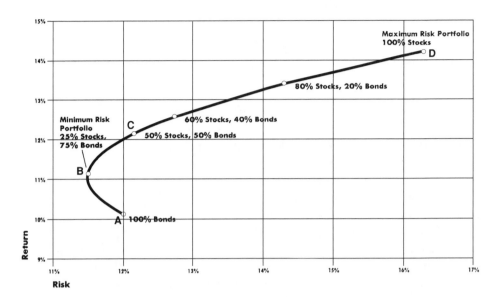

**FIGURE 3.3**  Modern Portfolio Theory uses complex mathematical formulas to create an efficient frontier showing what mix of assets would have produced the optimum level of returns for a specified level of risk. This example of a portfolio containing stocks and bonds clearly shows that a conservative investor could enjoy higher returns and less risk with a portfolio invested 75% in bonds and 25% in stocks than by investing in bonds alone. An aggressive investor seeking maximum returns (100% stocks) would have to take on the most risk. *Source:* Calculated by Kreitler Associates using information and data presented in Ibbotson Investment Analysis Software, ©1999 Ibbotson Associates, Inc. All rights reserved. Used with permission.

investor who is 100% in bonds (A) could move to a mix of 75% bonds and 25% stocks (B) to have a portfolio with less risk and higher performance.

This may seem counterintuitive to investors who have long heard that bonds are less risky than stocks. But as a riskier asset (stock) is added to a portfolio of conservative bonds the risk of the portfolio drops because they move differently; that is, they have low correlation. Not only does risk drop but, with a 25% allocation to stocks, returns also increase. Again, this is the magic of diversification with low correlation.

Or the investor could move to 50% bonds and 50%

stocks (C) to have a portfolio with the same risk as one 100% invested in bonds but achieve 2% better performance. Moving further up the efficient frontier to 100% stocks (D) would increase both risk and return.

Asset allocation provides investors with a great deal of control over risk and performance of their portfolios. Portfolio theory explains why asset diversification works. Its concepts provide investors with a major tool for controlling risks and returns. Investors do not need to know portfolio theory's various mathematical formulas nor use sophisticated computer software in order to apply the concepts to their portfolios. Those who understand these concepts and the advantages of a portfolio containing multiple asset classes are better prepared to understand The Island Principle.

## Owning Stocks in Multiple Markets

The application of portfolio theory to non-U.S. markets has encouraged many investors to drop their bias against foreign investing and expand into global markets to further diversify their portfolios.

Figure 3.4 shows an efficient frontier curve plotted for U.S. and non-U.S. stocks as though they were two asset classes. Typically, investors use the S&P 500 index and the EAFE index to do this. Because the lowest risk occurs at the point where assets are allocated 25% to international (foreign) stocks and 75% to U.S. stocks, this chart has been a major factor in convincing many investors that approximately 25% of their stock portfolios should be foreign stocks. Once again, a portfolio whose allocation of U.S. stocks and non-U.S. stocks that is not on the efficient frontier curve can be improved to reduce risk or increase returns just by changing the portfolio's allocation to move it to this line.

*Investors can reduce the risk of a portfolio 100% invested in U.S. stocks by adding foreign stocks to it.*

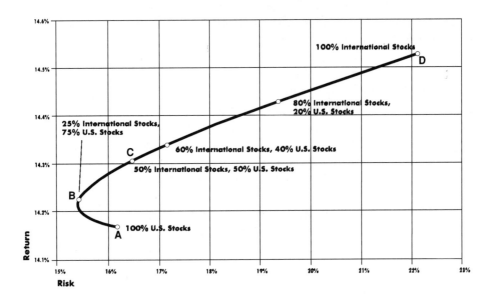

**FIGURE 3.4** This efficient frontier shows the optimum mix of U.S. and international (or foreign, non-U.S.) stocks from 1970 to 1998 at various levels of risk. It shows that, over that historical time period, a portfolio invested 25% in international stocks and 75% in U.S. stocks offered higher returns with less risk than a portfolio of U.S. stocks alone. *Source:* Calculated by Kreitler Associates using information and data presented in Ibbotson Investment Analysis Software, ©1999 Ibbotson Associates, Inc. All rights reserved. Used with permission.

The problem remains, however, that this chart encourages investors diversifying into non-U.S. markets to treat U.S. and non-U.S. as though the world offered them only two asset classes. In 1968, Herbert G. Grubel took the work of Markowitz and Tobin and expanded it to international markets. He concluded that a stock portfolio diversified to *11 countries* increased returns or reduced risk versus an all-U.S. portfolio. Grubel's work got little attention. The Island Principle suggests that investors have more choices than 11 countries.

Again, it may seem counterintuitive to investors who have been reminded over and over again by their advisers about the "special risks" of "foreign investing" to include non-U.S. stocks in a portfolio in order to reduce risk. However, this follows the same logic that tells investors it is less risky to own multiple stocks than it is to own a single stock and less risky to own multiple asset classes rather than a single asset class, even if some of those stocks or assets are riskier. The Island Principle says that owning stocks in multiple countries (markets) is less risky than owning stocks in a single market. It also says that using multiple decision makers to choose those markets is less risky than using a single decision maker.

# Chapter 4

# **Mapping Goals**

T he Island Principle is a means to an end, not a goal in itself. It is a risk management strategy suited to investors whose goal is long-term appreciation with a better than average level of returns. Because it allows investors to control their portfolios' volatility, The Island Principle also gives investors the option to include a greater proportion of stocks or select some riskier investments which may, in turn, increase their portfolios' overall returns. It is an ideal strategy for many individual investors but it is not appropriate for everyone.

> *The Island Principle gives investors the option to include a greater proportion of stocks or select some riskier investments which may, in turn, increase their portfolios' overall returns.*

To develop and carry through any investment plan like The Island Principle, investors first need to understand just what kind of investors they are. Many investors do not fully acknowledge the motives behind their investment choices. These motives, as well as investors' long-term goals, are critical in determining what level of risk they can tolerate, what level of returns they need to achieve to meet their goals, and what investment strategy will be appropriate for them. Understanding their motives is necessary before they can take several key steps toward meeting their financial objectives:

✔ Investors must set appropriate risk and return goals that will meet their real financial needs.

✔ Investors must choose a strategy that is likely to meet their goals.

✔ Investors must implement that strategy.

✔ Investors must monitor the progress of their investment plan.

These steps look simple on paper. Each one, however, can be a challenge. Sticking to an investment strategy over the long term can be really difficult. Volatility affects investors psychologically. It can create doubt and uncertainty that make them abandon an otherwise good strategy before it has a chance to work. Peer pressure from relatives, friends, and coworkers who approach investing as a competitive sport makes it hard to resist going after short-term bragging rights about individual investment killings. The media bombards us with business news hype that tempts investors into frequent buying and selling, even risky day trading.

Getting away from these distractions to the perspective of our hypothetical island allows investors to take an objective look at some typical investment motives and goals as well as the strategies investors use to pursue them. Depending on an individual investor's personal investment goals, The Island Principle may or may not be an appropriate strategy for reaching those goals. A fresh perspective also enables investors to think about their personal approach to risk and returns. They need to define their risk and return objectives in order to implement an investment strategy they are comfortable with and then use them to monitor the progress of their investment program. Here are goals of some typical investors.

# GOAL: INVESTING FOR SPORT

Many people invest for the sport or fun of it. They partici-
pate in investing as a game of risk, somewhat akin to gam-
bling. Their goal is to be in on the action. The sport
investor's basic strategy is to follow his or her gut feeling
or a hot tip from the guy in the elevator. They do not understand that they are buying a real company—what it
does or makes, its management expertise, or its expected
financial outlook. Stocks are just numbers printed in the
newspaper which happen to be printed in the financial
section rather than in the sports section with the race results. The more frequently they trade, the more their
adrenaline flows and the more rewarding their investing
becomes to them.

Sport investors are a stockbroker's delight because
their frequent trading puts more money in the broker's
paycheck. Their recurrent multiple transactions help discount houses flourish. The sport investor's *trading costs*
and taxes can be significant, and these eat into any profits
they may realize.

People who buy stocks for sport are often drawn
into the market at exactly the wrong time. Sport investors easily get swept up in the great enthusiasm that
accompanies a fast-rising bull market. Friends boast
about the money they are making. The press beats the
drums about how well the market is doing and makes it
look as though it is riskier to be standing on the sidelines than to be in the market. Buying is easy and fun.
The advent of easy, fast Internet trading is just what
these stock junkies ordered.

Most investors fail to realize it is normal to want to
buy stocks in periods of euphoria. Everyone wants in
when the market is hot. The increased demand pushes
stock prices higher and higher. It is also normal for investors to want to sell when the market is depressed. The
increased selling pushes prices down further, which, in
turn, encourages more selling. Sport investors are particularly vulnerable to this psychological trap. Like a flock of
sheep, they typically follow the market and stock prices

 **trading
costs**
the cost of buy-
ing and selling a
stock, typically
commissions.

up and down, accelerating the trends by their very normal psychological reactions to them.

In a rising market, sport investors are likely to attribute any gains to their skill because they don't recognize that the market is lifting *all* portfolios, not just theirs. When the market drops and profits are harder to come by, the sport investor tends to leave the market and move to other activities. They stay out of the market during the dreary days when stocks are hitting lows, precisely the time that disciplined, long-term investors are hunting for bargains to build their portfolios.

---

*An adrenaline rush from frequent trading is the sport investor's goal.*

---

The sport investor's goal is a short-term coup on an individual stock. A long-term investment strategy like The Island Principle that focuses on favorable overall returns on invested capital seems dull and slow to this kind of investor. These investors are too impatient to stick with and benefit from any long-term strategy. Unless they change their short-term focus, these investors are unlikely to gain anything from The Island Principle.

## GOAL: MATCHING THE MARKET

Many investors and even investment professionals believe that matching or beating a particular market index is very important. They make the mistake of thinking that matching the market is their investment goal when it is really only a strategy. This thinking is ingrained in many investors.

In practice, matching the market is a very easy goal to accomplish. The strategy is simple and straightforward. All an investor has to do is buy a mutual fund that tracks the particular stock market index such as the S&P 500 that they want to match. In one easy step, market matchers can achieve their goal. No other buying or selling decision is required.

There are, however, three problems with this approach to investing. First, investors really only want to achieve this supposed goal when a market is moving up, not as it moves down. Typically, investors choose the strategy of matching a market index near the end of a bull market when it appears, looking backward, that investing in the index has worked for many years. Looking forward, everyone is predicting the trend will continue and the strategy of matching an index will continue to work. They forget that bear markets always follow bull markets. Most market matchers do not have the stomach to follow their strategy during prolonged bear markets. Think of the impact on an investor using an index-matching strategy during the 1929 market crash.

Second, it is deceptively easy to pick the right index after the fact. All an investor has to do is look at the historical data and choose the index with the best performance record. Picking the best-performing market index in advance is luck. Fickle investors may change their benchmark index every few years and find to their frustration that they are never using the right one.

Third, investors forget that the composition of an index changes over time. This change may be counter to what an investor is trying to achieve, and the investor has no control over the change. When an index is originally created, it contains a group of stocks chosen to be representative of the market. Over time, the original mix changes, primarily because indexes are weighted by capitalization. That means that to calculate the value of the index (the *index capitalization*), analysts multiply the value of each stock times the number of shares of that stock in the index.

For example, the S&P 500 index was originally designed as a broad-based index of large company stocks in the United States. Due to the explosive growth in the technology sector, however, by September 1999 technology stocks represented 21% of the total value of the S&P 500 (at the same time, the technology sector contributed only about 5% of the gross domestic product).

 **index capitalization** the total value of all of the stocks in an index, calculated by taking the market price of each stock in the index times the number of shares, and then adding them all together.

**index fund**
a mutual fund that has a portfolio designed to simulate the movement of a particular market index.

So investors who bought an *index fund* tracking the S&P 500 in 1993 thinking they were buying a well-rounded portfolio of large company stocks would have found their portfolios heavily weighted by much riskier technology stocks.

The role of Japan in the EAFE index is another example of how an index can be skewed by capitalization. The EAFE index is considered the benchmark for most non-U.S. stock portfolios. In 1970, Japan comprised 14% of the EAFE index. At the top of the Japanese market bubble in 1990, Japanese stocks accounted for 58% of the index. Investors trying to match the EAFE index while the bubble was building would have loaded their portfolios with more and more overpriced Japanese stocks and set themselves up for the Japanese market crash. Non-U.S. fund managers found it difficult to match the EAFE index when the Japanese market was rising without a large exposure to Japanese stocks. After the Japanese stock market fell, it became easier for them to match or beat the EAFE index. By January 1999, Japan's portion of the EAFE index had dropped to 21%.

Finally, and most important, investors who think matching the market is their goal are confusing means with ends. Matching an index has no direct relationship to an investor's current financial objectives or future needs. Matching a market index can be a *strategy* for reaching an investment goal. But in and of itself, it has no relevance to an investor's financial needs or aspirations.

*Matching or beating the market is an investment strategy, not a goal.*

Matching the market through one of its indexes should not be a goal for most investors. It is a strategy. Investors who try to match a market index are saying they accept 100% of that market's volatility and they are satisfied with whatever rate of return it provides.

They are letting the market determine their financial well-being.

Market matchers who rethink their investment goals will find that The Island Principle offers them a better strategy for achieving real, long-term goals. It allows them to enjoy less risk while maintaining their level of returns or to maintain the same level of risk while they go after higher returns. Their financial future is no longer determined by a single market index.

## GOAL: PRESERVING CAPITAL

Retaining every dollar of their capital is the goal set by some investors. Their strategy is to put their money into savings accounts and safe investments like bank certificates of deposit or U.S. Treasury bills.

These investors are extremely risk averse. If they have $50,000 now, they want to be guaranteed that they will still have that $50,000 tomorrow, the next day, and a year from now. They never want the value to drop below $50,000.

This makes sense for investors who need to have their money available on relatively short notice. For example, they may want cash available to pay college tuition bills in a year or they may want money available for financial emergencies such as medical expenses or a job loss.

For investors with a longer time horizon, however, the objective of preserving capital is actually self-defeating. The fear of losing capital over the short term almost guarantees that these investors will have poor returns over the long term.

Since 1925, funds held safely in investments like savings accounts have grown at 3.8% per year while U.S. large company stocks have grown at 11.2%, according to *Ibbotson Associates, Inc.* At these rates over a 20-year time horizon, $1,000 invested in a savings account would grow to $2,108 while $1,000 in large cap stocks would grow to $8,358, approximately four times the value of the savings account.

**Ibbotson Associates, Inc.** a consulting firm located in Chicago, Illinois, that collects and distributes comprehensive historical stock market data and provides consulting services to investment professionals and institutional clients.

*Keeping funds in low-yielding savings or money market accounts is an inefficient use of capital and may prevent investors from reaching their long-term goals.*

The Island Principle uses global diversification to control volatility and risk so investors who want to preserve capital can feel more confident about putting that capital into stocks and other vehicles with potentially higher returns. It can increase the comfort level of risk-averse investors so that they can dare to do better with their portfolios.

## GOAL: FIXED INCOME

The objective of other investors, frequently retirees, is to receive a fixed level of income for the rest of their lives. Their typical investment strategy is to put their entire portfolio into long-term bonds with fixed interest rates. Another strategy is to purchase an immediate annuity providing a fixed monthly income for life. A company pension works the same way as an immediate annuity except that the investor's former employer makes the annuity purchase to fund the retiree's pension. Many retirees stay away from stocks because they perceive them as too risky.

Investors seeking fixed income are typically long-term investors. They need sufficient lifetime income for themselves and often for a spouse as well. That's a period of time that can easily be 30 years or more. It is crucial for these investors to understand how inflation can erode the real value of both their periodic payments and their principal over those decades (Table 4.1).

For example, an annual cash flow of $30,000 in today's dollars will be worth only about $20,000 in real dollars after 20 years given 2% inflation. If inflation were 4%, their buying power would drop to the equivalent of less than $13,700 in today's dollars.

| TABLE 4.1   Future Buying Power of $30,000 after 20 Years | |
|---|---|
| Inflation Rate | Buying Power in Terms of Today's Dollars |
| 1% | $24,586 |
| 2% | $20,189 |
| 3% | $16,610 |
| 4% | $13,692 |
| 5% | $11,307 |
| 6% | $ 9,354 |
| 7% | $ 7,752 |
| 8% | $ 6,436 |
| 9% | $ 5,353 |
| 10% | $ 4,459 |

*Note:* As investors plan for future needs, they must stay aware of the effects of inflation on their future buying power. This table shows the future buying power of $30,000 in today's dollars at various rates of inflation over 20 years. *Source:* Kreitler Associates.

*The goal of receiving fixed income leaves investors exposed to the risk of reduced buying power over time.*

Investors seeking a fixed income over a long period of time can benefit from The Island Principle's strategy of using a diversified global portfolio to achieve higher total returns without increasing overall risk. Historically, a bond portfolio with some stocks has had less volatility than a portfolio 100% in bonds. Psychologically, anything that can be done to reduce the volatility they must face when holding stocks will increase the willingness of these investors to use stocks in their portfolios. By diversifying their stock holdings across multiple markets, The Island Principle not only makes it possible for these investors to reduce the risk (volatility) in their portfolios but also gives them the opportunity to increase their returns.

## GOAL: GROWING INCOME

Other investors want income from their portfolios but they want that income to increase over time to protect their future buying power from effects of inflation. These investors need a portfolio with some capital growth that will generate increasing income over time. Typically their strategy is to include dividend-paying stocks, real estate, and possibly inflation-indexed bonds in their portfolios. All of these investments historically have provided either growing income or protection against inflation.

In contrast to the investor seeking a fixed annual income, investors who want income plus capital growth to offset inflation realize they must sacrifice some income in their earlier investing years in order to have more income in the future. Part of their portfolio's total returns must remain in the portfolio so their capital can grow.

For example, if long-term quality bonds are yielding 6%, a $500,000 investment will provide $30,000 annual income. If, however, an investor put that same $500,000 into a mixed portfolio of stocks and bonds providing an 8% total return, he or she could take out 4% ($20,000) as current income and add the rest of the dividends and interest to capital. This would allow the capital base to grow at a rate of 4%. If the investor continues this pattern of returns and distributions, in 20 years annual income will grow to $43,800 while capital more than doubles.

Table 4.2 and Figure 4.1 show how a portfolio managed for a steady level of income compares to a portfolio managed for growing income over time. Investors interested in income from their portfolios obvi-

| TABLE 4.2 Comparison of the Results of Investing $500,000 for Income versus Growth | | |
|---|---|---|
| | *Invested for Level Income* | *Invested for Growing Income* |
| Total portfolio return | 6% | 8% |
| Original investment | $500,000 | $500,000 |
| Current yield | 6% | 4% |
| Current income | $30,000 | $20,000 |
| Portfolio annual growth | 0% | 4% |
| Portfolio value in 20 years | $500,000 | $1,095,000 |
| Income in 20 years | $30,000 | $43,800 |
| *Source:* Kreitler Associates. | | |

ously need to make a crucial decision as to whether they want:

✔ Level income that will be higher in the earlier years but may not keep up with inflation over time, or

✔ Growing income that may be less initially but which will grow over time to offset inflation.

---

*Investors who want income plus growth must sacrifice some current income in order to have more income in the future.*

---

The Island Principle's global perspective on investing can help these investors see the trade-offs they must make between current income and future income more clearly. The Island Principle can help them manage the risk of their portfolios so that they are more comfortable holding a larger proportion of stock or holding riskier stocks, either of which can provide them with higher long-term returns.

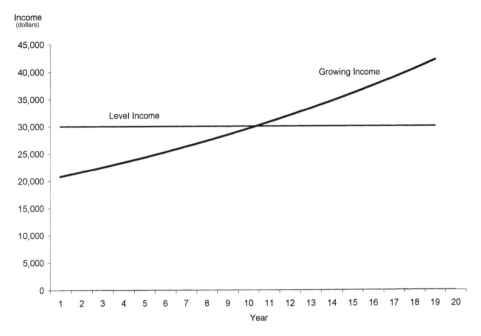

**FIGURE 4.1** Graphing the data from Table 4.2 makes the difference between investing for level income and investing for growth more evident. *Source:* Kreitler Associates.

## GOAL: TOTAL RETURNS

Traditionally, many investors regard portfolio income and portfolio growth as separate categories and treat them differently. They consider interest and dividends as income and appreciation in the value of the stocks or bonds in their portfolios as growth. Traditional investors are willing to spend income but they religiously reinvest any capital growth in their portfolios. "Never use capital" is often their mantra.

Investors who focus on total portfolio return differ from these traditionalists in a subtle but important way. They do not distinguish between income and growth. Instead, they concentrate on the combined total from both and its effect on the overall portfolio. Psychologically this is very hard to do because we are warned never to spend capital.

In the previous example of an investor seeking

growing income, the portfolio's total return was 8% with 4% coming from dividends and interest and 4% coming from capital appreciation. The investor focusing on total return would base the decision regarding how much to withdraw from the portfolio on how much current income versus how much future portfolio growth he or she wants. Withdrawing 2% of the income permits the portfolio to grow at 6%. Withdrawing 4% permits the portfolio to grow at 4%. Since *annual return* and annual portfolio value fluctuate from year to year, investors focusing on total returns could use a three-year moving average to calculate the base they use to determine how much they want to withdraw.

Concentrating on total portfolio return provides investors much more flexibility in selecting their investment strategies. A stock's dividend or a bond's interest becomes less important when making investment decisions. Instead the investor seeks opportunities for total returns.

---

*Investors whose goal is to achieve superior overall portfolio returns concentrate on the total and ignore the split between income and capital growth.*

---

Investors seeking total returns can benefit from The Island Principle because it expands their ability to seek higher total returns while limiting risk. It is a logical extension of diversification strategies already used by these investors.

 **annual return**
the return of portfolio or mutual fund when adjusted to an annual basis, typically calculated as a geometric return. The actual calculation can be very complicated particularly if there have been cash contributions or disbursements. The calculation assumes that the returns for all years are the same.

## GOAL: AGGRESSIVE GROWTH

Accumulating maximum capital is the primary goal of some investors. They choose to ignore risk as they pursue their objective. These investors have a long time horizon. They need to understand that the big rewards they seek do not come without equivalent risks.

Their strategies include buying volatile stocks, providing venture capital for business start-ups, and leveraged real estate deals in order to seek above-average returns. Their potential losses are as great as their potential gains. Their investments may be very illiquid and they may be unable to change their investment strategy quickly if their personal situation changes.

Investors seeking aggressive growth face two major risks in achieving their goal. First, their portfolios are subject to large and frequent short-term market fluctuations. Investors often believe they can tolerate these price fluctuations when a large drop occurs, but the reality is they may panic and abandon their investment strategy—assuming they can even get out of the market.

Second, the high risk inherent in aggressive growth means the final outcome of following an aggressive strategy is very uncertain. These investors often fail to understand the true range of potential long-term outcomes they face. As they try to balance risk and reward, aggressive growth investors tend to think their eventual return will be a statistical mean. Their expected portfolio performance, however, is a wide range of possible outcomes.

If an aggressive growth investor's long-term goal is to parlay $100,000 into $1 million, he or she may be just as likely to realize $140,000 or $2 million. There is a high probability that this investor will fall short of his or her investment goal over the long term. The initial investment may even be lost. Few investors can tolerate such a high level of risk.

---

*Along with their potential for above-average returns, aggressive growth investment strategies have a high potential for failure. The range of expected outcomes is very wide.*

---

The global diversification of The Island Principle can significantly reduce the high risk these investors face and narrows the range of expected outcomes. This increases their chances of reaching their financial objectives. These investors can gain a great deal by adopting The Island Principle.

## STRATEGY: THE ISLAND PRINCIPLE

The Island Principle enables long-term investors to manage risk. They can enjoy a lower level of portfolio risk or they can maintain their original level of risk while seeking higher returns. It can help many, though not all, investors. Depending on their goals, some investors could benefit from it by shifting their perspective and reevaluating their investment objectives.

Typically island investors seek steady capital growth and they are often total return investors. Because market diversification helps control the risk and volatility of their overall portfolios, island investors can choose individual global investments with potential for above-average gains that, considered alone, they might feel were too risky. Another major benefit is that they can also increase their portfolio allocation to stocks versus other asset classes in order to raise total returns.

Island investors want their capital working for them and they take a long view about making money. They share several characteristics:

- ✔ Island investors expect to keep their investments in place for at least five but more likely 10 years or more.
- ✔ They want good returns but they also want to dampen the volatility that makes them uncomfortable.
- ✔ They recognize that inflation or devaluation are real risks when all of a portfolio is in a single market.
- ✔ They are comfortable buying stocks in foreign countries.
- ✔ They are able to abandon the United States as the focus of their investing.

✔ They are willing to turn market and stock choice decisions over to global experts.

The Island Principle allows investors to select the relationship between risk and return in their portfolios. They can choose to have less portfolio risk with the same returns, go for higher portfolio returns without increasing risk, or take on more risk while seeking higher returns.

*Chapter*

# 5

# Casting Off

---

I sland investors are true global investors. They set
sail in search of investment opportunities around
the world. They chart multiple investment possibilities and see the United States as only one of many ports
of call they can choose among. They put together portfolios containing stocks from many geographic markets
to create diversity that helps them manage portfolio
risk.

*The Island Principle is a global investment strat-
egy for investors who want to control portfolio
volatility and protect themselves against the real,
long-term risks every investor faces.*

## THE ISLAND PRINCIPLE

The Island Principle puts the power of diversification
to work for investors in new ways. It extends the
asset allocation principles of portfolio theory to global
markets. It can be summarized as a series of paired
concepts:

85

✔ It provides two levels of diversification—diversification of the countries in the investor's portfolio and diversification of the decision about which countries to invest in.

✔ This diversification provides dual portfolio benefits—it reduces risk and it enhances returns.

✔ Risk is reduced two ways—investors face less normal portfolio volatility (those up-and-down market swings that often scare investors into abandoning otherwise sound investment strategies), and they decrease the likelihood that the long-term risks that threaten every investor will ruin their chances of achieving their investment objectives.

✔ With risk under control, investors can enhance their portfolio returns two ways—they can increase their overall portfolio allocation to stocks versus lower-yielding cash or bonds or they can increase the proportion of higher-risk but higher-returning stocks in their portfolios.

*Island investors invest their portfolios in multiple markets around the world chosen by professional money managers.*

## AN ISLAND INVESTOR PROFILE

The Island Principle makes sense for investors whose goal is to optimize the balance between risk and return. Island investors also share several key characteristics:

**1.** *They are long-term investors.* Island investors plan to be in the market for a minimum of five or preferably 10 years. Markets are always volatile. They go up and down. There will be years when a market posts back-to-back losses. Investors who are in the market for only a few years may not even get their original investment back, much less realize any gain. Although following The Island Principle helps reduce the psychological impact of short-term volatility in any single market on your portfolio, volatility will always exist, and swings may sometimes be greater than investors expect. Investors should not follow The Island Principle—or even invest in stocks—unless they expect to keep their investments in place for at least five or preferably 10 years.

**2. *Their investment goals include enhancing returns, managing risk, or both.*** Improving a portfolio's risk and return is the objective of modern investment strategies. Although this sounds obvious, there are many investors who consciously or unconsciously pursue investment strategies with other objectives. These include the gamblers who enjoy the adrenaline rush of active trading. They are always buying and selling stocks because, for them, the act of transacting counts more than long-term performance. Since short-term trading is more important than long-term portfolio performance, The Island Principle will not work for these investors.

Similarly, it is not a good strategy for investors focused on maximum returns regardless of risk. These investors are after that singular stock, the killing, that will allow them to retire early or drive a fancy car or buy a huge house. The Island Principle uses geographic market diversity and decision-making diversity to dampen the effects of market volatility on a portfolio. That, in turn, permits investors to seek out investments with above-average returns that, when considered alone, might be considered very risky. However, this is not the same as the big, once-in-a-lifetime investment coup these investors are after.

**3. *They are willing to own stocks outside the United States.*** Island investors are comfortable owning non-U.S. securities. They may read, travel abroad, and continue to educate themselves about other countries and cultures so that foreign markets no longer seem unfamiliar or alien. Perhaps their ancestors came from Japan, the United Kingdom, Germany, Norway, or Australia or they have friends who live outside the United States so that those markets feel more familiar. Applying The Island Principle means becoming as psychologically comfortable with other markets as one is with Wall Street.

**4.** *They are willing to abandon a fixation on the Dow or S&P 500.* Related to becoming comfortable with markets outside the United States is a willingness to stop thinking of investing in terms of beating or matching the U.S. stock market. The Standard & Poor's 500 Index and *Dow Jones Industrial Average* are only barometers of a single market, only one of many worldwide investment opportunities. Island investors deliberately diversify their portfolios so they will not behave like the U.S. market, since that is one of the risks they are trying to reduce. Comparing their portfolios against a U.S. market index or any other single market index therefore is not meaningful. As island investors, their goal is consistent, long-term returns, not matching or beating an arbitrary index.

**5.** *They want to protect their future buying power.* The danger of losing future portfolio buying power is a major threat to all long-term investors. Inflation or fluctuations in currency values become an even greater threat when a portfolio is invested in a single market. When all or even most of a portfolio's investments are in a single market, the investor is exposed to the risk that a single government's policies can erode the portfolio's future purchasing power. A portfolio containing stocks from multiple markets in multiple currencies provides diversification to reduce this risk. An investor is no longer held hostage to the policies of a single government.

**6.** *They are willing to share decision making about where to invest.* Island investors acknowledge that they cannot do all the necessary research and analysis to select the best market mix themselves. They do not try to make the crucial decision about which markets they should invest in alone. Letting go of day-to-day decisions and individual stock picking can be very difficult for some investors. Island investors not only recognize that they lack the expertise to make global stock or market picks but also that it is extremely risky for a single decision maker to determine the geographic distribution of a portfolio. Whether that decision maker is the investor or a professional portfolio manager makes no difference.

**Dow Jones Industrial Average**
a weighted index of U.S. blue chip stocks. Historically, a very popular measure of the U.S. stock market.

# ADDING MARKET DIVERSIFICATION

Extending the diversification techniques investors already use for stocks and sectors to geographic markets is The Island Principle's chief strategy for reducing risk and enhancing returns. Examining how a series of efficient frontiers shifts with increasing levels of market diversification illustrates how this works. As a reminder about how to read an efficient frontier curve, remember that risk is measured on the horizontal axis as standard deviation while rate of return expressed as a percentage is measured on the vertical axis. Each point along the curve is the best return obtainable for a given risk level. The mix of assets at each point is the optimum selection that provides this return. The appropriate point on the efficient frontier curve will be different for each investor depending on the returns they are after and their tolerance for risk.

Figures 5.1 and 5.2 show how the efficient frontier curve shifts upward as more markets are added for greater diversification. A higher curve means greater returns for a given level of risk or less risk for a given return, both desirable goals. It takes at least two markets (or two assets) to create an efficient frontier curve. The more markets, the greater the diversity and the higher the curve. However, after the market mix reaches about 10 markets, there is only a small increment of risk reduction provided by each additional market. Markets with high expected returns and low correlations create efficient frontiers that provide the best returns for the level of risk taken. (While this series of efficient frontiers clearly demonstrates the benefits of global diversification, investors need to remember that they are constructed from historical data. Each point on the curve represents a single decision made one time and unchanged for 29 years, from 1970 to 1998. In real life, investors would change their mix of markets from time to time with the hope of improving their returns, reducing their risk, or both, compared to a one-time decision.)

As a starting point, Figure 5.1 shows an efficient frontier for two markets—United States and Japan. An

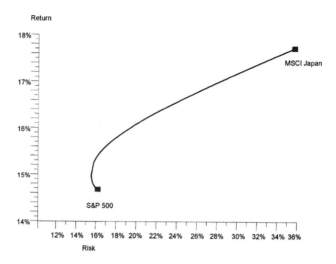

**FIGURE 5.1** An efficient frontier combining the U.S. and Japanese markets from 1970 to 1998. *Source:* Morgan Stanley Capital International.

investor seeking to maximize a given combination of risk and return would move along this curve changing the percentage of the portfolio invested in each market to achieve the objective. Moving along the curve to the left provides both lower risk and return levels while moving to the right provides higher returns but at higher risk levels.

In a way, this example is philosophically similar to the way many investors typically approach global investing. They build their portfolios as though there were only two market choices available to them—U.S. and foreign, them and us. The world, however, has many more than two markets and a global investor benefits by understanding this.

Figure 5.2 compares two efficient frontiers to demonstrate how more is better when it comes to market diversification. The upper curve represents choices among the world's 21 developed markets. The lower curve (which shows as a straight line at this scale) represents choices from either the U.S. market or the EAFE index, the two markets approach that individual investors typically use.

When "foreign" is broken into all the different devel-

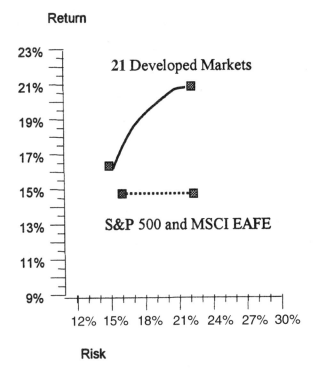

**Return**

**FIGURE 5.2** These two efficient frontiers show the benefits investors gain when they stop treating the world as though it consisted of just two markets (U.S. and foreign markets, shown on the lower curve) and begin treating all of the world's developed markets as the individual markets they are (the upper curve). *Source:* Morgan Stanley Capital International.

oped markets available to island investors, the efficient frontier shifts up. Studying these two curves shows how much better off the investor looking at the world as multiple markets, instead of just two markets, did from 1970 to 1998. Over that period of time, an investor on the 21-market efficient frontier would have earned a 2.5% higher rate of return (17.5%) than the investor limited to just two markets (15%), without taking on any more risk than that of being invested in the S&P 500. An investor willing to take on more risk than the S&P 500 could have significantly higher returns by investing in the 21 developed markets.

Again, when it comes to developing optimum market mixes and efficient frontier curves based on portfolio theory formulas, the more markets the better up to about 10, when there are diminishing returns from further additions. Comparing Figures 5.1 and 5.2 shows the significant potential for reduced risk or increased returns investors achieve when they increase the number of markets in their portfolios.

---

*Viewing "foreign" or non-U.S. investing as multiple markets rather than as a single market makes it possible for investors to reduce risk, increase returns, or do both.*

---

Low correlation among world markets makes it possible for geographic market diversification to work its risk-and-return magic. While shocks such as the market crash of 1987 affect markets around the world over the short term, world markets have surprisingly low correlation over the long term. Figure 5.3 shows the correlation of the developed markets with the United States from 1970 to 1998. Note that only Canada has a relatively close correlation (73%) with the United States.

Island investors will look for low correlation not only between the United States and other markets but also among all the markets where they invest. Table 5.1 shows that the markets in most countries have low correlation not only with the U.S. market but also with each other. This makes it relatively easy for island investors to achieve diversification in their global portfolios.

Although a study by Charles Wang found that world market correlations are increasing (not surprising considering the globalization of the world's economy), long-term market movements should continue to have correlations low enough to benefit investors who diversify geographically. Local stock market performance is heavily influenced by the local economy, and local economies tend to move differently from each other. They are rarely in sync. Likewise, the stock markets associated with those

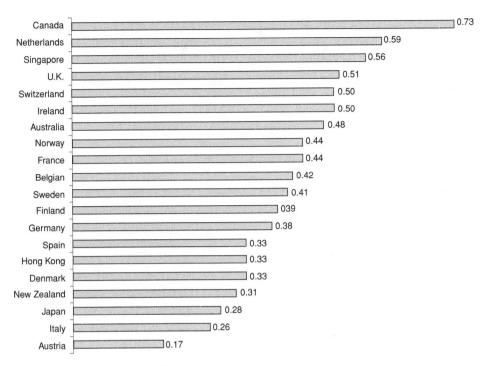

**FIGURE 5.3**   The correlations of the developed markets around the world with the U.S. stock market. *Source:* Morgan Stanley Capital International.

economies tend to be out of sync. Even if geographic markets continue to become more closely correlated, there are enough differences among markets that geographic diversification will continue to be a powerful tool for investors to manage risk and seek higher returns.

## HOW THE ISLAND PRINCIPLE REDUCES RISK

The Island Principle's strategy of investing in multiple markets around the world helps island investors manage risk. It provides a way for investors to minimize the odds that short-term market volatility will make them so nervous or uncertain that they abandon their investment strategies. It also helps investors address the very

| TABLE 5.1 Historical Correlations among the World's 21 Developed Markets | | | | | | | |
|---|---|---|---|---|---|---|---|
| | Aust. | Aus. | Belg. | Can. | Den. | Fin. | Fr. | Ger. |
| Australia | 1.00 | | | | | | | |
| Austria | 0.18 | 1.00 | | | | | | |
| Belgium | 0.32 | 0.44 | 1.00 | | | | | |
| Canada | 0.58 | 0.23 | 0.38 | 1.00 | | | | |
| Denmark | 0.27 | 0.35 | 0.48 | 0.32 | 1.00 | | | |
| Finland | 0.41 | 0.31 | 0.30 | 0.44 | 0.34 | 1.00 | | |
| France | 0.37 | 0.43 | 0.67 | 0.44 | 0.40 | 0.29 | 1.00 | |
| Germany | 0.30 | 0.58 | 0.66 | 0.33 | 0.46 | 0.38 | 0.61 | 1.00 |
| Hong Kong | 0.36 | 0.25 | 0.30 | 0.35 | 0.28 | 0.34 | 0.28 | 0.29 |
| Ireland | 0.38 | 0.40 | 0.49 | 0.43 | 0.52 | 0.48 | 0.47 | 0.50 |
| Italy | 0.25 | 0.28 | 0.41 | 0.31 | 0.36 | 0.42 | 0.46 | 0.39 |
| Japan | 0.30 | 0.23 | 0.41 | 0.29 | 0.36 | 0.32 | 0.40 | 0.37 |
| Netherlands | 0.41 | 0.44 | 0.67 | 0.55 | 0.50 | 0.45 | 0.61 | 0.69 |
| New Zealand | 0.66 | 0.29 | 0.13 | 0.42 | 0.21 | 0.37 | 0.22 | 0.23 |
| Norway | 0.42 | 0.35 | 0.51 | 0.46 | 0.39 | 0.50 | 0.47 | 0.40 |
| Singapore | 0.55 | 0.35 | 0.28 | 0.56 | 0.31 | 0.34 | 0.45 | 0.40 |
| Spain | 0.35 | 0.34 | 0.43 | 0.33 | 0.38 | 0.50 | 0.43 | 0.41 |
| Sweden | 0.40 | 0.32 | 0.43 | 0.38 | 0.38 | 0.58 | 0.38 | 0.45 |
| Switzerland | 0.40 | 0.48 | 0.64 | 0.47 | 0.47 | 0.31 | 0.61 | 0.68 |
| United Kingdom | 0.48 | 0.27 | 0.52 | 0.52 | 0.39 | 0.42 | 0.55 | 0.43 |
| S&P 500 | 0.48 | 0.17 | 0.42 | 0.73 | 0.33 | 0.39 | 0.44 | 0.38 |

*Note:* Based on monthly returns from 1970 to 1998. *Source:* Morgan Stanley Capital International.

real investment risks they face over the long term, which were identified in Chapter 2, including:

✔ The normal range of potential future outcomes investors face is wider than they realize.

✔ Projecting current trends into the future can result in erroneous forecasts.

| H.K. | Ire. | It. | Jap. | Neth. | N.Z. | Nor. | Sing. | Sp. | Swed. | Switz. | U.K. | S&P |
|------|------|------|------|-------|------|------|-------|-----|-------|--------|------|-----|
| 1.00 | | | | | | | | | | | | |
| 0.34 | 1.00 | | | | | | | | | | | |
| 0.21 | 0.36 | 1.00 | | | | | | | | | | |
| 0.29 | 0.50 | 0.36 | 1.00 | | | | | | | | | |
| 0.42 | 0.63 | 0.38 | 0.43 | 1.00 | | | | | | | | |
| 0.34 | 0.33 | 0.26 | 0.33 | 0.42 | 1.00 | | | | | | | |
| 0.29 | 0.52 | 0.29 | 0.21 | 0.52 | 0.43 | 1.00 | | | | | | |
| 0.79 | 0.44 | 0.25 | 0.34 | 0.49 | 0.56 | 0.45 | 1.00 | | | | | |
| 0.27 | 0.57 | 0.42 | 0.40 | 0.43 | 0.49 | 0.33 | 0.53 | 1.00 | | | | |
| 0.28 | 0.57 | 0.36 | 0.38 | 0.48 | 0.52 | 0.44 | 0.44 | 0.44 | 1.00 | | | |
| 0.34 | 0.48 | 0.37 | 0.43 | 0.71 | 0.39 | 0.46 | 0.42 | 0.40 | 0.51 | 1.00 | | |
| 0.37 | 0.68 | 0.34 | 0.36 | 0.64 | 0.41 | 0.42 | 0.50 | 0.36 | 0.43 | 0.55 | 1.00 | |
| 0.33 | 0.50 | 0.26 | 0.28 | 0.59 | 0.31 | 0.44 | 0.56 | 0.33 | 0.41 | 0.50 | 0.51 | 1.00 |

✔ Investing in a single market means that market completely controls one's financial destiny.

✔ The future buying power of a single-market portfolio is dependent on the actions of a single government.

✔ The investor may choose the wrong markets for investment.

### *The Island Principle Manages Volatility Jitters, Unpredictability, and Investor Psychology*

Market volatility makes investors nervous. Psychologically, investors do not like to see the value of their assets on a roller coaster. High levels of volatility undermine their confidence in their investment strategies. They become concerned that the analysis they used as a basis for their investment choices was wrong. The future no longer seems as predictable as they thought. They begin to worry not only that they will fail to achieve their goals but also that they may lose their capital. When investors feel they are in uncharted waters, they may abandon their investment strategies, return to a familiar port, and fail to reach their long-term goals.

Diversification into multiple markets helps investors handle their psychological discomfort with short-term market volatility. Volatility or risk of a diversified portfolio is less than that of the individual stocks in it. The Island Principle extends this magic of diversification to markets.

Since the volatility of the portfolio as a whole is less than the volatility of most of the individual markets within it, island investors no longer feel panicky when any single market fluctuates widely from day to day or week to week. An investor who is diversified into multiple markets is less nervous about volatility in any individual market because no single market drives the portfolio's destiny.

Investing in multiple markets also helps island investors overcome their emotional reactions to unpredictable events. When all of an investor's portfolio is in a single market, an unexpected event that affects that market can undermine his or her confidence. Nagging doubt often leads single-market investors to abandon otherwise sound investment strategies.

Island investors, on the other hand, predict that the unexpected *will* occur in some market somewhere sometime. They hedge that risk by investing in multiple markets. An unforeseen event in a single market simply has less psychological impact on them because they have already anticipated it and taken steps to dampen its impact, both psychological and real. If a trend breaks, they do not get the jitters. If a government policy unexpectedly changes and devalues their stocks in that market, they do not panic. They are able to keep their long-term investment strategies in place. The more predictable they can make the future, the more confident investors can be.

---

*Investing in multiple markets helps island investors discount market volatility or unexpected events in any single market.*

---

## The Island Principle Makes Long-Term Investment Performance More Certain

Financial advisers sometimes use normal market volatility data to project a portfolio's range of expected future rates of return. This creates the trumpet charts (Figure 5.4), introduced in Chapter 2, which can give investors a false sense of security. They give the impression that investors face less risk in the future because the range of a portfolio's potential rates of return narrows over the long term. Investors use trumpet charts to assure themselves that the long term is more certain than the short term.

As was pointed out in Chapter 2, these charts do not show how uncertainty increases because, in fact, the potential range of outcomes in terms of actual portfolio value *increases* over time given normal market volatility. The future is less certain, not more certain. When the same normal market volatility data is plotted a different way (Figure 5.5), it becomes obvious the range of future values actually becomes larger. The reason why the range of future values is getting larger while the range of expected returns is narrowing is because of the effect of compounding over time. A small difference in expected returns over 10 or 20 years makes a very big difference in value.

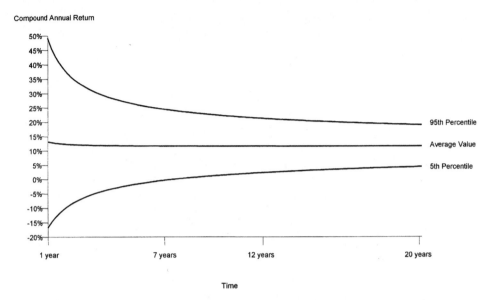

Compound Annual Return

**FIGURE 5.4** The expected rate of returns over 1, 7, and 12 years at 5% and 95% probability. The bands narrow over time, giving the impression that rates of return become more predictable over time. This is the trumpet chart many investors turn to as proof that buying stocks and holding them will provide better returns over the long term. *Source:* Kreitler Associates.

Portfolio value is a more meaningful measure for investors to use than rates of return. Investors do not live on their rates of return. Future portfolio value converts to a future standard of living. Even if their investment strategy works out as planned, the wide range of future outcomes that investors face despite a narrowing range of return rates is critical to their future well-being.

Following The Island Principle and investing in multiple markets reduces the short-term volatility within a portfolio. Since reducing the *short-term* volatility of a portfolio narrows the range of *future* outcomes an investor faces, investing in multiple markets makes it more likely that an investor will reach the financial goals that he or she set.

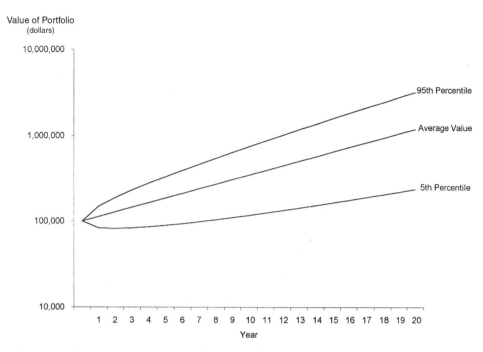

Value of Portfolio
(dollars)

**FIGURE 5.5** When the expected range of portfolio values (based on the same basic volatility data as Figure 5.4) is charted rather than expected rates of return, the future looks less certain. Over time, the 95% confidence range becomes wider, not narrower, indicating that investors face less certainty 20 years out than they do one year out. *Source:* Kreitler Associates.

> *Investing in multiple markets decreases the range of normal market volatility an investor faces. Reduced volatility narrows the range of future portfolio values the investor may eventually achieve, and increases certainty.*

## The Island Principle Reduces the Impact of Inaccurate Forecasts

Most of the projections investors rely on as they plan their investment strategies assume that historical trends will continue linearly into the future. But market behavior is a lot like the weather. Accurate weather forecasts are not based on a linear extension of past trends but on very complex nonlinear formulas that take into account feedback of the weather systems themselves. Investing is similar. Projecting current trends into the future can be very dangerous to one's financial health. An investor cannot predict which geographic market will be the best-performing one in 10, 20, or 30 years.

Normal weather may be pleasant some days and disagreeable on others, but it is the abnormal extremes like hurricanes or tornadoes that cause damage. Similarly, it is normal for the stock market to fluctuate up and down from day to day. But an extreme—a once-in-a-lifetime market crash—can cause great damage, even destroy an investor's portfolio. These deviations from the norm have long-term consequences and may keep investors from reaching their goals.

Investors in multiple geographic markets are protected, however, by the diversification in their portfolios. Unpredicted events usually do not affect all markets around the world the same way. In fact, an event that is a disaster for one market may even prove a boon for another. Following The Island Principle cannot completely protect investors from unforeseen events such as war or changes in governmental systems or new government policies that can derail projections of future market behaviors. However, investing in multiple markets can reduce the impact of these events, because the portfolio's future performance is no longer completely dependent on the future performance of a single market.

---

*Investing in multiple markets diversifies a portfolio, so that a financial disaster in any single market is less likely to destroy an investor's portfolio.*

---

Many investors will be investing for 30 to 50 years or more. A great deal can happen in that time. No one can predict which will be the leading countries. No one can accurately predict where a particular market will be after that length of time. A geographically diversified portfolio provides much greater assurance that the investor will survive and achieve his or her financial goals.

## The Island Principle Helps Investors Escape the Risk Inherent in Any Single Market

Most investors already use diversification to reduce the risk of owning a single stock (nonsystematic risk). They buy more than one stock. They not only pick stocks they think will go up in value but they also pick stocks in unrelated industry sectors that will be influenced differently by the same events or factors. This low correlation means that the prices of all the stocks in the portfolio do not move together. Low correlation reduces the volatility or short-term risk of the portfolio as a whole.

This diversification tactic fails, however, to protect the investor from the risk of the market itself (systematic risk). When all of their investments are in a single market, investors cannot escape their exposure to the risk inherent in that market.

Traditionally, investors who want to reduce the risk in their portfolios do this by diversifying into other asset classes such as bonds, real estate, or cash. While this reduces portfolio risk, it typically reduces returns as well because over time the returns from stocks have generally been higher than for other asset classes, such as bonds. The Island Principle applies the diversification techniques of Modern Portfolio Theory to markets. Just as investing in multiple asset classes can reduce exposure to the systematic risk of investing only in the U.S. stock market, investing in multiple markets around the world can accomplish the same objective.

Island investors are able to reduce the risk of owning stocks below the systematic risk of the U.S. market by diversifying their stock purchases into multiple markets with low correlations around the world.

*Investing in multiple markets around the world with low correlations reduces the investor's exposure to the systematic risk inherent in any single market.*

### The Island Principle Protects an Investor's Future Buying Power

Investors in a single market expose themselves to the risk that government actions in that market will erode their portfolios' value. Even though these investors may successfully stick to their strategy and achieve good returns, *currency devaluation* or inflation in that single market can bring financial disaster. It is impossible for investors to predict what the value of a particular currency will be in 20, 30, or more years when they begin calling on their portfolios for retirement needs or other financial objectives. They do not know what their portfolios' future buying power will be as they purchase goods and services from around the world.

The U.S. investor can protect future buying power against devaluation of the U.S. dollar by investing in international stocks valued in their local currencies. This diversification protects against U.S. government policies that might cause inflation or currency devaluation. Rather than letting a single government's decisions determine their financial future, island investors diversify into multiple currencies in order to gain more control over their financial destinies.

For example, investors with all of their assets valued in U.S. dollars are letting U.S. government policies determine the future buying power of their portfolios. This is an issue not only of U.S. inflation but also of the value of the U.S. dollar versus other world currencies and of the investors' ability to use their dollars to buy foreign goods and services.

When U.S. government policies lead to a weaker dollar, its consumers pay a higher price for foreign goods and services. The same effect occurs if a foreign country strengthens its currency versus the United States. A port-

**currency devaluation**

when a government lets the value of its currency drop (or encourages it to drop) versus other currencies. Usually done to increase competitiveness of the country's products in world markets, it reduces the buying power of the country's own citizens when they buy foreign goods and services.

folio invested in stocks valued in several currencies protects the future buying power of an investor's portfolio from the actions of a single government.

*Investing in multiple markets gives island investors currency diversification to protect the future buying power of their portfolios.*

## The Island Principle Protects against the Risk of Choosing the Wrong Markets

As island investors diversify into multiple geographic markets, the choice of which markets to invest in ultimately determines the future value of their portfolios. Because selection of markets is so important, island investors also diversify the decision-making process about which markets to invest in and how much of their portfolios to put into each of these markets. They understand that these market decisions will drive their portfolios' long-term performance so they seek help from *multiple* professional money managers to hedge the risk of making the wrong market selections.

Using the combined expertise of multiple decision makers means a much greater likelihood of being in the better markets or at least avoiding heavy concentration in the worst. No matter how good the stock picking within a given market or markets may be, an investor cannot overcome the handicap of being in the wrong markets. Even good stocks in an underperforming market will have trouble beating average stocks in a good market.

*Using multiple professional money managers protects island investors against the risk of choosing the wrong markets.*

Island investors diversify by using several global investment managers with different *styles*. Just as they

**style**
the bias of a mutual fund, its manager, or of an individual investor to hold stocks of a certain type such as those of large companies, mid-size companies, small companies, companies that appear to be good values based on their price ratios, or companies that appear to be candidates for strong future growth.

want markets with low correlation to help them reduce risk, they also want managers whose styles have low correlation. Once island investors select several global managers to help them make the decisions about which markets to be in and which stocks in those markets to select (using the selection criteria outlined in Chapter 6), their job becomes one of managing the managers. They monitor the managers' performances and they monitor the overall balance of markets and stocks within their portfolios rather than picking individual stocks or tracking individual markets. Mutual funds give individual investors ready access to global managers and make it possible for U.S. citizens easily to invest in non-U.S. markets for many reasons, which are described more fully later in this chapter.

## HOW THE ISLAND PRINCIPLE CAN HELP INCREASE RETURNS

When investors start thinking of the world as multiple markets rather than as just the U.S. market and everything else lumped into the "other" market, Figure 5.2 showed how this single decision can improve their returns without increasing the risk of their portfolios. Investors' ability to control risk gives them the flexibility to seek higher returns. The Island Principle opens opportunities for investors to improve portfolio performance in two ways:

1. They can invest more in riskier stocks with potential for higher returns.
2. They can invest a higher proportion of their portfolios in stocks.

### *Island Investors Can Choose Riskier Stocks with Potential for Higher Returns*

Investors must constantly balance their risk objectives against their return objectives. Keeping risk at a low level means compromising returns. Going for higher returns means taking on more risk than the investor may feel comfortable with.

Stocks have typically offered higher returns than other asset classes, and stocks with higher potential returns carry the highest risk. Investors in a single market trying to keep risk levels low are in a particular bind. They cannot reduce risk without reducing returns. When they choose low-risk stocks in order to keep the risk of the portfolio as a whole at an acceptable level, they also lower the portfolio's returns.

Island investors again use diversification among multiple markets with low correlation to help them solve this dilemma. The access to stocks in multiple markets provides them not only with investment options with good appreciation but also with correlations that are lower than if they owned only U.S. stocks. Within the stock portion of their portfolios investors can then choose more risky stocks with potential for higher returns without raising the risk of the portfolio as a whole.

---

*The Island Principle allows investors to choose stocks with potential for higher returns that otherwise would have been too risky to put into their portfolios.*

---

## Island Investors Can Invest a Higher Proportion of Their Portfolios in Stock

Stocks have traditionally provided higher returns than other asset classes. But a portfolio invested entirely in a single asset class like stocks carries all the risk of the market itself. To escape this risk, investors typically diversify their portfolios by investing in a mix of asset classes such as stocks, bonds, and cash that help them meet their particular risk and return objectives.

However, investors gain this risk protection at the cost of lower potential returns, because assets such as bonds and cash have traditionally had lower returns than stocks and drag down the portfolio's returns. The investor who wants less risk keeps a smaller percentage of the portfolio in stocks and must accept lower returns. The investor who wants higher returns may keep a higher proportion of the portfolio in stocks but then must accept more risk.

Instead of reducing portfolio risk by diversifying into multiple asset classes (and facing lower returns), The Island Principle helps investors break out of this box by using multiple markets around the world to add new opportunity for diversification. The Island Principle allows an investor to increase his or her portfolio's asset allocation to stocks in order to achieve a higher level of returns without increasing risk or even while decreasing it. Diversification into multiple markets lets an investor reduce the risk of equities (in effect reducing systematic risk).

*Investing in multiple markets reduces an investor's exposure to the risk of any single market in the same way that diversification to multiple asset classes reduces risk, but it accomplishes this risk reduction without reducing returns.*

## ISLAND BENCHMARKS

Because an island investor's portfolio is structured so differently from a traditional portfolio invested only or even primarily in U.S. stocks, it will also behave very differently. A U.S. investor's portfolio will track the U.S. market. An island investor's portfolio will not track any single market or even any single index. It is more likely to track the World Index than it is to track the Standard & Poor's 500 Index or the Dow.

*Island investors will not use the U.S. market as their benchmark for portfolio performance.*

During periods when the U.S. market is unusually strong, an island portfolio may underperform U.S. benchmarks. When the U.S. market is weak, the island portfolio should do better. It is impossible to predict exactly where an island portfolio will be in 20 or 30 years any more than one can predict accurately where the Dow or the S&P 500 indexes will be in 20 or 30 years, either. Over the long term, however, an island portfolio's market diversity should provide more stable, consistent growth with lower volatility than a portfolio of U.S. stocks alone.

Investors who shift away from a traditional portfolio of all U.S. securities to build global portfolios often feel the need to justify that decision. Island investors may feel considerable peer pressure because their portfolios do not perform the same as those of their friends who are invested primarily in the United States. There may be times when it is hard to feel satisfied with 14% returns when those friends are boasting of 20% returns. Institutional money managers have a similar problem. Their boards and trustees are familiar with the U.S. market. When they monitor a money manager's performance, they compare it to U.S. indexes. There is little incentive for a money manager to deviate from a traditional portfolio of U.S. stocks when his or her job is on the line.

At least one investment expert feels the shoe should be on the other foot. Putnam Investments senior vice president Stephen A. Gorman argues that the case for global investing is so compelling that the burden should be on investors to explain why they are *not* diversified around the world. He believes that while better returns should be expected from investing globally, the primary benefit of global investing is risk reduction.

---

*The benefits of investing in multiple markets are so great that the burden should be on investors who are holding traditional portfolios full of only U.S. securities to explain why they are following such a limiting investment strategy.*

---

Many portfolio managers spend a great deal of time worrying about allocations to value stocks versus growth stocks or small companies versus large companies in their portfolios of U.S. stocks. Gorman observes that the benefits of all their fine-tuning are small in comparison to the benefits to be gained from true global diversification.

## SETTING REALISTIC RETURNS GOALS

Island investors need to set goals that include a reasonable, achievable annual rate of return. They want to know when they are on course toward their goals and when they need a course correction because their portfolio is underperforming.

The 1986 and 1991 studies by Brinson and coauthors of U.S. money managers and the more recent Ibbotson study (Chapter 3) showed that asset allocation determined almost all of a portfolio's movement, not stock picking or market timing. Planning to beat the market over long periods is not realistic.

Striving to achieve the long-term performance of the market is a more reasonable goal. Ibbotson Associates, Inc., reports that from 1926 to 1998 large company U.S. stocks provided a 11.2% compounded annual rate of return. From 1970 (when reliable information on foreign markets became available) to 1998, the compounded annual rate of return from various indexes ranged between 12.4% and 15.2% (Table 5.2).

| TABLE 5.2 Compounded Annual Rates of Return, 1970 to 1998 | | |
|---|---|---|
| *Market* | *Index* | *Return* |
| United States | S&P 500 | 13.5% |
| Foreign | MSCI EAFE | 12.4% |
| World | MSCI World | 15.2% |
| *Source:* Morgan Stanley Capital International. | | |

Based on past performance of markets around the world (using the MSCI World Index as the benchmark), a return rate of 12% to 13% would be a reasonable long-term objective for a typical island investor. A conservative island investor might use the U.S. long-term rate of 11.2% as a target. Remember that these returns apply to the stock portion of your overall portfolio and would not be the objective for an entire portfolio of stocks, bonds, cash, and other assets.

> *A return rate of 12% to 13% would be a reasonable long-term objective for a typical island investor.*

These rates may sound disappointing to investors who enjoyed the recent spike in U.S. returns. The extraordinary rate of return on U.S. stocks from 1988 to 1997 distorted reality for many investors. During this unusual 10-year period U.S. stocks provided an 18.18% annual rate of return. Many investors want to believe they can consistently achieve high returns, and they point to this period as proof. But investors who consider this rate of return normal and believe it is a realistic long-term objective are setting themselves up for a major disappointment.

Investors naturally hope to make as much money from their investments as possible. In setting investment goals, being realistic about potential rates of return can be critical. Late-starting investors who want to retire in 10 or 15 years and need to achieve an 18% or 20% compounded annual rate of return to maintain today's living standards in retirement would have to assume a great deal of risk. They face a paradox that while they need high rates to achieve their objectives, they are short of resources and can least afford to lose what they have. They are not being realistic in setting such a high rate of return goal. They face the very real possibility that they will fall far short of their financial goals, which would be very painful.

On the other hand, if they assume as little risk as

possible they may wind up with only a 4% or 5% compounded annual rate of return. They then face the certainty that their portfolio will not grow fast enough for them to reach their financial goals. They should reduce their goals and strive for reasonably achievable returns rather than taking on too much risk.

Extending portfolio theory to world markets, The Island Principle contends that much of an island portfolio's performance will be determined by the markets where it is invested. Investors who think that superior stock selection skills will provide them with exceptional returns are also not being realistic. Many professional money managers feel they are doing well if they can beat the market by even 1% over the longer term.

Whatever rate of return investors choose, they should be aware that the number is deceptive, because a mathematical quirk affects rate calculation over time and enters into goal setting and monitoring. An investor who wants to achieve a long-term compounded rate of return of about 12.4% (equal to that of the foreign market from 1970 to 1998, as measured by the EAFE index) actually needs to achieve an average 13.6% rate of return on a year-to-year basis. That extra 1.2% is the difference between a geometric calculation of the rate of return needed to meet long-term goals and an arithmetic calculation of it (Table 5.3).

When returns fluctuate from year to year, the average *arithmetic rate of return* is higher than the *geometric rate of return* for the period. When investors project the long-term portfolio returns they want, they geometrically calculate the rate of return they need to achieve that level of returns. This means there is often a gap between what investors think they need to achieve on a long-term basis and what they actually need to achieve each year. Over time, this gap has averaged a little over 1%, which is quite significant.

*To achieve a particular rate of return over the long term, investors must aim to achieve a higher rate of return on a year-to-year basis, on average, than their long-term goal.*

---

**arithmetic rate of return** the average (mean) of the annual returns. For example, to determine the arithmetic return over a 10-year period, add the annual return for each of the 10 years and divide by 10. Unless the returns for each year are exactly the same (they usually are not), the arithmetic return will always exceed the geometric return.

**geometric rate of return** rate of return at which an investment compounds over a period of years; compounded rate of return.

| | Arithmetic Rate | | Geometric Rate | |
|---|---|---|---|---|
| Year-End | Percent | Principal | Percent | Principal |
| 1969 | | $ 10,000 | | $ 10,000 |
| 1970 | −1.98% | 9,602 | 12.41% | 11,241 |
| 1971 | 19.56 | 11,719 | 12.41 | 12,637 |
| 1972 | 23.55 | 14,479 | 12.41 | 14,206 |
| 1973 | −14.51 | 12,375 | 12.41 | 15,959 |
| 1974 | −24.46 | 9,346 | 12.41 | 17,952 |
| 1975 | 34.50 | 12,573 | 12.41 | 20,181 |
| 1976 | 14.71 | 14,423 | 12.41 | 22,686 |
| 1977 | 2.00 | 14,711 | 12.41 | 25,502 |
| 1978 | 18.22 | 17,391 | 12.41 | 28,868 |
| 1979 | 12.67 | 19,595 | 12.41 | 32,227 |
| 1980 | 27.72 | 25,027 | 12.41 | 36,228 |
| 1981 | −3.30 | 24,201 | 12.41 | 40,726 |
| 1982 | 11.27 | 26,926 | 12.41 | 45,782 |
| 1983 | 23.28 | 33,197 | 12.41 | 51,465 |
| 1984 | 5.77 | 35,113 | 12.41 | 57,855 |
| 1985 | 41.77 | 49,779 | 12.41 | 65,037 |
| 1986 | 42.80 | 71,084 | 12.41 | 73,111 |
| 1987 | 16.76 | 82,998 | 12.41 | 82,167 |
| 1988 | 23.95 | 102,876 | 12.41 | 92,391 |
| 1989 | 17.19 | 120,581 | 12.41 | 103,861 |
| 1990 | −16.52 | 100,644 | 12.41 | 116,754 |
| 1991 | 18.98 | 119,746 | 12.41 | 131,249 |
| 1992 | −4.66 | 114,166 | 12.41 | 147,543 |
| 1993 | 23.13 | 140,573 | 12.41 | 165,860 |
| 1994 | 5.58 | 148,417 | 12.41 | 186,450 |
| 1995 | 21.32 | 180,059 | 12.41 | 209,597 |
| 1996 | 14.00 | 205,268 | 12.41 | 235,818 |
| 1997 | 16.23 | 238,582 | 12.41 | 264,869 |
| 1998 | 24.80 | 297,751 | 12.41 | 297,751 |
| Average | 13.60% | | 12.41% | |

**TABLE 5.3 Geometric Rates of Return versus Arithmetic Rates of Return**

*Source:* Morgan Stanley Capital International.

### Geometric versus Arithmetic Rates of Return

A *geometric rate* of return assumes an investment will grow at exactly the same rate each year, compounding steadily from the beginning to the end of the investment period as it does. Most people use financial calculators to compute geometric rates. These are programmed to compound the value of the original investment moving forward or backward over a specified time period.

Bankers use geometric rates going forward to figure annual and monthly mortgage payments. Market analysts calculate geometric rates going backward to describe how a market has performed, on an annual basis, over a multiyear period.

When analysts say that a market grew 12% annually from 1980 to 1990, they do not mean that it grew at that same rate in each and every one of those 10 years. They mean that, looking back over that period of time, it would have taken a 12% rate of return compounded annually to produce the returns achieved.

In reality, of course, the market does not perform at exactly the same rate each year. Its actual return rate fluctuates, sometimes widely, from one year to the next.

The *arithmetic rate* is the average of all of the annual rates in whatever period the investor may be looking at. For example, an investor who wanted to know the arithmetic rate of his or her portfolio's returns for the past 10 years would add up the rates of return for each of those years and divide the total by 10. Losses in one year can be offset by gains in another and vice versa.

For mathematical reasons, the arithmetic rate of return over a period of years is higher than the geometric rate if the returns fluctuate from year to year. For example, Table 5.3 shows an investment of $10,000 in 1970 that grew to $297,751 by the end of 1998. The column of arithmetic returns shows the actual rate of return of the EAFE index in each of those years. The column to its right shows the actual dollar value of the portfolio in each year, based on the annual rate of return.

Looking back over that time period, the portfolio's growth to $297,751 represents a 12.41% return compounded annually. The fourth numerical column shows what the value of the portfolio would have been if, each year, the portfolio had grown exactly 12.41%.

When the annual arithmetic rates of return are totaled and averaged, the portfolio's arithmetic rate of return from 1970 to 1998 is 13.6%. That is about 1.2% greater than the geometric rate required to achieve the same portfolio returns.

Since their long-term goal is calculated geometrically, investors should use an arithmetic rate of return about 1% higher than that long-term goal as their target when they evaluate their portfolio's performance on an annual basis. If their goal is to achieve returns at least equal to the EAFE index's 12.4% long-term performance from 1970 to 1998, investors must actually achieve an average 13.6% return each year. Put another way, in a year that an investor's portfolio achieves a 12.4% rate of return, he or she is underperforming the 13.6% arithmetic average actually needed each year to achieve his or her goal.

Whatever rate an investor chooses as a long-term objective, the reality is that he or she needs to aim for a *higher* rate each year to compensate for this mathematical quirk. Otherwise, the long-term objective will not be met. Understanding the impact of fluctuating year-to-year rates of return and compounding on the portfolio's long-term rate of return is important as investors set their goals and monitor their progress toward them.

There's a second mathematical quirk investors should be aware of as they decide what long-term rate of return is a realistic objective. Like the idiosyncrasies of compounding,

**survivor bias**

the tendency of long-term performance records for mutual funds or stock indexes to be biased upward because funds or stocks in an index that have failed or merged with others are no longer included. Performance data and records for global indexes also may be biased because they include only data from successful countries and exclude data from countries viewed as less successful.

it makes reaching your objective more difficult. Investment analysts call it *survivor bias*. Reporting of long-term mutual fund performance is biased upward because funds that have failed or merged with others are eliminated from databases. Data also becomes biased when an index includes only data from successful countries and excludes data from countries viewed as less successful. This survivor bias gives investors an overly optimistic view of what is normal and makes it even more challenging to achieve what appear to be reasonable investment goals.

---

*Survivor bias must be factored into expectations for long-term portfolio returns.*

---

## SETTING RISK LEVEL OBJECTIVES

Investors must constantly balance the returns they would like to achieve against the risk they will face in order to achieve those performance goals. Most investors have very little idea how much risk they are actually taking or how to quantify risk in their portfolios.

Fluctuating market value or volatility is the risk investors most often fret about. The degree of volatility they are individually comfortable with is something investors constantly struggle to quantify. The market or portfolio fluctuation that one investor ignores may completely terrify another. As a rule of thumb, island investors can strive to keep the volatility of their portfolios lower than the volatility of the U.S. market and lower than the volatility of the world market. There are many other risks investors face, but they are even more difficult to quantify than normal market volatility.

---

*Island investors should strive for portfolio volatility lower than that of either the U.S. market or the world market.*

---

Investors who prefer doing things by the seat of their pants can watch the fluctuation or volatility of their portfolios versus the markets they are invested in. If fluctuations in individual markets create equal fluctuations in the investor's portfolio, the portfolio is too closely correlated with that market. The portfolio should not have the ups and downs of the S&P 500 or the Dow and ideally should fluctuate less than the World Index.

Investors who prefer more technical analysis can use standard deviation. Market volatility can be measured using standard deviation. The investor who prefers less short-term volatility should design a portfolio with a lower standard deviation than the market or markets that person is invested in; the more aggressive investor with a higher tolerance for volatility should design a portfolio with a higher standard deviation.

Table 5.4 shows the standard deviation of the Standard & Poor's 500, the EAFE index, and the World Index from 1970 to 1998. Services such as *Morningstar* report standard deviation of specific mutual funds and various indexes, and the more sophisticated ones can even calculate it for individual portfolios. Individuals would find this difficult to calculate on their own. A typical investor might want to keep the standard deviation of his or her

**Morningstar**
a reporting service based in Chicago, Illinois, that specializes in collecting and distributing information on mutual funds.

| TABLE 5.4 Standard Deviation of Major Market Indexes, 1970 to 1998 | |
| --- | --- |
| Index | Standard Deviation |
| S&P 500 | 16.21% |
| MSCI EAFE | 21.86% |
| MSCI World | 16.09% |
| MSCI Japan | 29.03% |
| MSCI Germany | 25.63% |

*Source:* Calculated by Kreitler Associates using information and data presented in Ibbotson Investment Analysis Software, © 1999 Ibbotson Associates, Inc. All rights reserved. Used with permission.

portfolio below 16, which was the approximate standard deviation of the S&P 500 from 1970 to 1998.

The concept of standard deviation is hard to understand and use just looking at this raw data. Standard deviation begins to take on some meaning when investors use it to project the range of expected portfolio performances they face over both short and long terms. Over the long term, investors should be more concerned with the range of expected long-term portfolio values they can expect after investing for many years (shown in Figures 2.4 and 2.5) than they are with rates of return, because those values translate directly into their future buying power. Investors need to take a close look at this range and ask whether the entire range would be acceptable and would enable them to reach their financial objectives. If the range is too broad, they should seek investments with lower risks (lower standard deviations) to narrow it.

*Lower standard deviation indicates lower volatility and means the investor faces a narrower range of potential portfolio values over the long term. Greater standard deviation indicates higher volatility, which means the investor faces a wider range of potential portfolio values over the long term.*

As investors determine what levels of short-term risk are tolerable and what range of expected future outcomes is acceptable, they cannot forget one of the fundamental rules of investing: Risk and return are linked. Seeking higher returns means accepting higher risk. Seeking less risk means accepting lower returns.

Figures 2.4 and 2.5 graphically show that investors face greater uncertainty (more risk) about the final outcome of their investing efforts than most investors realize. When investors adopt a more conservative strategy, they gain greater certainty that they will achieve a particular investment objective and lower their risk, but they also achieve lower returns. The Island Principle's strategy is to increase the slope of these curves so investors not only can achieve higher returns but they also can reduce risk by narrowing the range of expected outcomes. Using The Island Principle, an investor faces less volatility and more certainty about long-term portfolio returns.

Once investors have determined their objectives, set realistic returns goals to reach those objectives, and defined their personal tolerance for risk, the next step in building an island portfolio is to diversify into markets around the world. The next chapter explains how to select several experienced mutual fund managers with good track records in global markets to help investors decide which markets to invest in and how much of their portfolio to put in each one.

## THE MUTUAL FUND SOLUTION

Determining the optimum mix of markets to put into an island portfolio is a challenge. It is a complex analytical process calling for a great deal of knowledge and guesswork in predicting the future. There is always the risk of choosing the wrong mix. No expert will be right all the time. Hindsight is 20/20. It is easy to look back and see which markets would have been the best bets in the past. Looking forward to make that decision requires a great deal of knowledge, experience, judgment, and luck.

Using computer models to create efficient frontier curves that tell investors what combination of geographic markets is best for meeting particular risk and return objectives sounds simple and straightforward, but there is a catch—only historical data is certain. But in order to model an efficient frontier predicting future portfolio behavior, analysts have to enter data on *projected* returns, *projected* standard deviations, and *projected* correlation coefficients. The model will be only as accurate as these projections. And the projections will be only as good as the people making them. Unlike historical data, future data is uncertain.

Typically, investment analysts use both historical data and their professional opinions to project future portfolio performance. If an analyst believes that the outstanding 16% growth rate of the United Kingdom from 1970 to 1997 will continue, he or she will use that data as input for creating the optimum mix. If the analyst believes that high growth rate is not sustainable, he or she will use the alternative projections. The analyst's future projections for each market around the world determine the efficient frontier and its optimum mixes generated by the computer model.

In real life, most professional money managers rely on their own judgment rather than computer models to decide what is the best mix of markets. No matter how much data is available or how good the computer models are, human judgment is the most important factor. This is the art of investing.

*Investing is not a precise science. It involves a high degree of informed judgment.*

One reason many investors are more comfortable investing in the U.S. market is that they are comfortable in that market. They trust their judgment about it. They live in it; they feel they understand what makes it tick and can predict how it will respond to various events and happenings. Most individual investors are not global stock experts, nor do they have the time or resources (even with the Internet) to become knowledgeable about companies in 21 different developed markets, much less in the over 50 existing markets around the world. Buying and selling stocks in non-U.S. markets means engaging in complicated trading transactions that are beyond the ability of most investors to execute. To implement a global investing strategy, they need to hire global investment experts.

While large investors with, say, $50 million could hire six to eight private global money managers to advise them, that is not a very practical approach for most individual investors. Private money managers tend to work with very large portfolios, typically pension funds and institutions. Many do not deal with individual investors at all, especially those with smaller portfolios.

Fortunately, global mutual funds (*world funds*) offer island investors access to top professional money management. The decision of mutual fund companies to expand their horizons and invest in stocks in non-U.S. markets has made it possible and practical for U.S. investors to become global investors. Island investors seek out true global mutual fund managers. A *regional fund* manager does not have the freedom to search for the best markets around the world because of the limitations the fund's structure places on choices. Similarly, managers of *international funds* or *foreign funds* are restricted from including the U.S. among their market choices. True global diversity means selecting mutual funds whose managers have discretion to buy in any market in the world. As of this writing, Morningstar *Principia Pro* lists 271 global mutual funds. Many of these have only short track records, but 24 have been in existence for more than 10 years, and seven have performance records stretching back 20 years or more (Table 5.5).

**world fund**
a mutual fund with holdings throughout the world including the United States; the same as a global fund.

**regional fund**
a mutual fund that invests in stocks in only one region of the world.

---

*Global mutual funds offer individual investors with even modest portfolios access to top professional portfolio managers with global experience and the resources to back them up.*

---

Global investment analysis can entail research in other languages and analysis of data gathered under unfamiliar accounting systems. Global stock transactions mean dealing with currency exchange and different transaction customs in markets around the world. Using mutual funds simplifies these things enormously for individual investors.

High-quality global mutual fund managers are backed by worldwide research staffs and have access to analysts who understand those foreign accounting systems. Global mutual funds have experience with international transactions and know how to handle currency issues. On the whole, mutual funds are very popular with

**international fund**
a mutual fund that owns securities throughout the world except in the United States; the same as a foreign fund or non-U.S. fund.

**TABLE 5.5  Global Mutual Funds Available to Investors as of December 1999 with Track Records Spanning at Least 10 Years**

| Fund Name | Fund Family | Year Started |
|---|---|---|
| Templeton Growth A | Templeton Group | 1954 |
| Phoenix-Aberdeen Wldwde OppA | Phoenix Funds | 1960 |
| Alliance Global Sm Cap A | Alliance Capital Funds | 1966 |
| Putnam Global Growth A | Putnam Funds | 1967 |
| Oppenheimer Global A | Oppenheimer Funds | 1969 |
| New Perspective | American Funds Group | 1973 |
| Templeton World A | Templeton Group | 1978 |
| First Invest Global A | First Investors Group | 1981 |
| Templeton Global Small Co A | Templeton Group | 1981 |
| Merrill Lynch Global Holdg A | Merrill Lynch Group | 1984 |
| Prudential World Global B | Prudential Mutual Funds | 1984 |
| GAM Global A | GAM Funds | 1986 |
| Hancock Global B | John Hancock Funds | 1986 |
| MFS Global Equity B | MFS Family of Funds | 1986 |
| Scudder Global | Scudder Funds | 1986 |
| Dreyfus Global Growth | Dreyfus Group | 1987 |
| Elfun Global | Elfun Mutual Funds | 1987 |
| Lexington Global Corp Lead | Lexington Group | 1987 |
| Midas U.S. & Overseas | Bull & Bear Group | 1987 |
| Evergreen Global Opport A | Evergreen Funds | 1988 |
| Lord Abbett Global Equity A | Lord Abbett Family of Funds | 1988 |
| Merrill Lynch Global Holdg B | Merrill Lynch Group | 1988 |
| Prudential Global Genesis B | Prudential Mutual Funds | 1988 |
| Founders Worldwide Growth | Founders Funds | 1989 |

*Source:* Morningstar, Inc. www.morningstar.com or 800-735-0700.

individual investors and for good reason. They offer several important benefits:

✔ Instant diversification.

✔ Professional management.

✔ Low investment minimums.

✔ Verifiable historical returns and easy monitoring.

✔ Modest fees and charges.

✔ Direct access to non-U.S. stocks.

## *Instant Diversification*

A mutual fund frequently holds over 100 stocks. With a single decision—to buy the fund—an investor obtains far more diversification than most individual investors could reasonably provide in a personal stock portfolio.

## *Professional Management*

Fund managers are highly trained (most hold professional designation as a Chartered Financial Analyst) and typically are backed by worldwide research capability that individual investors cannot match.

Through mutual funds, even an investor with only a modest-sized portfolio can hire several high-quality professional money managers. For most investors, there is no other affordable way to obtain this kind of professional management and diversification.

## *Low Investment Minimums*

Private money managers typically require $100,000 or more before they will open a new account. Many set minimums of $1 million to $5 million. If island investors want to diversify decision making using six professional money managers, this means they would need a minimum of $600,000 in order to hire the global experts they need to help them implement The Island Principle. Finding six different quality money managers willing to handle accounts of $100,000 would be difficult. Most private money managers are unwilling to handle accounts of this size.

Mutual fund accounts, on the other hand, can frequently be opened with as little as $1,000 to $2,000. This puts a diversified global portfolio within the reach of most investors. Even a modest $12,000 portfolio could be

 **foreign fund**
a mutual fund that can invest in the stocks of countries around the world except the United States; the same as an international fund.

 **Principia Pro**
premium reporting service from Morningstar available to individual investors through subscribing investment analysts; it is capable of summarizing a portfolio containing multiple mutual funds.

**management fee**
an amount charged by a mutual fund company to manage a fund; excludes loads and the commission charges when the fund buys and sells securities.

**private portfolio manager**
an investment specialist who manages a portfolio (not a mutual fund) for a fee.

**American Depositary Receipt (ADR)**
a certificate of receipt tradable in the United States indicating ownership in a foreign company stock that is being held by a U.S. trust company or bank.

diversified into six different global mutual funds to develop an Island Principle portfolio.

### Verifiable Historical Returns and Easy Monitoring

Checking a mutual fund's track record and monitoring the portfolio manager's performance is relatively easy. There is a great deal of public information about each fund and its managers. Investment magazines and newspapers track the mutual fund industry closely. Reporting services such as Morningstar provide large quantities of data about individual funds.

### Modest Fees and Charges

*Management fees* for mutual funds are usually lower than the fees for an actively managed individual account. A typical global stock fund will have internal management charges of 1% to 2.5%. Management expenses for global mutual funds do, however, tend to be higher than those for a mutual fund invested only in U.S. stocks because of the added costs of conducting global research and managing money internationally.

### Direct Access to Non-U.S. Stocks

Mutual funds have another unique advantage for U.S. investors buying non-U.S. stocks. Buying and holding non-U.S. stocks is very complicated. From a practical standpoint, direct ownership of non-U.S. stocks is almost impossible under current securities laws for many investors. Because of the complexities, individual investors or *private portfolio managers* typically do not invest directly in non-U.S. stocks. Instead, they invest through *American Depositary Receipts (ADRs)* or through *World Equity Benchmark Shares (WEBS)*, which are indirect ways to own overseas stocks.

American Depositary Receipts are available only for major non-U.S. companies, and they are traded only in the United States and not in other markets. An investor using ADRs to invest globally does not have access to all non-U.S. stocks or markets. The price of an ADR may or may not move exactly with the price of the company it represents. Mutual fund companies are the preferred alternative. They are set up to handle the many complexities of the outright purchase of stocks in companies outside the United States. They are not limited to owning those companies with ADRs.

WEBS are investment vehicles designed to simulate buying an entire country stock market index. There are 17 of these WEBS, which are traded like a stock on the American Stock Exchange. Each is designed to perform like the *MSCI* index for that country. For example, an investor interested in the Austrian market would buy a WEBS for Austria. A WEBS is similar to a *Standard & Poor's Depositary Receipt (SPDR or "spider")*, which is an investment vehicle that simulates the S&P 500. From the standpoint of an island investor, WEBS do not offer the stock or geographic diversity available through global mutual funds that helps them reduce their portfolios' risk.

---

*For many investors, buying mutual funds investing in non-U.S. stocks may be the only way they can directly buy shares of stock in companies outside the United States.*

---

## TAXING ISSUES

Mutual funds, of course, have disadvantages as well as advantages. Their primary drawback is that someone else is controlling the investor's *tax liability*. With a mutual fund, each investor's funds are merged with every other investor's funds. When investors purchase shares in a mutual fund, they buy into some investments that already have appreciated in value. That means that new investors inherit gains from other investors who have been in the fund a longer time. This is not a problem if the mutual

**World Equity Benchmark Shares (WEBS)** a tradable security that simulates a market index, available for 17 foreign country markets.

**MSCI** an abbreviation for Morgan Stanley Capital International, a company that provides benchmark products and services to the investment community.

**Standard & Poor's Depositary Receipt (SPDR or "spider")** a tradable security that simulates the Standard & Poor's 500 Index.

**tax liability**
income taxes individual investors must pay when mutual fund managers sell stocks and which reduce the investor's net returns.

**capital gain**
the gain in value of a stock or mutual fund when it is sold versus what an investor paid for it including the cost of subsequent investments or reinvestments of dividends or other distributions; taxed by the federal government at a lower rate than ordinary income, typically 20%.

fund is part of an IRA, 401(k), or other qualified plan with special tax treatment. But it can be a problem in taxable portfolios.

A painful example of how this can affect an investor occurs when a new investor buys mutual fund shares toward the end of the year and almost immediately receives an unexpected *capital gain* distribution that triggers taxes.

*Allowing someone else to make decisions that affect an investor's tax liability is a disadvantage of investing through mutual funds.*

Sharing gains is a benefit if an investor is on the other side of the sharing arrangement, of course, but most investors are not aware of or ignore this benefit. In fast-growing funds, existing shareholders pass on part of their annual tax problem to new shareholders and end up deferring gains until later when they eventually sell their shares in the fund. This deferral turns the tax problem into a benefit.

*Sharing the tax burden with new investors in a rapidly growing mutual fund turns a tax problem into an advantage for existing fund shareholders.*

Island investors (and any other mutual fund investors) can significantly reduce this tax problem by selecting tax-efficient mutual funds. That means there is low turnover of stocks within the fund or that the fund uses other management techniques such as keeping track of the costs on various lots of shares purchased and then, when selling, selling those lots that will have the lowest tax impact for investors. Unfortunately, many mutual fund and portfolio managers ignore tax consequences when they buy and sell stocks. Hopefully, this will change as investors demand that portfolios be managed in a tax-efficient manner not just for pretax returns.

Many investors are unaware of a small tax advantage enjoyed by owners of non-U.S. stocks. Some foreign governments levy taxes on dividends paid by companies under their jurisdiction. The Internal Revenue Service allows shareholders in these overseas companies a dollar-for-dollar tax credit for these taxes. This credit flows through a mutual fund company to its shareholders (mutual fund companies report the tax credit to shareholders annually on Form 1099-DIV along with interest, dividends, and capital gains).

Although these foreign tax credits are typically small amounts, a tax credit is the equivalent of real income and is worth much more than a deduction. To receive the credit, the taxpayer must either complete IRS Form 1116 (Foreign Tax Credit) as part of annual federal income tax filing, or, if one meets certain requirements, claim the foreign tax credit on Form 1040.

## SHIFTING TO A GLOBAL PORTFOLIO

The Island Principle asks investors to start thinking like citizens of a tiny island with no market of its own. It invites them to become true global investors. Island investors shift their investment perspective and take two related actions to increase their long-term odds for investment success:

✔ They invest in multiple markets around the world, not in a single market like the U.S. market, nor in just two markets—U.S. and foreign.

✔ They use multiple decision makers to help them choose these markets.

Investors following The Island Principle accomplish both actions by buying shares in six to eight global mutual funds (those that can invest everywhere around the world, including the United States). The funds are specifically chosen not only because they have successful *management styles* but also because their management styles are different—that is, they have low correlations.

**management style**
a term describing whether a mutual fund manager buys small company stocks, large company stocks, value stocks, or growth stocks.

These global mutual funds create a portfolio that is diversified geographically around the world. Because their styles are different, the decisions of the investors' individual mutual fund managers create a mix of markets with low correlation in their portfolios. This market diversification reduces both the short-term volatility of their portfolios and the real, long-term risks that threaten the ability of investors to achieve their financial objectives.

The benefit of this diversification is that no single market controls an investor's future. Island investors should strive for a risk (volatility) lower than either the MSCI World Index or the S&P 500.

Typically, the amount of an island portfolio allocated to U.S. stocks will range between 25% and 50%. Fifty percent invested in any single market, even the U.S. market, can be considered aggressive investing in that market. This larger allocation to the U.S. versus other markets can be justified because of the advantages of investing in a home market, the diversity of the U.S. market, and the strength of the U.S. economy. At times when U.S. stocks are overpriced, however, even a 25% allocation to U.S. stocks may be too much and investors should choose lower allocations. These allocations may appear radical to a U.S. investor but quite normal to an island investor.

Though annual returns will vary significantly from one year to the next, island investors should strive to achieve average annual returns of 13% to 14% for the stock portion of their portfolios. These are arithmetic averages to use as an annual goal. Calculated on a long-term basis, a 13% to 14% arithmetic return rate works out to a 12% to 13% geometric return rate over time.

Island investors should monitor their portfolios on a quarterly basis (annually at a minimum). Each mutual fund was chosen for a reason, and investors should watch to make sure each is fulfilling its purpose in the portfolio and that the portfolio as a whole is performing as planned. Corrections or changes typically will be small (as discussed in Chapter 7).

Following The Island Principle will require a considerable shift from where most portfolios are right now, and this shift is best made gradually. For example, if an investor currently has 20% of a stock portfolio in non-U.S. holdings, the first step might be to buy one or more global mutual funds and move that level to 35% (however, since a global fund can hold U.S. stocks, the transition to a particular level of non-U.S. holdings may be slower than the investor expects).

As an investor becomes more comfortable with higher levels of non-U.S. securities, he or she can shift more assets into global mutual funds the following year and move the portfolio to an allocation of 40% or 50% non-U.S. stocks. Ultimately, an island investor's portfolio of global mutual funds might contain 50% to 75% non-U.S. stocks and 50% to 25% U.S. stocks. The investor's original allocation to U.S. and non-U.S. securities is now reversed. From an island perspective, allocating 50% of a portfolio to a single market is a large allocation.

A second approach to developing a global portfolio, though one that does not provide the full benefits of The Island Principle, is to buy shares in one or more foreign funds. Because these funds have no U.S. holdings, the investor's portfolio will shift to a global position more rapidly.

This approach has a significant drawback. It may have considerable tax consequences at a later date if the investor decides to shift from foreign funds to global funds in order to fully implement The Island Principle, because the investor may have a large gain to realize on the sale of the foreign fund. The investor may be reluctant to make this change and incur that cost.

The Island Principle is not a scheme to avoid taxes or protect assets from creditors in an offshore bank. It is a long-term global investment strategy. It encourages investors to shift to a new perspective in order to enlarge their investment horizons. It provides them with a simple method of building their global portfolios. By investing as if they were world citizens instead of citizens of a single country, island investors gain a new perspective on investment success.

# Choosing
# Individual Managers

T he Island Principle adds new levels of diversification to the portfolio risk management techniques
most investors already use. First, island investors
add geographic market diversity. They understand that all
stock investing involves risk and that includes investing
in the United States. They see the United States as only
one of many markets around the world. They understand
the risk of investing in a single market. Instead of holding
only U.S. stocks in their portfolios, they include stocks
from multiple markets around the world.

Second, island investors add decision diversity. They
understand that relying on a single person to make the
portfolio's geographic distribution is risky in the same
way that putting only a single stock in a portfolio would
be risky. Instead, they put together a crack crew of global
experts who share the responsibility for choosing both the
right markets and the right stocks within those markets
that together are most likely to meet the investor's personal financial goals.

Understanding what kind of investors they are, what
level of risk they can tolerate, and what level of returns
they want to achieve to meet their goals are critical first
steps. Island investors use these parameters to help them

pick professional managers whose styles, combined within a global portfolio, are most likely to meet the investors' goals.

---

*Island investors hire a team of global experts to help them decide what markets to be in and what stocks to buy in those markets.*

---

Just as choosing stocks or markets with low correlation is key to making the magic of diversification work, choosing managers with different styles is also important for portfolio diversification. The market and stock choices of individual managers the investor chooses should have low correlation to one another if the managers' styles are different. This gives island investors the decision-making diversity they want.

As captain of the overall portfolio, the island investor's responsibilities are:

- ✔ Choosing several true global managers with different styles.
- ✔ Setting up a system for tracking the consolidated portfolio.
- ✔ Monitoring portfolio results on a regular basis and measuring those results against the investor's personal risk and return parameters.
- ✔ Deciding when to change managers or portfolio allocation among the investor's managers.

## GLOBAL VERSUS FOREIGN VERSUS REGIONAL FUNDS

Island investors look for true global managers with a world perspective. Managers of global or world funds have the freedom to choose stocks from around the world. Their portfolios are not restricted to any particular region or country, nor do they exclude any particular country from consideration. The mutual fund's stated objectives and guidelines, as outlined in its prospectus, give the portfolio manager flexibility to seek investment opportunities throughout the world. This provides the greatest potential for the risk-reducing geographic diversification the island investor wants (Figure 6.1).

By contrast, a foreign or international fund manager invests anywhere around the world *except* the United States. Many investors just beginning to shift from a U.S.-only stock portfolio to one with some global stocks may want to do so by investing part of their portfolio with an international or foreign money manager. This is a convenient way for investors to begin investing globally, but it

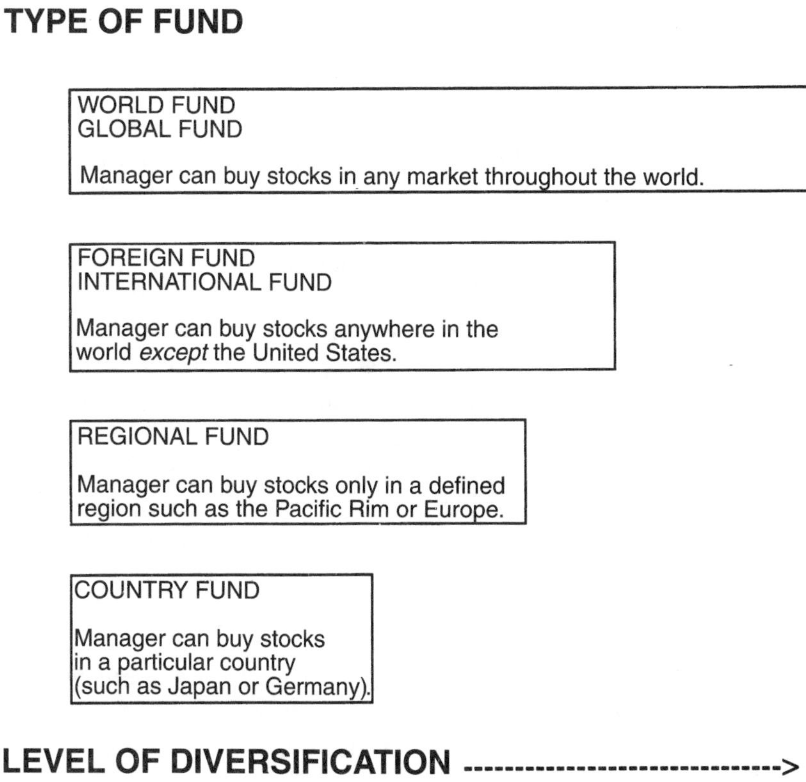

## TYPE OF FUND

WORLD FUND
GLOBAL FUND

Manager can buy stocks in any market throughout the world.

FOREIGN FUND
INTERNATIONAL FUND

Manager can buy stocks anywhere in the world *except* the United States.

REGIONAL FUND

Manager can buy stocks only in a defined region such as the Pacific Rim or Europe.

COUNTRY FUND

Manager can buy stocks in a particular country (such as Japan or Germany).

## LEVEL OF DIVERSIFICATION ------------------------------->

**FIGURE 6.1**   To gain the broadest benefits from diversification around the world, island investors look for true global mutual funds that have no limitations on where their fund managers can invest. *Source:* Kreitler Associates.

has disadvantages when it comes to true global diversification. When an investor chooses a foreign mutual fund, the investor actually is making a decision about how much of the portfolio should be invested in the United States versus in non-U.S. stocks. That means that this crucial market allocation decision is riding on the expertise of a single individual—in this case, the investor. By choosing global mutual funds instead, island investors leave that market allocation decision to experts.

*By choosing a foreign manager instead of a global manager, the investor makes the crucial decision of how much to invest in U.S. versus non-U.S. stocks rather than leaving that decision to global experts.*

 **country fund**
a mutual fund that invests in stocks in only one country.

Similarly, investors who purchase regional mutual funds or *country funds* that invest only in particular regions such as Europe or the Pacific Rim or countries such as Japan or Germany are also making market allocation decisions on their own. Since the fund manager has no choice except to invest in stocks in that area, the investor will never know if the manager might have preferred to be investing money elsewhere around the world. The same thing is true of funds that specialize only in emerging markets. Unfortunately, the investment community focuses on foreign investing rather than global investing, and this is reflected in the funds it offers investors. Morningstar lists only 271 global funds while it lists 1,196 foreign, country, and other specialized non-U.S. funds (excluding hybrid funds).

*The investment community bias is toward foreign (non-U.S.) or regional or country-based mutual funds rather than true global funds.*

Selecting regional managers defeats the geographic decision-making diversification island investors want in their portfolios. Investors who put 20% of their capital with a manager specializing in a particular region such as Europe or the Pacific Rim have effectively made a geographic allocation decision on their own.

Some investors have a hard time giving up control of the geographic allocation of their portfolios. Rather than using true global managers, they prefer choosing the geographic mix of funds—U.S., foreign, or regional funds—so they are determining the overall portfolio's global allocation themselves. These investors can benefit from The Island Principle's increased exposure to global markets. However, they will not benefit from the diversification that comes with using multiple decision makers to choose the market mix.

A crucial tenet of The Island Principle is that since the geographic allocation decision drives much of a portfolio's performance, this allocation is too important for a single person to decide no matter how highly qualified that individual may be. Additionally, most individual investors lack the global expertise to choose the right market. Diversifying this decision among multiple global managers reduces the risk of choosing the wrong markets.

*Island investors choose true global managers and then allow those managers to make the crucial decision about how much to invest in various markets throughout the world.*

## RESEARCHING SUPERIOR GLOBAL FUNDS

The Ibbotson and Kaplan study (Chapter 3) determined that both asset allocation and stock selection are important factors in portfolio performance. Since global managers both choose the markets (a form of asset allocation) as well as pick the individual stocks in those markets, an island investor should choose his or her global managers carefully. Their skill and expertise will clearly determine most of the island portfolio's performance.

Fully researching a mutual fund means doing a lot of old-fashioned homework. The more research investors do, the better they will become at reading between the lines and making informed judgments. This is an ongoing and never-ending process. While investors can get hard data on fund performance and even on how much risk a particular fund will add to their portfolios from several sources, they also need to find soft data about management philosophy and styles, which will have significant long-term impact on their portfolios' success.

Information is available from a variety of sources, some better than others. Keep in mind that by the time it reaches users, most mutual fund data is already several months old. By the time articles are researched, written, and printed, the information in most magazines or newsletters is several weeks or months old when subscribers read it. Similarly, data may be several weeks old by the time mutual fund companies send it to reporting services or brokerage houses whose reports on individual funds may be updated only quarterly or even less frequently. This data delay may not be significant if a fund has a consistent approach to investing. However, if a fund changes its direction, it may be a while before the reports investors rely on catch up with the shift.

The financial press is the place most investors start their research. Keep in mind that most press coverage is very performance oriented, and performance is only one part of the total picture. Popular newsstand magazines are fond of making lists of the best-performing funds. This sells subscriptions. They are fun to read but investors should not attach much significance to them. The "best" fund typically changes from year to year, and investors should be looking for funds that perform well consistently over many years, not just in a given year.

Careful reading of interviews with fund managers in both the financial press and the popular press can uncover information about the philosophy and style of the fund manager and the fund or *fund family* itself. This soft data

**fund family**
a company that manages a group of mutual funds.

is important for investors seeking diversification in fund styles, but it is often difficult to obtain.

Investment newsletters are an important niche within the financial press. They often provide more detailed information than investors can find in newsstand publications. However, if investors use them, they should be sure they understand the particular biases of the newsletters' editors. Editors filter any information they have through those personal biases when making their recommendations. None currently focuses exclusively on global mutual funds.

Marketing materials put out by the funds themselves also tend to be performance oriented, but they often contain information about philosophy, details about the managers, and other useful facts. The fund's prospectus outlines the fund's history, basic philosophy, and other background information. Annual and *quarterly reports* provide essential data on things like the fund's largest stock holdings, *sector weighting*, which markets the fund currently invests in, and its cash position. Most funds also have web sites that contain information about the fund and how to buy shares in it. Many investors forget that they always have the option of calling a fund directly for information. They can ask the fund for a Statement of Additional Information or SAI, which contains a wealth of information. They can also ask for specific information such as the manager's biography or *currency hedging* practices (the answers they receive to some questions may be limited because of NASD regulations).

Mutual fund reporting services are a popular and efficient way to obtain information about individual funds. They provide a great deal of basic data that makes it possible for individual investors to do a lot of their own research. These services have the ability to gather data from mutual fund companies that is hard to get from any other source. Most mutual fund companies will go out of their way to provide the services with data because they know that they influence investors' decisions to buy or sell their funds. The reporting services are not directly regulated by the NASD so they can be a bit more opinionated about what they say.

 **quarterly report**
a document prepared by the mutual fund company for shareholders describing the activities of the fund over the prior three months.

 **sector weighting**
amount of a mutual fund or a portfolio that is allocated to various market sectors.

 **currency hedging**
a transaction that offsets the changes in foreign currency values so changes do not affect the value of non-U.S. stock holdings in a portfolio.

Morningstar is the most popular service available. Morningstar reports consolidate a great deal of information in one place and are a good starting point for investors who want to do their own research. A print version of Morningstar's reports on individual funds is available in many libraries. Morningstar also offers some limited free data on its Internet web site (www.morningstar.com). For a nominal monthly fee of about $10, it provides online subscribers with a great deal of information on both individual mutual funds and the management styles of fund families. An example of a Morningstar report on an individual fund and how an island investor might scrutinize the data in it follows at the end of the chapter.

At still another level, investment advisers often subscribe to the more expensive Morningstar Principia Pro service, which allows them to rank and manipulate several sets of data to form and analyze hypothetical portfolios invested in multiple funds, stocks, and variable annuities. CDA Wiesenberger is another service providing mutual fund data to investors.

Many professional investment advisers also subscribe to asset allocation software and data services such as Ibbotson Associates and Wilson Associates. These subscriptions are too pricey for most individual investors but those who do use the services of these investment professionals can gain access to this more detailed information. Their advisers can help these investors understand how to use and interpret it. Many brokerage houses are now using their extensive research capabilities to develop mutual fund reports that they make available to their clients. The more advanced reports are based on face-to-face discussions with fund managers and contain important information (that soft data) about the fund managers' style and philosophy that is unavailable elsewhere.

Some investors who begin investing globally look for research shortcuts. They search for a single criterion or a simple marker that will enable them quickly to choose the right funds for their portfolios. For example, some investors think they can just pick three or four global mutual funds that have earned high star ratings from

Morningstar to create a diversified global portfolio. However, many of these services rely heavily on short-term performance data rather than in-depth analysis of performance over time. Their rankings are often based on a very limited number of factors or on criteria that are not very important to long-term performance. They seldom include any of the soft data that is also critical to consider when selecting good managers. Chapter 7 compares two sample portfolios to show investors how to apply The Island Principle to develop a diversified global portfolio that reduces overall portfolio risk.

---

*Investors need to do a lot of old-fashioned homework pulling information from multiple sources in order to intelligently identify global mutual fund candidates for their island portfolios.*

---

## ASKING THE RIGHT QUESTIONS

As investors research individual global mutual funds, they should keep several key points in mind. For starters, investors should focus on long-term data, not short-term performance. Investors have no way of telling whether the manager's short-term performance was due to skill or luck. Looking at the manager's five- or 10-year track record is a more meaningful yardstick of his or her ability. It is also critical for investors to understand that risk and return go hand in hand. Besides looking at a manager's performance record, they also need to understand what kind of risks he or she typically takes.

As they research funds and managers, investors should be aware that the performance and risk of a fund and its manager may not always be one and the same. The manager may have just recently joined the fund so the track record is not his.

Finally, while mutual fund information services focus on hard data that can be reported objectively in absolute numbers, investors also need soft information about style issues like currency hedging or the latitude that a fund allows its manager that can be harder to get. Investors will have to read interviews and reports in the financial press closely to learn this information.

As investors research a potential mutual fund investment, they need a variety of information that will help them select a mix of global funds that will meet their long-term risk and return objectives (Table 6.1). Among the questions their research should answer are:

✔ What is the basic philosophy and style of the fund or fund family?

✔ How has the fund performed over time?

✔ Who manages the fund?

✔ What are the costs of running the fund?

✔ How does the fund handle currency fluctuations?

### What Is the Fund's Basic Philosophy and Style?

Investors should pay close attention to the philosophy and style a mutual fund outlines in its prospectus and that is reported through interviews in the financial press. Is the fund conservative or aggressive, does it favor large companies or small companies, does it keep large amounts in cash, does it tend toward investing in developed markets or in countries that are considered developing or emerging markets?

If the fund is part of a mutual fund family, investors should research the underlying philosophy and culture of the family of funds, if any, that owns that mutual fund. Some fund families allow individual managers quite a lot of autonomy. Other fund families require that all their fund managers follow a particular investment philosophy. In this case, researching this parent organization will probably tell investors a great deal about the style and philosophy of a fund in that family.

Mutual fund management changes are a fact of life. Within some fund families, managers seem to change every two or three years while managers have long

| TABLE 6.1   Questions to Ask about Global Mutual Funds and Their Managers with Suggested Research Sources | |
| --- | --- |
| *Questions to Ask* | *Information Sources* |
| **What is the fund's basic philosophy and style?**<br>Is it aggressive (favors growth stocks, small companies, developing markets)?<br>Is it conservative (favors undervalued stocks, large companies, developed markets)?<br>Is it part of a family of funds that may influence its style or management?<br>What is its correlation with other funds the investor is considering? | Popular and financial press<br>Mutual fund newsletters<br>Morningstar reports<br>Brokerage house mutual fund reports<br>Fund prospectus<br>Fund Statement of Additional Information<br>Web site |
| **How has the fund performed over time?**<br>How many years has the fund been in existence?<br>What is its philosophy and style?<br>How has it performed in bull markets?<br>How has it performed in bear markets?<br>How has it performed over three, five, and ten-year periods?<br>What are its standard deviation, alpha, beta, and Sharpe ratio (measures of risk)? | Fund prospectus<br>Fund Statement of Additional Information<br>Fund annual report<br>Morningstar reports<br>Web site |
| **Who is the fund manager?**<br>What is the manager's personal philosophy and style?<br>   Is the manager aggressive or conservative?<br>   Does the manager hedge currencies?<br>   How often does the manager turn stocks over?<br>   What percent of cash does the manager hold?<br>How long has the manager been managing money?<br>How long has the manager been with this fund?<br>How consistently has the manager performed?<br>How is the manager paid?<br>What kind of research resources does the manager have available? | Popular and financial press<br>Annual and quarterly fund reports<br>Fund Statement of Additional Information<br>Manager biography from fund<br>Brokerage house mutual fund reports<br>Morningstar reports<br>Web site |
| **What are the fund's costs?**<br>What are the costs of buying the fund?<br>What are the costs of selling the fund?<br>What are the fund's management fees? | Fund prospectus<br>Fund Statement of Additional Information<br>Morningstar reports<br>Web site |
| **How does the fund handle currency fluctuations?**<br>Does the fund hedge at all?<br>Does the fund hedge a portion of its total portfolio? | Annual and quarterly fund reports<br>Fund Statement of Additional Information<br>Morningstar reports |

*Source:* Kreitler Associates.

tenures at others. When managers are replaced, drastic style changes are possible. A new manager who rearranges a portfolio may create large taxable distributions to shareholders. Likewise, investors who decide to sell the fund because they do not want to use the new manager may face large taxable gains.

Consistent management style within a fund family can be a real advantage when managers change. A fund family with consistent management style will arrange for a smooth transition from the old to the new manager. The new manager's style is more likely to be compatible with that of the old. If investors chose the fund because they wanted that particular style in their portfolios, they can remain confident that the fund will continue to add that style to their portfolio mix. The new manager is less likely to liquidate a substantial portion of the fund's stocks and generate a large tax liability for its shareholders.

Markets also change. That is one of the few things that can be guaranteed in investing. Short-term fund performance, therefore, is less relevant than the philosophy of the organization, which will have a tremendous impact on a fund's long-term performance through both up and down markets. This basic style can sometimes be more important than the personal style of the fund's manager.

*A fund's basic philosophy and style determine its long-term performance.*

## How Has the Fund Performed over Time?

Island investors concentrate on long-term performance. They understand that focusing on short-term performance would be a big mistake in selecting their global mutual funds. Betting on a winning manager based on his or her short-term performance is a little like backing a winning craps player at a casino. At some point, the player's luck will run out and the backers will lose their money. Before investing with a winning mutual fund, investors need to understand whether the manager has just been lucky or if there really is something special about that management style. Good research will discover the reason for his or her success.

An investor's goal should be to own funds with consistently good five- to 10-year or even longer track records. Investors should look for funds that are consistently in the top quartile of their peers. A fund that stays in the top quartile over a period of several years will rise to the top of the performance list when investors look at five- and 10-year periods. This is meaningful performance.

In terms of benchmarks, there really is no completely appropriate index to compare individual global fund performance against. Morgan Stanley Capital International's EAFE index is a popular index used as a benchmark for portfolios containing only non-U.S. stocks. It includes 19 developed markets around the world but excludes Canada and the United States. This exclusion is a major problem for island investors who are looking for an index of all developed markets.

The Morgan Stanley Capital International World Index, the most commonly used benchmark for global portfolios, is a much broader index than the EAFE index. It includes the United States and Canada and also includes many developing countries. Island investors should use the World Index as their primary benchmark. Various financial publications including the *Wall Street Journal* and *Barron's* publish the World Index and the EAFE index.

Popular indexes all have the problem that they are weighted by capitalization. This overemphasizes the performance of large countries and companies and underweights that of smaller ones. A benchmark based on capitalization is distorted, so most indexes must be viewed with skepticism when comparing a fund's performance against them.

The Appendix chart showing the annual returns of all developed markets from 1970 to 1998 (Table A.1) includes a column showing the average of these developed markets. This is a simple average that is not weighted by capitalization and, ironically, this number is higher for the period than any of the global indexes. Unfortunately, no one tracks and reports this number, which would be an ideal benchmark for many island portfolios.

Another meaningful benchmark is the average return of all other global stock mutual funds. They are all competing in the same universe and have access to the same investments. This is reported by Morningstar and periodically by the financial press.

> *The World Index and the average of all global mutual funds are good benchmarks to compare a fund against.*

Investors should remember that returns must be balanced against risk as they evaluate funds. Investors also need to ask how the fund manager has done on a *risk-adjusted basis*. Beating the market by 10% is not such a great accomplishment if the manager took on 25% more risk to achieve it. Investors should look for managers who can achieve superior returns with less risk. If investors take on more risk than the market, they should expect to obtain higher returns to compensate for taking that extra risk.

As with managers, investors often judge a fund's risk by the seat of their pants using the information they have learned about a particular fund's investment style. Investors can measure risk in more specific terms, however.

 **risk-adjusted basis** a method of evaluating a mutual fund manager's performance that combines the amount of risk he or she took on to achieve a certain level of returns with that level of returns.

> *Investors must pay attention to the level of risk a portfolio manager takes on as well as his or her performance.*

Standard deviation is the most popular benchmark for volatility. It measures how much the fund's return varied over a given period of time versus its average return. Morningstar mutual fund reports include a fund's standard deviation. Comparing a fund's volatility (standard deviation) to that of the market as a whole is another way of measuring the fund's overall risk level. In this case, the World Index would be the benchmark.

*Alpha* is a measurement used by financial analysts that combines return and risk that is reported by Morningstar and other reporting services. An alpha of greater than 1.0 means that, on a risk-adjusted basis, the manager's performance is better than its relevant benchmark. That means he or she is adding value to the portfolio. An alpha under 1.0 means the manager is doing worse than the benchmark and the management decisions are not adding any value to the portfolio.

Some funds are consistently more volatile or less volatile than the market because of the particular stocks they own. If the market is up 10%, a volatile fund may be up 15%. Conversely, if the market is down 10%, that volatile fund may be down 15%. Investors want to compare the volatility of their funds versus the market.

Mutual fund reporting services also include a measurement called *beta*, which is used to measure this relative volatility. A beta of 1.0 means the fund is likely to move with and have the same risk as a market. A beta of less than 1.0 means that a fund is less volatile than the market, while a beta greater than 1.0 means the fund has more volatility than the market. A conservative investor will emphasize funds with lower betas. An aggressive investor will seek out funds with higher betas.

The *Sharpe ratio* is another measure of the risk of a fund or portfolio. Developed by William Sharpe, who has contributed much to the development of Modern Portfolio Theory, this ratio divides excess return by standard deviation (excess return is calculated as the return of the fund or portfolio compared to 90-day Treasury bills). The higher the resulting number, the better the performance of the fund or portfolio on a risk-adjusted basis. The Sharpe ratio is a good measure to use when comparing two funds or two portfolios against one another.

## Who Manages the Fund?

Remember that the manager's performance and the fund's performance may or may not be one and the same

**alpha**
a factor that measures fund performance on a risk-adjusted basis; an alpha of 1.0 means that a fund manager's performance on a risk-adjusted basis matches the market while alphas above or below 1.0 mean that the manager is doing better or worse than the market, respectively.

**beta**
a factor that shows a fund's sensitivity to market movements. A beta of 1.0 means its volatility is the same as the market. A beta in excess of 1.0 means the fund is more volatile than the market. A beta less than 1.0 means the fund is less volatile than the market.

**Sharpe ratio**
a formula developed by Nobel prizewinning economist William Sharpe to show risk-adjusted performance.

depending on how long the manager has been with the fund. So investors may need to consider the fund's track record separately from that of its current manager. Since the allocation of their capital among markets around the world will be the biggest single factor in their portfolios' performance, how a fund manager makes those crucial style decisions is critical.

While performance and risk can be measured using specific benchmarks, there is a lot of information about a fund's management that is much harder to quantify. This is the soft data that takes diligent research on the investor's part but which will be very important to the portfolio's long-term outcome.

Investors should ask themselves whether the fund is run by people they would like to have managing their money through good times and bad. How the manager behaved in both up and down markets in the past is an indicator of how he or she will behave in the future. A fund manager is a real human being who is making decisions to buy and sell in the same good or bad markets as everyone else. Investors want someone who is a real pro at making intelligent decisions, finding the best opportunities, and managing their money when negative emotions may be running high.

Investors should find out how long the manager has been investing money, whether with the fund they are looking at or at other funds. Investors should look for managers with a minimum of five years of experience. Ten years is better. Fund managers who have been through bear markets like those we experienced in 1973–1974 and in 1987 will have a different perspective than managers who have only made decisions during a strong bull market.

*Investors should feel confident that a fund manager is someone they would like to have managing their money through both up and down markets over the long term.*

Another very useful piece of information is to find out how a fund manager is paid. This is some of that soft data that can be very hard to find. Some funds pay managers based on just the past year's performance, while others compensate their managers based on a longer term. How the manager is paid is going to influence his or her behavior. Some compensation systems may encourage managers to take unnecessary risks. If an investor is investing for long-term performance, the fund manager's compensation should be based on long-term performance.

Managers can only be as good as the research teams supporting them. Investors should find out if a fund's research analysts actually go out and meet face to face with the management of the companies they own or are considering. For global mutual funds, this can be quite a logistical challenge, but it is critical for managers to have firsthand information on which to base decisions. Investors should be skeptical if a portfolio manager only picks stocks from around the world from a suite of offices somewhere in the United States using second-generation reports and information developed by others.

Reviewing the qualifications of an individual manager in depth may be less essential when they are within a fund family whose managers are required to follow the same *investment style*. This guarantees a certain level of consistency. If the investor is confident that the fund family's recruiting program and compensation package assure high-quality managers, then the credentials of individual managers do not need to be scrutinized as closely. But investors should be aware that even within fund families there can be wide variation among the styles and philosophies of individual fund managers.

## What Are the Costs of Buying, Selling, and Owning the Fund?

The most obvious cost of a mutual fund is any *front-end load* paid when an investor buys a fund or the *back-end load* when the investor sells it (a *load* is a sales charge).

**investment style**
the overall style a manager uses in managing a portfolio such as value, growth, large company, or small company.

**front-end load**
a sales charge levied when mutual fund shares are purchased; typically calculated as a percentage of the value of the shares purchased.

**back-end load**
a sales charge paid when an investor sells mutual fund shares.

**load**
a sales charge
levied either
when an investor
buys a mutual
fund or when the
investor sells it,
based on a per-
centage of the
investor's
purchase.

**share
classes**
separate classes
of the same mu-
tual fund which
have different
sales loads and
expenses.

**no-load
fund**
a mutual fund
that does not
charge a commis-
sion to buy or
sell shares.

Typically, the maximum sales charge is approximately 5.5% and the load scales down as the amount purchased increases. Loads cover the mutual fund's costs for market-ing and distribution including commissions to brokers or investment advisers.

Investors dislike paying loads. So the mutual fund industry has responded by creating different classes of shares, typically called A, B, and C shares. These differ-ent *share classes* have varying expense charges, which are used to cover the cost of marketing and some admin-istration expenses. These new classes replace all or some of the up-front load with early redemption fees and on-going charges that typically are not easily visible. Many fund families have two or three classes of shares for the same mutual fund. Complicating matters, many *no-load funds* have imposed sales charges to cover the cost of marketing.

The latest trend in the investment industry is to make funds available through a wrap fee program with an investment adviser or through programs such as OneSource at Charles Schwab. Schwab makes mutual funds available without a load because the investment house has negotiated a separate fee with the mutual fund company to cover costs of marketing and of servic-ing the account. Most brokerage houses now offer wrap programs in one form or another. Under a wrap pro-gram, an adviser charges a fee for investment advice but all transactions are free or at a minimal charge. Eventually these programs may make large up-front loads obsolete.

Less obvious than a load but just as important are a fund's *internal management costs*, the cost of running the fund. Investors frequently have to dig to find these costs because they are buried in the prospectus or in reports published by services such as Morningstar and CDA Wiesenberger. Internal costs can add up over long periods of time. A small difference in annual returns can make a significant difference in long-term investment returns. For a long-term investor, the cumulative cost of annual internal management costs are more important than a fund's initial sales charge.

*Internal management costs can have a large impact on portfolio value over the long term.*

Management costs are actually much more predictable than fund performance. While future performance is very difficult to predict, historical costs are a relatively good predictor of future costs. Internal management costs may be as low as 0.6% or as high as 2% (a cost of 0.6% is referred to as 60 *basis points*; a cost of 2% is 200 basis points). These are based on the value of the fund. Over longer periods, a difference of 0.6% is important.

Over 20 years $100,000 at 8% will grow to $466,095. If the return is only 7.5% because management costs of one fund are 50 more basis points than another, the total return will only grow to $424,785. This is a 9% difference. In a retirement portfolio, this would mean the investor with the higher return would have a 9% higher retirement income stream. That is why fund management costs are important.

An investor's tax liability also varies from fund to fund depending on many factors including how often a manager turns stocks over and whether the fund makes any effort to actively manage the tax liabilities of its shareholders. Frequent buying and selling of stocks may trigger gains to be taxed at short-term rates rather than long-term rates. Unfortunately, relatively few managers pay attention to the tax problems they pass on to investors.

**internal management costs**
a mutual fund's costs to operate the fund including overhead, salaries, and other business expenses. By tradition does not include the commissions paid when funds buy and sell securities.

**basis point**
a hundredth of 1%; 100 basis points equals 1%. Used in calculating investment fees or bond yields.

## How Does the Fund Handle Currency Fluctuations?

Currency hedging is an example of how managers (or fund families) may differ in style. There is no consensus on the best approach to fluctuations in currency values, even among the academics. Some portfolio managers hedge the *currency exposure* in their portfolios; others do not. Some experts hedge their position on the issue by recommending that an investor hedge half one's assets in U.S. dollars and leave the other half unhedged.

**currency exposure**
the currencies that a fund's assets are held in. A high exposure in foreign currencies increases the volatility of the portfolio but, over the long term, hedges the portfolio's buying power.

The Island Principle strategy includes some portfolio managers who do no currency hedging or only minimal hedging because a partially unhedged diversified portfolio protects an investor's global buying power. Since currencies are volatile, hedging currencies reduces short-term volatility of a portfolio. However, currency hedging is a costly management technique and many argue that it actually reduces long-term returns. On balance, a portfolio denominated 50% in U.S. dollars and the other 50% diversified in other currencies is a good position for an island investor.

*Currency exposure helps to protect an investor's long-term global purchasing power.*

An investor's goal should be to protect his or her long-term buying power, not necessarily to maximize the value of the portfolio in U.S. dollars. One of the benefits of a global portfolio denominated in local currencies is that it protects the global purchasing power of a portfolio and hedges its value against changes in the U.S. dollar.

The investor who tracks everything in U.S. dollars and does not want to face the additional volatility (in U.S. dollars) provided by unhedged portfolios should favor portfolio managers who hedge their portfolios. This is certainly better than avoiding global stocks entirely. This at least provides the benefits of global investing even though it does not provide the additional benefits of protecting global buying power.

## SOFT DATA—SOME EXAMPLES

Researching a fund family's style can help investors make better individual fund decisions. Here are short profiles of three leading global mutual fund families. Each profile is an amalgam of a great deal of soft data about overall philosophy and management styles gleaned from articles in the financial press, reporting service reports, and brokerage house reports. There is no single source investors can rely on for this information. Much of it can be discovered only through personal research and careful reading.

### American Funds

Has senior managers with long-term experience in many different types of market conditions.

Uses multiple, independent managers for each fund.

Compensates managers on multiyear performance.

Bottoms up stock selection.

Has worldwide research capability with analysts visiting a company before it is purchased and then annually after being purchased.

Uses value style in selection of stocks.

Seems to care about shareholders and has aggressively kept expenses low.

Has low loads and extremely loyal shareholders.

Has several high-quality global funds, which to date can only be bought with a load.

### Fidelity Funds

Has excellent research capability.

Marketing of the firm is excellent.

Managers and staff support are very talented.

There is extreme competition among managers, who are selected based on performance.

Managers tend to be moved frequently or to leave the company to take other positions.

Managers tend to be young and may lack experience in different types of markets.

Style and performance of funds are related to style of manager at the time and can change when managers change.

### Templeton

Is part of Franklin-Templeton.

Has global expertise.

Looks for bargains.

Prefers to buy stocks at times of extreme pessimism, which is psychologically very difficult to do.

Will not follow the crowd.

Buy-and-hold requires multiyear commitment.

May get out of a bull market too early, then buy into a depressed market too early.

Has low turnover.

Investment strategies used by retiring Sir John Templeton have been successfully passed on to new managers.

Traditionally a *load fund* family, though some funds can be purchased without a sales charge through Class C shares, which have higher annual charges and an early redemption charge, or as part of a wrap program.

**load fund** a fund that requires that investors pay a sales charge or load when they either buy (a front-end load) or sell (a back-end load) the fund.

## HARD DATA—AN EXAMPLE

Morningstar reports on individual mutual funds can be one of an island investor's most useful fund evaluation tools because they consolidate a great deal of information in a single place. The example here shows investors how to locate and interpret the information in these reports. Figure 6.2 provides a key to the mutual fund information on a sample Morningstar report on a global mutual fund—in this case, the New Perspective Fund. Table 6.2 explains which parts of the report provide investors with information on specific areas such as style, performance, management, and others discussed in the text. A more detailed explanation of how to interpret and use each section follows. The information in a Morningstar report answers many of the questions island investors should ask about a fund's style and philosophy as well as its performance, its management, the costs to own the fund, and how it handles currency hedging before selecting it for their portfolios. (Keep in mind that this example represents past data. The current Morningstar report on the

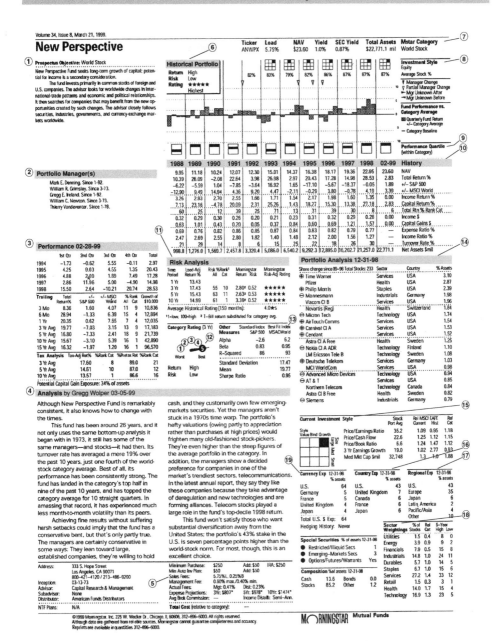

**FIGURE 6.2** Morningstar reports on individual mutual funds contain much useful information for island investors researching and evaluating global funds. This key shows investors where to look for specific hard data on style (philosophy), performance, management, fund costs, and hedging practices when selecting the global funds to put into their portfolios. The numbers coordinate with the text explanation. *Source:* Morningstar, Inc. www.morningstar.com or 800-735-0700.

---

### TABLE 6.2   Where to Find Key Information in a Morningstar Report

| Style | Performance | Management |
|---|---|---|
| Prospectus Objective (1) | Performance (3) | Portfolio Manager(s) (2) |
| Analysis (4) | Historical Profile (6) | |
| Morningstar Category (7) | Performance Quartile (9) | *Costs* |
| Investment Style (8) | Risk Analysis (11) | Sales Fees (5) |
| History (10) | Category Rating (12) | |
| Portfolio Analysis (14) | Other Measures (13) | *Hedging* |
| Current Investment Style (15) | | Currency Exposure (19) |
| Country Exposure (16) | | |
| Regional Exposure (17) | | |
| Sector Weightings (18) | | |

*Note:* This chart shows which parts of a Morningstar report will give investors information they can use to evaluate a fund's style, performance, management, costs, and hedging practices. The numbers are keyed to the Morningstar report in Figure 6.2 and the explanations in the text. *Source:* Kreitler Associates.

---

New Perspective Fund will be different from the example provided here.)

**1.** *Prospectus Objective.* The New Perspective prospectus states it is a world stock fund that seeks long-term capital growth with income a secondary consideration (Figure 6.2a). "World" and "global" have identical meaning.

**2.** *Portfolio Manager(s).* This list (Figure 6.2a) shows the names of the fund managers and how long each has been with the fund. Some funds have single managers; others have multiple managers. This report shows that New Perspective has five portfolio managers, two of whom joined the fund in 1992 while the other three have been there over 20 years. Based on industry standards, these are long tenures. Investors may also find informa-

Volume 34, Issue 8, March 21, 1999.

 **New Perspective**

**Prospectus Objective:** World Stock
. . . . . . . . . . . . . . . . . . . . . . . . . . . . . . . . . . . . . . . . . . .
New Perspective Fund seeks long-term growth of capital; poten-
tial for income is a secondary consideration.

    The fund invests primarily in common stocks of foreign and
U.S. companies. The advisor looks for worldwide changes in inter-
national-trade patterns and economic and political relationships.
It then searches for companies that may benefit from the new opportunities created by such changes. The advisor closely follows
securities, industries, governments, and currency-exchange markets worldwide.

②

**Portfolio Manager(s)**

    Mark E. Denning. Since 1-92.
    William R. Grimsley. Since 3-73.
    Gregg E. Ireland. Since 1-92.
    William C. Newton. Since 3-73.
    Thierry Vandeventer. Since 1-78.

**FIGURE 6.2a** The New Perspective Fund's prospectus
objective and portfolio managers.

tion about the fund's managers in the analysis section of
the report (4).

    **3. *Performance.*** The most useful information here
(Figure 6.2b) are the trailing 3-, 5-, 10-, and 15-year returns. Trailing geometric returns, which compound the
fund's returns over various periods of time, are more
meaningful to island investors than the quarterly returns.
The report also shows how the fund's trailing returns
compared to those of the MSCI World Index and how it
ranked versus other world funds. New Perspective has
done very well for all periods versus other world funds.
The comparison with the S&P 500 is less important to an
island investor.

    The tax analysis section gives investors information
on how the fund has performed on an after-tax basis. It reports a fund's annualized, after-tax total returns for three-,
five-, and ten-year periods. To calculate this figure, Morningstar makes three assumptions: that all income and

③

**Performance** 02-28-99

| | 1st Qtr | 2nd Qtr | 3rd Qtr | 4th Qtr | Total |
|---|---|---|---|---|---|
| 1994 | −1.73 | −0.62 | 5.55 | −0.11 | 2.97 |
| 1995 | 4.25 | 9.03 | 4.55 | 1.35 | 20.43 |
| 1996 | 4.88 | 2.09 | 1.89 | 7.49 | 17.28 |
| 1997 | 2.86 | 11.96 | 5.00 | −4.90 | 14.98 |
| 1998 | 15.50 | 2.64 | −10.21 | 20.74 | 28.53 |

| Trailing | Total Return% | +/− S&P 500 | +/−MSCI World | %Rank All | %Rank Cat | Growth of $10,000 |
|---|---|---|---|---|---|---|
| 3 Mo | 8.36 | 1.60 | 4.07 | 11 | 9 | 10,836 |
| 6 Mo | 28.94 | −1.33 | 6.39 | 15 | 4 | 12,894 |
| 1 Yr | 20.35 | 0.62 | 7.65 | 7 | 4 | 12,035 |
| 3 Yr Avg | 19.77 | −7.03 | 3.15 | 13 | 9 | 17,183 |
| 5 Yr Avg | 16.80 | −7.33 | 2.41 | 18 | 9 | 21,739 |
| 10 Yr Avg | 15.67 | −3.10 | 5.39 | 16 | 1 | 42,890 |
| 15 Yr Avg | 16.32 | −1.97 | 1.20 | 16 | 1 | 96,570 |

| Tax Analysis | Tax-Adj Ret% | %Rank Cat | %Pretax Ret | %Rank Cat |
|---|---|---|---|---|
| 3 Yr Avg | 17.60 | 8 | 89.0 | 21 |
| 5 Yr Avg | 14.61 | 10 | 87.0 | 12 |
| 10 Yr Avg | 13.57 | 1 | 86.6 | 16 |

Potential Capital Gain Exposure: 34% of assets

**FIGURE 6.2b**  New Perspective's performance.

short-term capital gains distributions are taxed at the maximum federal rate of 39.6% at the time of distribution, that long-term capital gains (gains on stocks held longer than one year) are taxed at a 20% rate, and that after-tax income is reinvested in the fund. State or local taxes are ignored. This particular report shows that New Perspective's after-tax performance ranking versus its peers is good.

**4.** *Analysis.* A Morningstar analyst provided his commentary on the fund's philosophy and investment style (Figure 6.2c). This is some of the valuable soft data that investors sometimes have a hard time finding, but they should understand that this part of a Morningstar report contains the analyst's personal views. The report does not give any information about the analyst's background or credentials.

**5.** *Sales Fees.* This section lists information from the fund's prospectus. It shows that the maximum load an investor would pay when buying the fund is 5.75%. It does not show how the load scales down for larger purchases. This section also shows that there is a 0.25% charge for *12b-1 fees.*

**12b-1 fee**
a fee mutual fund companies pay to brokers for servicing an account (advertising, marketing, and distribution). A typical 12b-1 fee for a stock fund is 0.25%.

④

**Analysis** by Gregg Wolper 03-05-99

Although New Perspective Fund is remarkably consistent, it also knows how to change with the times.

This fund has been around 26 years, and it not only uses the same bottom-up analysis it began with in 1973, it still has some of the same managers—and stocks—it had then. Its turnover rate has averaged a mere 19% over the past 10 years, just one fourth of the world-stock category average. Best of all, its performance has been consistently strong. The fund has landed in the category's top half in nine of the past 10 years, and has topped the category average for 10 straight quarters. In amassing that record, it has experienced much less month-to-month volatility than its peers.

Achieving fine results without suffering harsh setbacks could imply that the fund has a conservative bent, but that's only partly true. The managers are certainly conservative in some ways: They lean toward large, established companies, they're willing to hold cash, and they customarily own few emerging-markets securities. Yet the managers aren't stuck in a 1970s time warp. The portfolio's hefty valuations (owing partly to appreciation rather than purchases at high prices) would frighten many old-fashioned stock-pickers. They're even higher than the steep figures of the average portfolio in the category. In addition, the managers show a decided preference for companies in one of the market's trendiest sectors, telecommunications. In the latest annual report, they say they like these companies because they take advantage of deregulation and new technologies and are forming alliances. Telecom stocks played a large role in the fund's top-decile 1998 return.

This fund won't satisfy those who want substantial diversification away from the United States; the portfolio's 43% stake in the U.S. is seven percentage points higher than the world-stock norm. For most, though, this is an excellent choice.

| Address: | 333 S. Hope Street | | Minimum Purchase: | $250 | Add: $50 | IRA: $250 |
|---|---|---|---|---|---|---|
| | Los Angeles, CA 90071 | | Min Auto Inv Plan: | $50 | Add: $50 | |
| | 800–421–4120 / 213–486–9200 | | Sales Fees: | 5.75%L, 0.25%B | | |
| Inception: | 03-13-73 | ⑤ | Management Fee: | 0.60% max./0.40% min. | | |
| Advisor: | Capital Research & Management | | Actual Fees: | Mgt: 0.41% | Dist: 0.23% | |
| Subadvisor: | None | | Expense Projections: | 3Yr: $807* | 5Yr: $978* | 10Yr: $1474* |
| Distributor: | American Funds Distributors | | Avg Brok Commission: | — | Income Distrib: Semi-Ann. | |
| NTF Plans: | N/A | | **Total Cost** (relative to category): | — | | |

©1999 Morningstar, Inc. 225 W. Wacker Dr., Chicago, IL 60606, 312–696–6000. All rights reserved.
Although data are gathered from reliable sources, Morningstar cannot guarantee completeness and accuracy.
Reprints are available in quantity. 312–696–6100.

**FIGURE 6.2c** Analysis and costs of the New Perspective Fund.

**6. *Historical Profile.*** Morningstar's original star system appears in the historical profile box (Figure 6.2d) and, like the category rating (12), is based on risk-adjusted returns. However, the star system compares a fund against all other funds in its asset class. So, in the star ranking, a world or global stock fund will be compared with thousands of dissimilar stock funds. From the standpoint of an island investor seeking globally diversified funds, the star system is not a meaningful comparison. [The star rating is different from both the Morningstar category (7) and the category rating (12).]

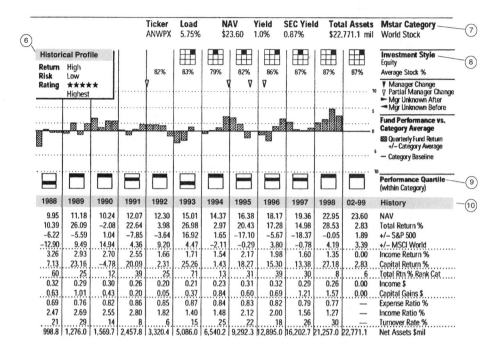

| | Ticker ANWPX | Load 5.75% | NAV $23.60 | Yield 1.0% | SEC Yield 0.87% | Total Assets $22,771.1 mil | Mstar Category World Stock |
|---|---|---|---|---|---|---|---|

| 1988 | 1989 | 1990 | 1991 | 1992 | 1993 | 1994 | 1995 | 1996 | 1997 | 1998 | 02-99 | History |
|---|---|---|---|---|---|---|---|---|---|---|---|---|
| 9.95 | 11.18 | 10.24 | 12.07 | 12.30 | 15.01 | 14.37 | 16.38 | 18.17 | 19.36 | 22.95 | 23.60 | NAV |
| 10.39 | 26.09 | -2.08 | 22.64 | 3.98 | 26.98 | 2.97 | 20.43 | 17.28 | 14.98 | 28.53 | 2.83 | Total Return % |
| -6.22 | -5.59 | 1.04 | -7.85 | -3.64 | 16.92 | 1.65 | -17.10 | -5.67 | -18.37 | -0.05 | 1.89 | +/- S&P 500 |
| -12.90 | 9.49 | 14.94 | 4.36 | 9.20 | 4.47 | -2.11 | -0.29 | 3.80 | -0.78 | 4.19 | 3.39 | +/- MSCI World |
| 3.26 | 2.93 | 2.70 | 2.55 | 1.66 | 1.71 | 1.54 | 2.17 | 1.98 | 1.60 | 1.35 | 0.00 | Income Return % |
| 7.13 | 23.16 | -4.78 | 20.09 | 2.31 | 25.26 | 1.43 | 18.27 | 15.30 | 13.38 | 27.18 | 2.83 | Capital Return % |
| 60 | 25 | 12 | 39 | 25 | 71 | 13 | 31 | 39 | 30 | 8 | 6 | Total Rtn % Rank Cat |
| 0.32 | 0.29 | 0.30 | 0.26 | 0.20 | 0.21 | 0.23 | 0.31 | 0.32 | 0.29 | 0.26 | 0.00 | Income $ |
| 0.63 | 1.01 | 0.43 | 0.20 | 0.05 | 0.37 | 0.84 | 0.60 | 0.69 | 1.21 | 1.57 | 0.00 | Capital Gains $ |
| 0.69 | 0.76 | 0.82 | 0.86 | 0.85 | 0.87 | 0.84 | 0.83 | 0.82 | 0.79 | 0.77 | — | Expense Ratio % |
| 2.47 | 2.69 | 2.55 | 2.80 | 1.82 | 1.40 | 1.48 | 2.12 | 2.00 | 1.56 | 1.27 | — | Income Ratio % |
| 21 | 29 | 14 | 8 | 6 | 15 | 25 | 22 | 18 | 26 | 30 | — | Turnover Rate % |
| 998.8 | 1,276.0 | 1,569.7 | 2,457.8 | 3,320.4 | 5,086.0 | 6,540.2 | 9,292.3 | 12,895.0 | 16,202.7 | 21,257.0 | 22,771.1 | Net Assets $mil |

**FIGURE 6.2d**  Historical profile, Morningstar category, investment style, performance quartile, and historical data of the New Perspective Fund.

**7.** *Morningstar Category.* Morningstar's analysis of how the fund was invested, not just how the fund says it invests, also classified New Perspective as a world fund. It is a red flag when the prospectus objective and the Morningstar analysis are different. However, there is consistency here. (Note that the Morningstar category is not the same as the category rating discussed further on.)

**8.** *Investment Style.* These miniature boxes show how the fund's style has changed over time. In 1994, 1995, and 1997 the fund had a blended style of growth and value. Some investors prefer that portfolio managers stick strictly to a style without varying from it so investors can control style in their portfolios. The island investor is likely to be more flexible and appreciates a portfolio manager willing to shift holdings when the manager thinks it is appropriate. Frequent shifts, however, could signal unstable management.

**9.** *Performance Quartile.* These boxes visually display on a year-by-year basis how New Perspective performed versus other world funds.

**10.** *History.* This part of the report provides 10 years of historical data. The most important types of data to track are:

✔ Total return (dividends, interest, and capital gains distributed, plus unrealized gains and losses).

✔ Return versus the MSCI World Index.

✔ How much of the return comes from income distributed versus capital appreciation or loss.

✔ The ratio of fund expenses to the value of a share.

✔ Portfolio turnover.

✔ Net assets of the fund.

This data shows, for example, that New Perspective had a very low expense ratio of 0.77% and a low 30% turnover rate (compared to the 50% to 100% turnover typical of many mutual funds). With $22 billion in net assets, it is one of the largest global mutual funds.

**11.** *Risk Analysis.* The comparison of New Perspective's risk to that of other funds in its world fund category is useful information (Figure 6.2e). A "10" means that the New Perspective Fund was in the top 10% (lowest risk) over three years versus other world stock funds.

**12.** *Category Rating.* This rating compares how a fund has performed on a risk-adjusted basis versus other funds in its Morningstar category (7). New Perspective is categorized as a world stock fund, so it is compared against other world or global funds. The comparison covers a three-year time period and New Perspective's five-star rating is the highest available.

Both the category rating (12) and the star rating (6) may give too much weight to risk (rather than performance) for the island investor. Both of these rating systems give better ratings to funds with low volatility. Island investors, however, are more concerned about the volatility of their portfolios as a whole than they are about the volatility of an individual fund. In seeking higher performance, they may tolerate a riskier (higher-volatility) fund

⑪

| Risk Analysis | | | | | |
|---|---|---|---|---|---|
| Time Period | Load-Adj Return % | Risk %Rank[1] All | Cat | Morningstar Return Risk | Morningstar Risk-Adj Rating |
| 1 Yr | 13.43 | | | | |
| 3 Yr | 17.43 | 55 | 10 | 2.80[2] 0.52 | ★★★★★ |
| 5 Yr | 15.43 | 63 | 11 | 2.63[2] 0.53 | ★★★★★ |
| 10 Yr | 14.99 | 61 | 1 | 3.39[2] 0.52 | ★★★★★ |

Average Historical Rating (159 months): 4.0★s

[1]=low, 100=high  [2] T-Bill return substituted for category avg.

⑫ **Category Rating (3 Yr)**

Worst ② ③ ④ Best
① ⑤

Return   High
Risk     Low

| Other Measures | Standard Index S&P 500 | Best Fit Index MSACWorld | ⑬ |
|---|---|---|---|
| Alpha | –2.6 | 6.2 | |
| Beta | 0.83 | 0.95 | |
| R–Squared | 86 | 93 | |
| Standard Deviation | | 17.47 | |
| Mean | | 19.77 | |
| Sharpe Ratio | | 0.95 | |

**FIGURE 6.2e**  Risk analysis, category rating, and other measures of the New Perspective Fund.

**large cap**

short for large capitalization stocks; a style of portfolio management that emphasizes stocks of larger companies.

**small cap**

short for small capitalization stocks; a style of portfolio management that emphasizes stocks of smaller companies.

**value style**

a style of investing that chooses undervalued stocks. Value is frequently measured using ratios such as price to earnings, price to book value, and price to sales.

if it has low correlation to other funds in their portfolios and thus does not increase the risk of the portfolio as a whole.

**13.** *Other Measures.* This section lists the fund's risk factors including alpha, beta, standard deviation, and Sharpe ratio. This data is usually not available from the fund companies.

**14.** *Portfolio Analysis.* This list (Figure 6.2f) shows the fund's top 20 stock holdings. A plus or minus sign indicates whether the manager was increasing or reducing the position in various stocks. The list includes both U.S. and non-U.S. companies. An investor should feel comfortable with the types of companies listed.

**15.** *Current Investment Style.* Morningstar uses a style box to classify a fund's investment style as growth or value, *large cap* or *small cap*, or blends of these pairings (Figure 6.2g). Value and growth are portfolio management styles. A portfolio manager with a *value style* picks stocks he or she feels are undervalued, stocks other managers are ignoring. A manager with a *growth style* picks stocks with growing earnings. Typically, growth stocks are more expensive because investors are willing to pay more for stocks with a proven track record. Morningstar uses the ratio of stock price to cash flow when classifying

growth style
an investment style under which managers primarily buy stocks with a pattern of consistently growing earnings or sales.

(14)

**Portfolio Analysis** 12-31-98

| Share change since 09–98 Total Stocks: 233 | Sector | Country | % Assets |
|---|---|---|---|
| ⊕ Time Warner | Services | USA | 3.10 |
| Pfizer | Health | USA | 2.87 |
| ⊕ Philip Morris | Staples | USA | 2.39 |
| ⊖ Mannesmann | Industrials | Germany | 1.98 |
| Viacom Cl B | Services | USA | 1.96 |
| Novartis (Reg) | Health | Switzerland | 1.84 |
| ⊖ Micron Tech | Technology | USA | 1.74 |
| ⊕ AirTouch Comms | Services | USA | 1.54 |
| ⊕ Carnival Cl A | Services | USA | 1.53 |
| ⊕ Cendant | Services | USA | 1.52 |
| Astra Cl A Free | Health | Sweden | 1.25 |
| ⊖ Nokia Cl A ADR | Technology | Finland | 1.10 |
| LM Ericsson Tele B | Technology | Sweden | 1.08 |
| ⊕ Deutsche Telekom | Services | Germany | 1.03 |
| MCI WorldCom | Services | USA | 0.98 |
| ⊖ Advanced Micro Devices | Technology | USA | 0.94 |
| ⊖ AT & T | Services | USA | 0.85 |
| Northern Telecom | Technology | Canada | 0.84 |
| Astra Cl B Free | Health | Sweden | 0.82 |
| ⊖ Siemens | Industrials | Germany | 0.79 |

**FIGURE 6.2f** Portfolio analysis of the New Perspective Fund.

funds with non-U.S. stocks as growth, value, or a blend. This is a different method from the one Morningstar uses to classify U.S. stock funds, and it recognizes that foreign companies frequently do not use the same accounting standards.

From left to right the style box shows value versus growth. From top to bottom it shows the size of the companies held—large, medium, and small. Morningstar defines size of international stocks based on market capitalization. Large companies have $5 billion capitalization and above, medium (*mid-cap*) are between $1 billion and $5 billion, and small are below $1 billion.

Here, New Perspective's style was classified as large-cap growth. This section of a Morningstar report also shows traditional financial *price ratios* such as *price/earnings ratio*, *price/cash flow ratio*, and *price/book ratio*. Investors also get information about three-year earnings growth and medium market capitalization.

**16.** *Country Exposure.* This list shows the top countries where the fund was invested as of the date of this report. The United States dominated New Perspective's portfolio with 43% of its assets invested there. The United

mid-cap
shorthand for medium capitalization stocks. A style of portfolio management that emphasizes medium-sized companies.

price ratios
comparisons of a company's price to other economic factors; used by investors to assess the company's value.

**price/earnings ratio**
the ratio that shows the price per share divided by the earnings per share, a factor useful in determining how fairly a stock is priced.

**price/cash flow ratio**
the ratio that shows the price per share divided by cash flow, a factor useful in determining how fairly a stock is priced.

**price/book ratio**
the ratio that shows the price per share divided by the book value, a factor useful in determining how fairly a stock is priced.

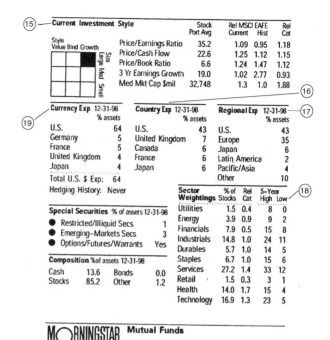

| Current Investment Style | | Stock Port Avg | Rel MSCI EAFE Current | Hist | Rel Cat |
|---|---|---|---|---|---|
| Price/Earnings Ratio | | 35.2 | 1.09 | 0.95 | 1.18 |
| Price/Cash Flow | | 22.6 | 1.25 | 1.12 | 1.15 |
| Price/Book Ratio | | 6.6 | 1.24 | 1.47 | 1.12 |
| 3 Yr Earnings Growth | | 19.0 | 1.02 | 2.77 | 0.93 |
| Med Mkt Cap $mil | | 32,748 | 1.3 | 1.0 | 1.88 |

Style: Value Blnd Growth / Size: Large Med Small

| Currency Exp 12-31-98 % assets | | Country Exp 12-31-98 % assets | | Regional Exp 12-31-98 % assets | |
|---|---|---|---|---|---|
| U.S. | 64 | U.S. | 43 | U.S. | 43 |
| Germany | 5 | United Kingdom | 7 | Europe | 35 |
| France | 5 | Canada | 6 | Japan | 6 |
| United Kingdom | 4 | France | 6 | Latin America | 2 |
| Japan | 4 | Japan | 6 | Pacific/Asia | 4 |
| Total U.S. $ Exp: 64 | | | | Other | 10 |
| Hedging History: Never | | | | | |

| Special Securities % of assets 12-31-98 | |
|---|---|
| ● Restricted/Illiquid Secs | 1 |
| ● Emerging–Markets Secs | 3 |
| ● Options/Futures/Warrants | Yes |

| Composition %of assets 12-31-98 | | | |
|---|---|---|---|
| Cash | 13.6 | Bonds | 0.0 |
| Stocks | 85.2 | Other | 1.2 |

| Sector Weightings | % of Stocks | Rel Cat | 5-Year High | Low |
|---|---|---|---|---|
| Utilities | 1.5 | 0.4 | 8 | 0 |
| Energy | 3.9 | 0.9 | 9 | 2 |
| Financials | 7.9 | 0.5 | 15 | 8 |
| Industrials | 14.8 | 1.0 | 24 | 11 |
| Durables | 5.7 | 1.0 | 14 | 5 |
| Staples | 6.7 | 1.0 | 15 | 6 |
| Services | 27.2 | 1.4 | 33 | 12 |
| Retail | 1.5 | 0.3 | 3 | 1 |
| Health | 14.0 | 1.7 | 15 | 4 |
| Technology | 16.9 | 1.3 | 23 | 5 |

M○RNINGSTAR **Mutual Funds**

**FIGURE 6.2g**  The New Perspective Fund's current investment style, country exposure, regional exposure, sector weightings, and currency exposure.

Kingdom came next with only 7% of the fund's assets, followed by Canada, France, and Japan with only 6% each.

**17.** *Regional Exposure.* The *regional exposure* list shows the top regions where the New Perspective Fund was invested. Japan is considered by Morningstar to be a region separate from the rest of the Pacific Rim countries. Here, the United States is also considered a region, although Morningstar frequently changes the structure of its reports and may consolidate the United States and Canada into a single region in the future. The United States and Canada are combined into a single regional market in the portfolio summary in the next chapter.

**18.** *Sector Weightings.* New Perspective has the largest chunk of its assets invested in the services sector. The second column compares New Perspective to the average percent of assets invested in various sectors by other world stock funds ("relative to the category"). The third column shows how the fund's sector weightings have changed over time. In the prior five years, New Perspective's weighting to the services sector was as high as 33% and as low as 12%. This shows that the portfolio managers have been willing to make changes in the portfolio to find what they consider to be the best stocks.

**19.** *Currency Exposure.* This section shows what currencies a fund's assets are denominated in. It shows that 64% of New Perspective assets were in U.S. dollars at the time of the report. More importantly, this section gives the fund's overall policy on currency hedging. The managers of New Perspective do not hedge their currency positions.

**regional exposure** amount of fund invested in a particular geographic region.

# Assembling the Crew
# and Staying on Course

I sland investors begin building their global portfolios
by evaluating and selecting individual mutual fund
managers. Their long-term goal, however, is not only
to select outstanding individual managers but also to
build a team of managers who will provide both the geographic and management diversity that will help them
reach their personal financial objectives.

Since island investors are seeking diversity, there is
no single criterion they can use to select the six or eight
best fund managers to put into their portfolios. Just as a
football coach does not want a team made up only of outstanding fullbacks, island investors do not want to set sail
from their island out into the world with a portfolio management crew composed only of the top first mates or the
best cooks. Investors want a well-balanced crew that can
take them to their financial objectives. Each portfolio
manager must be chosen for the particular strengths he or
she brings to the portfolio that the other managers may
not have.

Investors must look at their portfolios as a whole
and ask many of the same performance, risk, and style
questions they asked themselves when selecting individual funds. Investors can create multiple trial mixes and

comparisons using data they collect and summarize on computer spreadsheets or summary reports generated by one of the premium software programs available from mutual fund reporting services and through many investment advisers. Then they can select the mix that appears to be the best one to meet their personal objectives.

*Once an investor has researched individual fund managers, the next job is to select the mix of managers the investor wants to use in the portfolio.*

## HOW MANY MANAGERS TO USE

In researching individual global mutual funds, the island investor's goal is to select six to eight different global mutual fund managers to combine in a portfolio. As the example later in the chapter shows, choosing fewer than six managers does not provide enough diversification. However, having more than eight gives little additional diversification. As the number of managers increases, the job of selecting global managers who meet the investor's risk and return criteria also becomes more challenging.

Island investors choose each portfolio manager because that manager is an expert. An investor who has six global portfolio managers has six experts making the decision of how much to invest in the United States versus Europe versus the Pacific Rim versus other markets throughout the world. Even though each is an expert, each one will make mistakes from time to time and will have bad years as well as good years. With multiple managers, an investor reduces the odds of one expert's bad year completely ruining the portfolio's performance that year.

*Island investors use from six to eight different global money managers in order to diversify the decisions about which markets are best for investors.*

# STYLE AND CORRELATION

Island investors should deliberately seek out fund managers who have different styles so that the funds in their portfolios will have low correlations and move differently. One manager may be an expert on large company growth stocks around the world, another may buy small companies, and a third may specialize in companies that appear to be unpopular and, therefore, undervalued.

Taken together, the styles of the managers an island investor chooses should complement the investor's overall objectives. For example, if investors can tolerate higher levels of risk, they will tend to prefer more aggressive managers who are biased toward growth, favor small-cap stocks, and keep a larger proportion of their funds in developing markets. If investors are conservative, the managers they prefer will be biased toward undervalued companies, favor large-cap stocks, and concentrate more heavily in developed markets.

Assembling a portfolio of global mutual funds cannot be done completely by the numbers. Investors should purposely seek out managers with different investment styles, using their judgment as to which different styles balance one another out to create a portfolio whose overall style—aggressive or conservative, growth or value—is what the investor would like it to be.

Just as investors diversify because they want low correlation among the stocks, sectors, or assets in their portfolios, island investors want to choose managers with low correlation as well. When an event negatively affects one region in the world, investors do not want their entire portfolio reacting to this event the same way. Diversification of management styles reduces overall portfolio volatility while investors strive to achieve higher returns.

The advantage of an island portfolio is that it can include and benefit from different management styles without driving the portfolio as a whole in any one direction. Figure 7.1 is a scatterplot showing three-year risk and return results for eight global funds and comparing them to

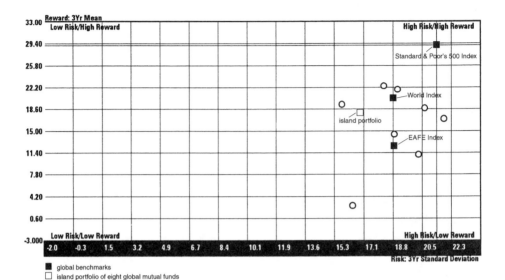

**FIGURE 7.1** This scatterplot from a Morningstar Principia Pro portfolio snapshot shows how a portfolio of eight global mutual funds compares both to various benchmarks and to each of the individual funds in it. The horizontal axis measures risk as three-year standard deviation. The vertical axis measures three-year mean (average) returns. The scatterplot shows that this portfolio had less risk than any of the benchmarks and also had much less risk than most of the individual funds themselves. *Source:* Morningstar, Inc. www.morningstar.com or 800-735-0700.

the consolidated risk and return results for the total portfolio. There is wide variation from one fund to another in terms of both risk and returns, but the net impact for the consolidated portfolio was lower risk without a major drop in returns.

Correlation coefficients for mutual funds show how one fund moves versus another. Figure 7.2 shows how several global funds are correlated with each other. A correlation coefficient of 1.0 means that two funds move together. A correlation coefficient of zero means that the

## Correlation of 60 Monthly Returns:
### Holdings from 07-01-1994 to 06-30-1999

Degree of Correlation

- .70 to 1.0  High
- .11 to .69  Moderate
- .10 to -.10  None
- -.11 to -.69  Moderate Negative
- -.70 to -1.0  Highly Negative

|   |                          | 1    | 2    | 3    | 4    |
|---|--------------------------|------|------|------|------|
| 1 | Janus Worldwide          |      | 0.77 | 0.79 | 0.85 |
| 2 | SoGen International A     | 0.77 |      | 0.93 | 0.87 |
| 3 | Templeton World A        | 0.79 | 0.93 |      | 0.93 |
| 4 | Capital World Growth & Inc | 0.85 | 0.87 | 0.93 |      |

**FIGURE 7.2** This table from a Morningstar Principia Pro portfolio snapshot shows the correlations among the global mutual funds in an island portfolio. In general, funds that have a correlation coefficient of 0.6 or 0.7 will move differently enough to provide the diversification island investors want in their portfolios. *Source:* Morningstar, Inc. www.morningstar.com or 800-735-0700.

two funds move completely independent of each other. As a rule of thumb, funds that have a correlation coefficient of 0.6 or 0.7 will move differently enough so investors may want to consider including them in their island portfolios. Funds with low correlations typically have managers with different investment styles.

————

*A portfolio diversified both geographically and in terms of management styles allows investors to lower risk without sacrificing returns.*

————

As they select managers, island investors should keep in mind that there may be philosophical or stylistic similarities among individual managers within a fund family. Mutual fund companies tend to be biased toward a particular investment style such as growth or value. Each of the fund managers in this fund family also tends to have this bias. This bias, combined with the fact that all of the managers base their decisions on the same research generated by the fund company's research arm, means it is common to see similar holdings among the funds in a given fund family. Therefore, investors should try to use at least two or three different fund families in their portfolios as well as diversifying among individual managers.

## HOW MUCH TO GIVE EACH MANAGER

When an island investor first assembles a global portfolio, the easiest thing is to assume that each fund chosen will have equal weighting in the portfolio. That is, if six funds are chosen, one-sixth of the portfolio's assets would be put into each one. From this starting point, the investor should fine-tune the fund allocation to meet his or her risk and return parameters.

For example, an investor might take the share of the portfolio allocated for aggressive management and split it among several different portfolio managers instead of giving all of it to a single manager. That way, a single aggressive manager cannot cause too much unwanted volatility in the portfolio. Similarly, the investor might place a greater proportion of the portfolio with a single conservative manager, one offering less risk. It might be normal to see a portfolio with several aggressive managers each managing small shares while fewer conservative managers manage larger shares. Customizing the portfolio this way produces a mix better suited to an investor's individual goals than giving each portfolio manager an equal share to manage.

*Island investors assign different amounts of their portfolios to each manager in order to fine-tune the portfolio to suit their personal risk and return goals.*

## AN ESSENTIAL NAVIGATIONAL TOOL

Creating an island portfolio is a multistep process. First, investors must analyze individual global mutual funds and their managers (as described in Chapter 6) and select several that appear to meet their investment criteria to put into an initial portfolio.

Next, investors should create a *portfolio summary* as a tool to analyze their initial choices. A portfolio summary takes the individual decisions of each mutual fund manager and combines them so that the investor can judge whether the portfolio as a whole is adequately diversified and still meets their performance and risk objectives.

**portfolio summary**
an analysis of all of the holdings within a portfolio.

Investors may change their initial mix of mutual funds several times before they put a portfolio in place that meets all of their objectives. They may change the number of funds in the portfolio, choose funds with different styles than they initially thought would work, or change the allocation among their different funds. A portfolio summary is a critical tool because investors need to focus on the performance and risk of the portfolio as a whole, not just of the individual funds in it.

Finally, investors need to periodically monitor their portfolio summary and revise their mutual fund selections as necessary to align the portfolio as a whole more closely with their performance and risk goals. Investing is a dynamic learning process. When investors look back on the portfolios they created six months earlier, they may want to modify their portfolios based on new ideas about investing, a change in fund managers or a fund manager's investment style, or a major change in their own lives.

Investors need to be comfortable with the combined results of their fund choices. When markets go crazy—and they will—investors must be comfortable enough with their decisions to ride through volatile times. If they are not comfortable when they put the portfolio together, they certainly will not be comfortable when other investors panic.

*A portfolio summary is an essential tool for evaluating an island investor's portfolio and for monitoring it over time.*

Analyzing a single mutual fund with assets in over a hundred stocks invested in multiple sectors and countries is a challenging task by itself. Until the advent of computers and sophisticated investment software, combining and summarizing the holdings of six or more different mutual funds was practically impossible. Morningstar's Principia Pro software, however, is a premium service from Morningstar that now makes this number crunching relatively easy. Principia Pro consolidates the information about all of the investor's fund choices into a portfolio summary. Each summary provides investors with a broad range of parameters to analyze the overall portfolio. At the time of this writing, the author is not aware of other services providing such summaries. While the cost of Principia Pro puts it outside the investment software budget of most individual investors, the portfolio summaries it generates are available through professional investment advisers who subscribe to the Morningstar service.

**portfolio snapshot**
what Morningstar calls its portfolio summaries.

The sample portfolio summaries in this chapter were analyzed using Principia Pro. Morningstar calls these summaries *portfolio snapshots* and, like a photograph, they only capture the information available at a given moment. Data collection and reporting by the mutual fund companies take time, and then the new numbers must be entered in Morningstar's software database. Those delays mean that the numbers used in Principia Pro's analyses may be several months old. Investors need to keep this in mind as they make decisions about changing the mix of global funds in their portfolios. Data from any reporting service can lag considerably behind what is currently happening in the market.

## ANALYZING INITIAL ALLOCATIONS

The following example shows how a hypothetical investor might analyze the summary of a portfolio of mutual funds chosen according to The Island Principle to see if it meets investment objectives. After analyzing the initial fund choices and mix, the investor modifies it to create the revised portfolio example. In actual practice, an investor might create and analyze several portfolios before selecting the one that best meets his or her needs.

To create an initial portfolio, our hypothetical island investor used the research criteria described in Chapter 6 to choose several global stock funds, and chose four highly rated global funds. This is fewer than The Island Principle suggests, but it is where this investor chose to start.

Figure 7.3 shows the snapshot of this investor's initial consolidated global portfolio created by Morningstar Principia Pro. The numbers in the figure are keyed to the following text explanations. While studying the portfolio summary, the investor asks some basic questions. There are no right or wrong, good or bad answers to these questions. Each island investor will answer them differently depending on personal investing experience and comfort levels. In analyzing the portfolio's summary, these are the questions an investor asks and the information the snapshot provides to help an investor answer those questions:

**1.** *Holdings. Is the investor satisfied with the funds included?* This list shows the four mutual funds our island investor selected for his portfolio: New Perspective, Putnam Global Growth, Templeton Growth, and Janus Worldwide. This part of the report also shows the dollar amount invested per fund and the percentage of the portfolio in each fund. Presumably the investor's homework on each of these individual funds has made the investor comfortable with each of the managers.

**2.** *Composition. Is the investor comfortable with the distribution of the portfolio among various asset classes?* The asset allocation of the portfolio is one of the most important things in the series of charts Principia Pro generates for a consolidated portfolio. Since asset allocation controls over 90% of a portfolio's return over time, investors must pay particular attention to it. The chart

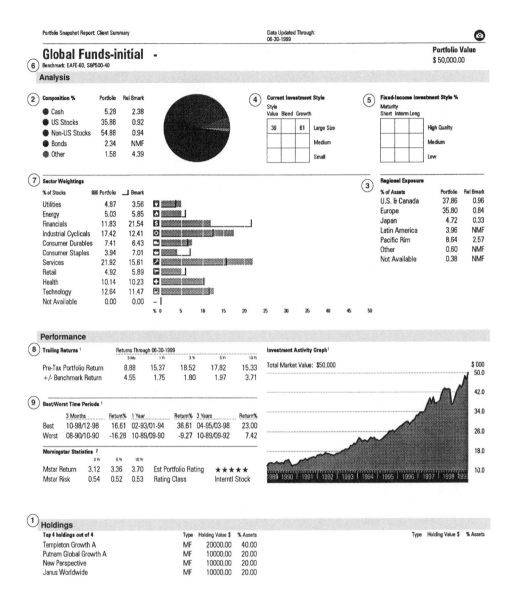

**FIGURE 7.3** This sample portfolio snapshot or summary generated by Morningstar Principia Pro consolidates the information on the initial fund selections in the sample island portfolio. The numbers are keyed to the explanation in the chapter text. *Source:* Morningstar, Inc. www.morningstar.com or 800-735-0700.

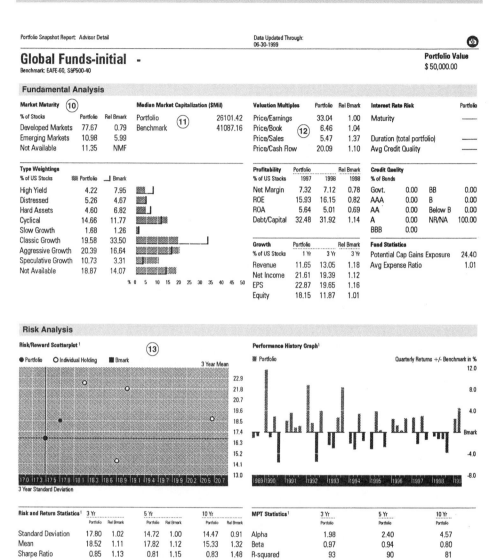

**FIGURE 7.3** (*Continued*)

shows the percentage of the overall portfolio that is in cash, U.S. stocks, non-U.S. stocks, bonds, and other assets. This provides a quick check on the U.S. versus non-U.S. holdings which, in this example portfolio, are 37.9% U.S. compared to 53.63% non-U.S. This is within the normal range of 25% to 50% allocated to the U.S. market under The Island Principle. Most portfolios typically con-

Portfolio Snapshot Report: Holdings

Data Updated Through:
06-30-1999

## Global Funds-initial -

Benchmark: EAFE-60, S&P500-40

**Portfolio Value**
$ 50,000.00

| Total 4 holdings | Type | Holding Value $ | % of Assets | Returns as of 06-30-1999 [1] | | | | |
|---|---|---|---|---|---|---|---|---|
| (14) | | | | 3 Mo | 1 Yr | 3 Yr | 5 Yr | 10 Yr |
| Templeton Growth A | MF | 20000.00 | 40.00 | 13.38 | 11.58 | 14.43 | 14.68 | 13.78 |
| Putnam Global Growth A | MF | 10000.00 | 20.00 | 4.68 | 15.24 | 18.73 | 16.48 | 13.23 |
| New Perspective | MF | 10000.00 | 20.00 | 6.92 | 22.84 | 22.40 | 20.05 | 16.14 |
| Janus Worldwide | MF | 10000.00 | 20.00 | 5.68 | 13.80 | 21.82 | 22.74 | NA |

MORNINGSTAR® Principia® Pro

**FIGURE 7.3** (Continued)

Graph:                                                    Release Date: 06-30-1999

⑮**Correlation of 60 Monthly Returns:**
**Holdings from 07-01-1994 to 06-30-1999**

Degree of Correlation

.70 to 1.0   High
.11 to .69   Moderate
.10 to -.10  None
-.11 to -.69  Moderate Negative
-.70 to -1.0  Highly Negative

| | | 1 | 2 | 3 | 4 |
|---|---|---|---|---|---|
| 1 | Janus Worldwide | | 0.90 | 0.93 | 0.72 |
| 2 | New Perspective | 0.90 | | 0.93 | 0.83 |
| 3 | Putnam Global Growth A | 0.93 | 0.93 | | 0.74 |
| 4 | Templeton Growth A | 0.72 | 0.83 | 0.74 | |

M**○RNINGSTAR**   **Principia™ Pro for Mutual Funds**

**FIGURE 7.3**   (*Continued*)

tain bonds and cash as well. However, for the purposes of this book's discussion, The Island Principle addresses only stock holdings.

In this sample portfolio, some investors may be surprised to see cash in a portfolio that has no cash accounts. The 5.17% cash reported here is the aggregate of the cash held in all of the funds together. Every manager holds some cash to meet shareholder redemptions, to purchase new stocks, or because the manager wants to keep some cash on the investment sidelines at the moment. Cash levels vary from fund to fund and managers may vary the levels of cash they hold through time. A level of 5% is relatively low. Similarly, investors may be surprised to find bonds here at all. However, the bond and other holdings are small because the investor chose stock funds.

**3.** *Regional Exposure. Is the investor comfortable with the portfolio's distribution among markets and regions?* Investors need to evaluate the proportion of their portfolios in various markets to see if they are comfortable with it. For example, if 40% of one investor's initial portfolio is in Japan, he or she might be uncomfortable with that much exposure to a single market. Another investor's initial portfolio summary might show that only 25% of the portfolio was invested in the United States, and the investor might not feel comfortable with this allocation.

Note that most of the sample portfolio's assets are in the United States, Canada, and Europe with smaller positions in the Pacific Rim, Japan (which Morningstar treats separately from the Pacific Rim), and Latin America. This is the kind of regional mix an island investor who wants to minimize exposure in less developed markets would like.

**4.** *Current Investment Style. Is the investor comfortable with the type of companies held in the portfolio?* Investors should look at their portfolio in terms of its emphasis on large companies or small companies, value stocks versus growth stocks. This style box shows a consolidated view of the types of stocks chosen by this island investor's four portfolio managers. The initial portfolio is all in large company stocks and is heavily weighted to growth stocks (76%) versus value stocks (24%).

This substantial allocation to large-cap growth stocks does not create a diversified portfolio. This is something the island investor needs to change in a revised portfolio because this heavy concentration is unnecessarily risky. This overemphasis on large cap companies happened because the investor used fund performance over the prior couple of years as one of the primary selection criteria for the four funds in the initial portfolio. Because large-cap growth stocks have done well on a worldwide basis over those years, the investor ended up overweighting large-cap growth. Putting too much weight on recent past performance is a common trap that many investors fall into.

**5. Fixed-Income Investment Style.** *Is the investor comfortable with the type of bonds the managers hold?* This box rates the style of any bonds in a portfolio. This portfolio has minimal bond holdings, so there is nothing shown.

**6. Benchmark.** *How is the portfolio performing compared to reasonable global benchmarks?* While periodically monitoring the portfolio's progress, the island investor needs to compare each of the global funds and the portfolio summary against some benchmark. As Chapter 6 pointed out, however, there is no single index that makes a good benchmark for an island portfolio. Island investors can use the World Index and the average of other global funds (reported by Morningstar and in the financial press). However, they do not want their portfolios to move exactly like an index. Global indexes are weighted depending on the level of holdings they have in a particular country or region. If an index is currently weighted 35% toward a given market and the island investor's personal portfolio contains only 10% holdings in that country, the portfolio will perform very differently from the index. There is nothing wrong with this.

Morningstar software permits some flexibility in selecting benchmarks that island investors can compare their consolidated portfolios against. At the time of this writing, however, Principia Pro does not give investors the option of selecting either the World Index or the average of other global funds. Either of those choices would be preferable to the EAFE index or the S&P 500 for island investors.

To get around this problem, this investor created a custom benchmark. Since the aim was about a 40/60 mix between U.S. and non-U.S. stocks in the consolidated portfolio, the investor created a benchmark of 40% of the S&P 500 and 60% of the EAFE index. This serves its function but is far from a perfect solution. The U.S. portion of this sample portfolio is 37.9%, which is relatively close to the 40% the investor chose in a custom benchmark.

**7.** *Sector Weightings. Are the portfolio's holdings diversified among industry sectors?* Achieving the right balance in the initial portfolio means analyzing the sector allocations within it, too. An investor may feel the consolidated portfolio is too heavily invested in technology stocks or industrial cyclicals, or services around the world. Changing these allocations will mean either changing the amount the investor has in each of the global mutual funds or, perhaps, choosing other funds.

This section of the investor's portfolio summary snapshot from Morningstar shows the percentage of various sectors within his initial portfolio. The heaviest concentration is in services, followed by technology. These sector weightings are compared against the investor's benchmark (which, in this case, is 60% of the EAFE index and 40% of the S&P 500). Remember, however, that index weightings are based strictly on market capitalization and The Island Principle argues that market capitalization is not a meaningful tool for portfolio choices. The primary benefits an island investor gains from comparing the consolidated portfolio to the benchmark weightings are that this comparison helps to spot overconcentration in one area and to explain why the portfolio performs differently than the benchmark.

**8.** *Trailing Returns. How would this combination of funds have performed over time?* Trailing returns tell our investor how the island portfolio would have performed historically (if it had existed). Although there is no certainty that past performance predicts future performance, historical data is the only certain information investors have to work with when they first put their portfolios together. The investor should ask oneself if the consolidated portfolio's 10-year return would have been acceptable. Shorter periods are not as meaningful.

Once again, the portfolio's performance is compared with the selected custom benchmark. For all periods, this initial portfolio shows above-normal returns that are higher than an investor should expect. It should be no surprise that the portfolio's historical return was above average, because returns were one of the parameters the investor used to select the four funds.

**9. Best/Worst Time Periods.** *Is the investor comfortable with the portfolio's volatility?* This section of the Morningstar report on the investor's portfolio shows its historical volatility over three months, one year, and three years. The portfolio's worst one-year period was a loss of 8.65% from October 1989 to September 1990. Over three years, its worst performance was a gain of 7.45% per year, which occurred between October 1989 and September 1992. The investor should feel that the portfolio's volatility appears to have a range the investor will be comfortable with over time.

**10. Market Maturity.** *Is the investor comfortable with the portfolio's distribution in developing markets?* This section tells an investor how much of his or her portfolio is in developed versus emerging markets. With 7.78% in emerging markets, this initial portfolio is slightly higher than the 5% recommended in Chapter 2.

**11. Median Market Capitalization.** *Again, is the investor comfortable with the type of companies in the portfolio?* The median size of the companies held in the portfolio compared to those held in the benchmark provides the investor with more style information. Remember, this initial portfolio is 100% in large cap stocks (defined as companies with $5 billion or more capitalization). The median capitalization in the portfolio is about $29 billion, however, versus $41 billion for the investor's 40/60 benchmark.

**12. Valuation Multiples.** *Is the investor comfortable with the relative price of the companies in the portfolio?* Many investors like to compare a stock's price using various measures of value. This section of the Principia Pro report gives the various ratios showing these valuations for the average stock in the portfolio. The price/earnings ratio of 35.37 is above that of the benchmark, meaning that the stocks in the portfolio are more highly priced than the benchmark. All of the other ratios show the same pattern.

**13. Risk Analysis.** *Is the investor comfortable with the level of risk in the portfolio as a whole?* The Island Principle's purpose is to improve the balance between risk and return within a portfolio. This risk/reward scatterplot shows that the investor's four-fund portfolio is significantly less risky than any of the four funds alone. The investor separately calculates that, on a three-year basis, the average of the standard deviations of the four funds was 19.23% while the consolidated portfolio has a standard deviation of 18.05%. This shows the magic of diversification to reduce risk.

The performance history graph shows that the consolidated portfolio outperformed the benchmark over the past three years. The portfolio's Sharpe ratio is considerably better than that of the benchmark.

The three-year returns and risk are both higher than the benchmark. The investor who created this initial portfolio loves the higher return but does not like the higher risk. Reducing the risk is something that needs to be addressed when revising the initial mix of global funds.

**14. Fund Performance.** *Is the investor satisfied with the performance of the individual funds in the portfolio?* This section of the report shows basic performance statistics for each of the four funds individually over three months, one year, three years, five years, and ten years. As investors make comparisons, they need to remember that they purposely selected managers with different investment styles. That means they should expect their funds to perform differently. If the investor seeks out funds with more variation when revising the portfolio, that will show here.

**15.** *Correlation of 60 Monthly Returns. Does the correlation among the funds within the portfolio show sufficient diversification?* This part of the report shows the correlation coefficients among the investor's four funds over five years. If all of the funds an investor has selected are moving together (that is, they have a correlation coefficient of 1.0), the investor has little diversification. Ideally, the investor has selected funds whose correlation coefficients are 0.6 to 0.7 (60% to 70%) or less so that they move differently.

Correlation coefficients above 90% don't provide much diversification so, in this initial portfolio, only Templeton Growth is providing any true diversification. The other three funds basically move together. The investor should see this as a reason to find other funds to add to this portfolio.

## REVISING THE INITIAL PORTFOLIO

In analyzing this initial portfolio composed of four mutual funds, the hypothetical island investor identified several things to be changed. Besides wanting more diversification (the historical return from this initial portfolio was great but the risk it carries is too high), the investor also does not like the high concentration in large-cap growth stocks.

The Island Principle recommends from six to eight different global managers for optimum diversification. So to create greater diversification and reduce the portfolio's risk, the investor adds four more funds to the portfolio's mix. One of the original funds could have been dropped because of the high correlation among them without reducing the portfolio's diversification. However, the investor likes each of the initial four picks and decides to keep them all. The new funds are Smallcap World growth fund, Templeton Global Small Company fund, GAM Global fund, and Capital World Growth and Income fund.

The investor chose Smallcap World growth fund and Templeton Global Small Company fund because both are small company stock funds. This is an area that was missing from the initial portfolio. These two new funds also have different styles. Templeton Global Small Company has a value bias while Smallcap World has a growth bias.

When compared to the universe of all funds, these two funds had below-average returns in recent years. However, this is primarily because small company stocks on the whole have not performed as well as large company stocks during the same period. Over longer periods of time, small company stocks have performed as well as or even better than large company stocks, though they frequently have been more volatile. The island investor wants both the diversification and the potential returns that small company stocks have historically added to portfolios. The investor expects to reduce the volatility of this portfolio by adding funds with low correlation to the large cap funds even though these new funds, considered by themselves, are more volatile.

Note that Morningstar has no category for "global small company" stock funds. Therefore, Principia Pro has trouble categorizing these two funds. It considers Smallcap World a small growth fund but categorizes Templeton Global Small Company as a world fund. This makes comparisons of these funds against their peers very difficult. In the world of investing, analysis is never perfect and investors have to use their creativity.

The investor chose GAM Global because of its low correlation with the other funds. Though the fund has had periods of stellar performance, it has recently underperformed. The investor adds it to the portfolio with the intention of watching its performance very carefully, particularly because the departure of an international manager who had been with the fund since 1990 adds to the uncertainty about its performance.

The investor's final addition to the revised portfolio is Capital World Growth and Income. Although this fund has a high correlation coefficient (95%) with New Perspective, its sister fund in the American Funds Group, the island investor chooses this fund because the style box in its Morningstar reports indicates it has a blended style compared to New Perspective's growth style. This indicates that it has a more conservative nature than New Perspective, which the investor feels is not reflected in their correlation coefficient. This is a judgment call, one of many investors must continually make as they design their portfolios.

Besides adding four new funds, the investor also decides to double the amount going to the Templeton Growth fund, wanting to push his revised portfolio more toward a value style and away from the heavy growth bias of the initial portfolio. The island investor notes the irony that Templeton Growth has a value bias, even though "growth" is part of its name.

Figure 7.4 shows how these decisions affect the investor's consolidated portfolio:

1. *Analysis.* The revised portfolio's asset allocation has changed relatively little from that of the initial portfolio.

2. *Current Investment Style.* The consolidated portfolio's style has changed dramatically. Large cap growth has dropped from 76% to 45%. Large cap blend has increased but, most importantly, small cap value and small cap growth have been added. The revised portfolio is a much more diversified portfolio, one of the investor's goals, and should have a lower risk.

3. *Regional Exposure.* The regional exposure of the revised portfolio is about the same as that of the initial one. The United States, Canada, and Europe still account for most of the holdings.

4. *Performance.* The historical performance of the revised portfolio has dropped relative to the initial mix of funds. This is because the revised portfolio has moved away from large cap growth, which has had outstanding recent returns. On a three- and five-year basis, the return of the revised portfolio is approximately equal to that of the investor's custom benchmark. On a 10-year basis, it is 2.6% above the benchmark.

5. *Median Market Capitalization.* In the revised portfolio, this has dropped from almost $30 billion to about $21 billion, reflecting the addition of small cap stocks.

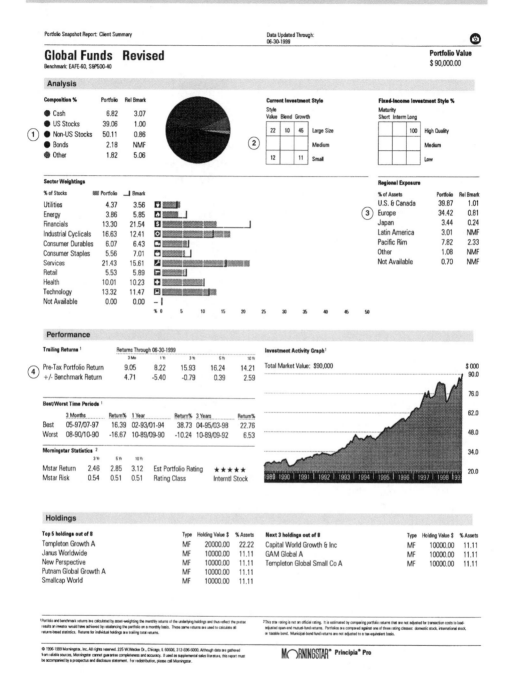

**FIGURE 7.4** This sample portfolio snapshot from Morningstar Principia Pro consolidates all of the information on the funds selected for the revised island portfolio. The numbers are keyed to the explanation in the chapter text. *Source:* Morningstar, Inc. www.morningstar.com or 800-735-0700.

Portfolio Snapshot Report: Advisor Detail

Data Updated Through:
06 30-1999

## Global Funds   Revised

Benchmark: EAFE-60, S&P500-40

**Portfolio Value**
$ 90,000.00

### Fundamental Analysis

| Market Maturity | | | | Median Market Capitalization ($Mil) | | | Valuation Multiples | | Portfolio | Rel Bmark | Interest Rate Risk | | Portfolio |
|---|---|---|---|---|---|---|---|---|---|---|---|---|---|
| % of Stocks | Portfolio | Rel Bmark | Portfolio | ⑤ | | 21170.57 | Price/Earnings | ⑥ | 31.04 | 0.94 | Maturity | | — |
| Developed Markets | 74.07 | 0.75 | Benchmark | | | 41087.16 | Price/Book | | 6.08 | 0.98 | | | |
| Emerging Markets | 7.87 | 4.30 | | | | | Price/Sales | | 4.93 | 1.24 | Duration (total portfolio) | | — |
| Not Available | 18.06 | NMF | | | | | Price/Cash Flow | | 19.48 | 1.06 | Avg Credit Quality | | — |

| Type Weightings | | | | | Profitability | Portfolio | | | Rel Bmark | Credit Quality | | | |
|---|---|---|---|---|---|---|---|---|---|---|---|---|---|
| % of US Stocks | ▓ Portfolio | ▭ Bmark | | | % of US Stocks | 1997 | 1998 | | 1998 | % of Bonds | | | |
| High Yield | 3.74 | 7.95 | | | Net Margin | 7.89 | 8.04 | | 0.88 | Govt. | 0.00 | BB | 0.00 |
| Distressed | 5.27 | 4.67 | | | ROE | 16.56 | 17.27 | | 0.88 | AAA | 24.49 | B | 0.00 |
| Hard Assets | 3.67 | 6.82 | | | ROA | 6.69 | 6.59 | | 0.91 | AA | 0.00 | Below B | 0.00 |
| Cyclical | 12.51 | 11.77 | | | Debt/Capital | 28.02 | 27.06 | | 0.97 | A | 0.00 | NR/NA | 75.51 |
| Slow Growth | 1.06 | 1.26 | | | | | | | | BBB | 0.00 | | |
| Classic Growth | 23.79 | 33.50 | | | **Growth** | Portfolio | | | Rel Bmark | **Fund Statistics** | | | |
| Aggressive Growth | 21.61 | 16.64 | | | % of US Stocks | 1 Yr | 3 Yr | | 3 Yr | Potential Cap Gains Exposure | | | 19.44 |
| Speculative Growth | 10.60 | 3.31 | | | Revenue | 12.93 | 15.20 | | 1.37 | Avg Expense Ratio | | | 1.09 |
| Not Available | 17.76 | 14.07 | | | Net Income | 14.51 | 15.87 | | 0.92 | | | | |

% 0   5   10   15   20   25   30   35   40   45   50

| | | | | |
|---|---|---|---|---|
| EPS | 15.20 | 15.68 | | 0.93 |
| Equity | 16.17 | 12.40 | | 1.05 |

### Risk Analysis

**Risk/Reward Scatterplot** ⑦

● Portfolio    ○ Individual Holding    ▪ Bmark

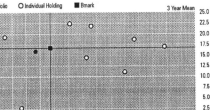

3 Year Standard Deviation

**Performance History Graph**

▓ Portfolio

Quarterly Returns +/- Benchmark in %

| Risk and Return Statistics | 3 Yr | | 5 Yr | | 10 Yr | | MPT Statistics | 3 Yr | 5 Yr | 10 Yr |
|---|---|---|---|---|---|---|---|---|---|---|
| | Portfolio | Rel Bmark | Portfolio | Rel Bmark | Portfolio | Rel Bmark | | Portfolio | Portfolio | Portfolio |
| Standard Deviation | 16.97 | 0.97 | 14.00 | 0.95 | 13.86 | 0.87 | Alpha | 0.22 | 1.49 | 3.83 |
| Mean | 15.93 | 0.95 | 16.24 | 1.02 | 14.21 | 1.22 | Beta | 0.92 | 0.88 | 0.75 |
| Sharpe Ratio | 0.73 | 0.96 | 0.76 | 1.07 | 0.78 | 1.41 | R-squared | 89 | 86 | 77 |

[1] Portfolio and benchmark returns are calculated by asset-weighting the monthly returns of the underlying holdings and thus reflect the pretax results an investor would have achieved by rebalancing the portfolio on a monthly basis. These same returns are used to calculate all returns-based statistics. Returns for individual holdings are trailing total returns.

[2] This star rating is not an official rating. It is estimated by comparing portfolio returns that are not adjusted for transaction costs to load-adjusted open-end mutual-fund returns. Portfolios are compared against one of three rating classes: domestic stock, international stock, or taxable bond. Municipal-bond fund returns are not adjusted to a tax-equivalent basis.

M⊙RNINGSTAR® Principia® Pro

**FIGURE 7.4** *(Continued)*

Portfolio Snapshot Report: Holdings

Data Updated Through:
06-30-1999

## Global Funds    Revised

Benchmark: EAFE-60, S&P500-40

**Portfolio Value**
$ 90,000.00

**Total 8 holdings**

| | Type | Holding Value $ | % of Assets | Returns as of 06-30-1999 [1] | | | | |
|---|---|---|---|---|---|---|---|---|
| | | | | 3 Mo | 1 Yr | 3 Yr | 5 Yr | 10 Yr |
| Templeton Growth A | MF | 20000.00 | 22.22 | 13.38 | 11.58 | 14.43 | 14.68 | 13.78 |
| Janus Worldwide | MF | 10000.00 | 11.11 | 5.68 | 13.80 | 21.82 | 22.74 | NA |
| New Perspective | MF | 10000.00 | 11.11 | 6.92 | 22.84 | 22.40 | 20.05 | 16.14 |
| Putnam Global Growth A | MF | 10000.00 | 11.11 | 4.68 | 15.24 | 18.73 | 16.48 | 13.23 |
| Smallcap World | MF | 10000.00 | 11.11 | 17.54 | 10.37 | 11.07 | 15.00 | NA |
| Templeton Global Small Co A | MF | 10000.00 | 11.11 | 10.93 | -9.74 | 2.68 | 7.34 | 8.66 |
| Capital World Growth & Inc | MF | 10000.00 | 11.11 | 7.35 | 14.37 | 19.35 | 18.54 | NA |
| GAM Global A | MF | 10000.00 | 11.11 | 1.35 | -14.61 | 16.99 | 15.12 | 13.08 |

[1] Portfolio and benchmark returns are calculated by asset-weighting the monthly returns of the underlying holdings and thus reflect the pretax results an investor would have achieved by rebalancing the portfolio on a monthly basis. These same returns are used to calculate all returns-based statistics. Returns for individual holdings are trailing total returns.

[2] This star rating is not an official rating. It is estimated by comparing portfolio returns that are not adjusted for transaction costs to load-adjusted open-end mutual-fund returns. Portfolios are compared against one of three rating classes: domestic stock, international stock, or taxable bond. Municipal-bond fund returns are not adjusted to a tax-equivalent basis.

**FIGURE 7.4** (Continued)

Graph: Release Date: 06-30-1999

## Correlation of 60 Monthly Returns:
**Holdings from 07-01-1994 to 06-30-1999**

Degree of Correlation

■ .70 to 1.0 High
■ .11 to .69 Moderate
▨ .10 to -.10 None
■ -.11 to -.69 Moderate Negative
■ -.70 to -1.0 Highly Negative

| | | 1 | 2 | 3 | 4 | 5 | 6 | 7 | 8 |
|---|---|---|---|---|---|---|---|---|---|
| 1 | Capital World Growth & Inc | | 0.56 | 0.85 | 0.95 | -0.89 | 0.84 | 0.83 | 0.91 |
| 2 | GAM Global A | 0.56 | | 0.54 | 0.58 | 0.64 | 0.43 | 0.45 | 0.44 |
| 3 | Janus Worldwide | 0.85 | 0.54 | | 0.90 | 0.93 | 0.81 | 0.73 | 0.72 |
| 4 | New Perspective | 0.95 | 0.58 | 0.90 | | 0.93 | 0.85 | 0.76 | 0.83 |
| 5 | Putnam Global Growth A | 0.89 | 0.64 | 0.93 | 0.93 | | 0.81 | 0.72 | 0.74 |
| 6 | Smallcap World | 0.84 | 0.43 | 0.81 | 0.85 | 0.81 | | 0.86 | 0.81 |
| 7 | Templeton Global Small Co A | 0.83 | 0.45 | 0.73 | 0.76 | 0.72 | 0.86 | | 0.89 |
| 8 | Templeton Growth A | 0.91 | 0.44 | 0.72 | 0.83 | 0.74 | 0.81 | 0.89 | |

 Principia™ Pro for Mutual Funds

**FIGURE 7.4** *(Continued)*

**6.** *Valuation Multiple.* The valuation ratios have dropped in all areas, reflecting the shift toward lower-priced stocks. The price/earnings ratio and price/book ratio are now below the benchmarks instead of being above them.

**7.** *Risk Analysis.* This shows that the new choices have enabled the island investor to achieve the goal the investor had in revising the initial fund mix. Risk has dropped. The standard deviation of the revised portfolio is now below that of the benchmark instead of above it. On a three-year basis, the revised portfolio's risk has a standard deviation of 16.97% compared to 18.05% for the initial portfolio and 18.91% for the average of the eight funds. The comparisons of risk over five years are also good. Over 10 years, risk falls to about 13% (below that of the benchmark, and 5% below that of the investor's initial portfolio).

In terms of diversification and risk, the island investor's revised portfolio shows a significant improvement over the initial fund mix. Not only has the investor lowered the portfolio's risk relative to the custom benchmark, but the revised portfolio also shows lower risk than either the EAFE index or the S&P 500 alone. The revised portfolio has a five-year standard deviation of only 14% compared to 14.9% for the EAFE index or 17.3% for the S&P 500.

In terms of returns, the revised portfolio's three, five, and ten-year returns of 15.93%, 16.24%, 14.21% respectively are better than the approximately 14% return in the global market from 1970 through 1998. While the return for 1998 was below average at 8.2%, investors should expect short-term variations like this.

Portfolio returns in excess of 14% and risks lower than the appropriate indexes are what most island investors should strive to achieve. If this island investor had held this portfolio over the past three, five, or ten years, the investor's goals would have been met according to this historical data. No one, of course, knows what the future will bring.

# COURSE CORRECTIONS

Monitoring a portfolio on a regular basis is critical in order to know if and when an investor should make mid-course corrections in the portfolio or overall investment strategy. No portfolio will be static. The investment world continually changes. Investors need to be prepared to make adjustments in their portfolios. If investors have a 15-year time horizon, for instance, they cannot wait 15 years to find out if their investment strategy is working. When investors design their portfolios thoughtfully, however, total restructuring is rarely necessary. Changes will typically be made on the margin.

A portfolio cannot do well unless each component within it is doing what it is supposed to do. Monitoring of both the investor's individual mutual funds and the portfolio as a whole to see if they are meeting the investor's performance and risk objectives is recommended. However, investors who like to look up mutual fund prices in the financial pages of the daily newspapers should think of that primarily as entertainment.

That said, closely watching how individual mutual funds move relative to the market can provide investors with useful information. For example, if an investor chose a particular fund manager because of his or her concentration in Europe and then notices that the fund does not react to a particular event the same way that the European markets do, the investor might want to find out why.

Investors are human and often have selective memories. It is easy to remember particularly good or bad quarters or years while losing track of the larger picture. Keep records of how a portfolio does over the years. Written records are critical for accurate confirmation of how the portfolio has done.

Investors should determine how their portfolios are doing quarterly or at least annually. A few poor quarters are not necessarily a sign that the portfolio is doing poorly. Even if an investor's annual return rate falls short of the goal he or she set in order to reach a long-term return objective, one first needs to remember that it is normal for the return to vary from year to year. Island investors should also not be concerned when their portfolios underperform a particular market. Each year, there can be only one country around the world with the best market. Investors cannot and should not have 100% of their portfolios in that single market any more than they should have all of their assets in the best-performing stock in a given year.

Before they assume their portfolios are doing poorly, island investors should check how the World Index and other global funds have done. If all of the relevant benchmarks have underperformed and the investors' portfolios did no worse than the benchmarks, then there is probably no reason for change.

On the other hand, if an investor's portfolio's return was significantly worse than the global benchmarks, it may be time to look at the individual mutual funds in the portfolio to see if one or more needs to be replaced or if the investor needs to change the allocation among the funds already held. As the portfolio begins to develop some history of its own, the investor can calculate the yearly and compounded annual rate of return and compare that to the performance objectives that have been set. The investor needs to remember, as explained in Chapter 5, that the average of the portfolio's annual returns (arithmetic rate) needs to be higher than the compounded rate (geometric rate) set as a long-term financial goal.

If the portfolio's risk level over a period of a year (investors can use the standard deviation reported in the portfolio's Morningstar snapshot to determine the portfolio's prior year volatility) exceeds what the investor set as an objective, the investor needs to ask why. The risk objective, for example, might have been to have 10% less standard deviation than the standard deviation of the World Index. Instead, over the prior year the portfolio might have been just as volatile as the index. This could mean that the managers selected were more aggressive than anticipated or that the correlation among the managers' styles was higher than the investor thought. Figure out what went wrong and decide whether it is a reason to make a change.

---

*Comparisons with the investor's risk and performance objectives are essential indicators signaling that all is well or that it may be time to make changes.*

---

Over short periods of time, some fund managers will underperform others, sometimes quite significantly. An island investor should expect this and tolerate it for even a year or two as long as the original reason for choosing this manager and mutual fund still exists. While one or even several of the investor's global mutual funds may be underperforming at a given point, perhaps because their philosophy of buying growth or value or small cap stocks is currently out of favor, the investor's primary focus should be on how the portfolio as a whole is doing.

As investors track their portfolios, they should pay particular attention to how they perform in *market corrections*. Watching how each of their mutual fund managers performs as well as how the portfolio as a whole performs during difficult times can vindicate their choice of fund managers or point out when it may be time for a change.

Investors may find, for example, that a particular portfolio manager is not performing as expected given his or her particular investment style. For instance, they may choose a portfolio manager who is expected to do well when world markets are weak. Then, when a correction occurs this fund drops as much as the others. This may be a sign that the investor needs to make a change in the portfolio.

Investors should reevaluate their choice of a particular fund whenever the mutual fund replaces its portfolio manager. Investors should investigate the new portfolio manager's background and make an educated decision to stay with the fund or move to another. What did the new manager do before? What is his or her track

 **market correction**
term used for a drop in stock prices after an advance, which assumes that the market advance got ahead of itself and which implies that the drop is temporary rather than a prolonged drop that could signal a bear market.

record? The investor should feel comfortable that this new manager meets the same standards and that the fund will continue to fill the role the investor intended in the consolidated portfolio. Investors do not want their money used as a training tool for someone just learning how to manage money.

As investors monitor their portfolios, they may find problems such as a large shift by one or more managers into a region where the investor is uncomfortable investing. The investor is going to have to decide whether to switch to a manager the investor is more comfortable with or to let the manager's decisions stand. The island investor should give the manager the benefit of the doubt.

Many investors who like to do their own asset allocation automatically replace a mutual fund manager who changes the country or regional allocation. These investors are making their own decisions about how much of their portfolios should be invested in the United States, Europe, or the Pacific Rim and have chosen mutual funds that specialize in these areas to implement their allocation decisions. When the manager of one of these funds changes and begins buying stock in other regions, the investor replaces the manager.

These investors may be global, but they are not island investors. Island investors use multiple managers to decide where to find the best stocks in the best markets. If a manager sees a reason to make a change, the island investor typically wants this change made. The change is not necessarily a reason to drop that fund.

---

*Investors should replace a manager when they have lost confidence in the manager's expertise, are uncomfortable with his or her decisions, or do not agree with those decisions.*

---

Finally, investors need to weigh the tax consequences of any decision to sell or reduce their positions in a particular fund. The costs of selling fund shares and paying taxes on any long-term gains can be significant.

However, investors should not let this tax problem immobilize them. If they give too much weight to tax issues when making decisions to sell, they run the risk of locking into investments that are no longer moving their portfolios closer to their goals. An investor with $100,000 in a particular fund who faces $10,000 in tax liabilities on selling needs to answer a basic question: Will the portfolio as a whole be better off if the $100,000 is left in the current fund or if $90,000 is invested in a different fund? That takes the investor back to basic fund research once again.

## MOVING TO AN ISLAND

For many investors, the most difficult thing about following The Island Principle will be moving away from their preoccupation with the performance of the Dow Jones Industrial Average or the S&P 500 index. Tracking these benchmarks is a deeply ingrained habit reinforced by the incessant reporting of the news media. While it is nice to hear on a daily basis how "the market" did, these benchmarks lose their significance for island investors. Their investment perspective has changed. Their attention is focused on a much broader investment horizon.

The Island Principle extends portfolio theory to global markets. No single market determines the long-term outcome of an island investor's investment strategy, because he or she has diversified away from the U.S. market. The portfolio is diversified not only globally, with a primary focus on the world's 21 developed markets, but also in terms of the decision process about which markets to invest in. No single individual makes this all-important determination.

The Island Principle's two-pronged diversification reduces portfolio risk or volatility. When investors have a strategy that minimizes volatility, they are much less likely to fall victim to the investment jitters that make investors panic when markets start moving unpredictably. Diversification also reduces the long-term risks all investors face and increases the likelihood they will achieve their long-term objectives.

When risk becomes more manageable, investors gain new options. Because of their additional diversification, island investors are able to increase their returns or to both decrease risk and enhance returns at the same time. Some may prefer to increase their holdings of riskier stocks with higher-potential returns. Others may prefer the strategy of increasing their portfolios' allocations to stocks versus lower-yielding asset classes such as cash or bonds.

Investors who mentally move to an island are not isolating themselves or narrowing their view of the world. To the contrary, they now look out and see an unlimited horizon unbounded by the borders of a single market. As they set sail into this investment world from their new perspective, they chart their way using new levels of diversity that mean a greater likelihood of reaching their investment goals. That is a destination every investor would like to reach safely.

# Appendix

**TABLE A.1   Total Returns of the World's 21 Developed Markets from 1970 to 1998, Expressed in U.S. Dollars**

|      | Australia | Austria | Belgium | Canada | Denmark | Finland |
|------|-----------|---------|---------|--------|---------|---------|
| 1970 | −19.41 | 11.46 | 7.16 | 14.87 | −6.50 | |
| 1971 | −1.19 | 8.03 | 21.69 | 13.98 | 10.10 | |
| 1972 | 23.52 | 37.76 | 32.77 | 33.39 | 112.34 | |
| 1973 | −13.95 | 24.66 | 13.83 | −2.64 | 5.39 | |
| 1974 | −32.25 | 15.07 | −14.32 | −27.02 | −11.12 | |
| 1975 | 48.94 | −2.80 | 16.10 | 15.32 | 24.41 | |
| 1976 | −10.32 | 15.47 | 6.61 | 9.96 | 7.18 | |
| 1977 | 12.14 | 4.93 | 9.37 | −2.06 | 2.34 | |
| 1978 | 22.00 | 16.45 | 30.68 | 20.56 | 9.58 | |
| 1979 | 43.62 | 19.61 | 18.89 | 52.94 | -2.75 | |
| 1980 | 54.85 | −11.76 | −21.23 | 21.27 | 18.54 | |
| 1981 | −23.74 | −21.88 | −7.24 | −10.02 | 25.17 | |
| 1982 | −22.40 | −8.72 | 2.29 | 2.60 | 2.79 | |
| 1983 | 56.48 | −2.05 | 24.61 | 32.20 | 69.45 | |
| 1984 | −12.63 | −3.53 | 11.88 | −7.12 | −35.40 | |
| 1985 | 20.54 | **176.90** | 78.68 | 16.24 | 61.19 | |
| 1986 | 44.22 | 34.52 | 83.02 | 10.76 | 2.18 | |
| 1987 | 10.36 | 3.97 | 15.85 | 14.84 | 14.68 | |
| 1988 | 38.09 | 0.29 | 44.65 | 17.81 | **52.75** | 14.14 |
| 1989 | 10.91 | **105.03** | 18.51 | 25.27 | 44.63 | −9.46 |
| 1990 | −15.99 | 6.63 | −9.73 | -12.20 | −0.40 | −31.01 |
| 1991 | 35.57 | −11.86 | 15.13 | 12.03 | 17.23 | −17.30 |
| 1992 | −9.97 | −10.54 | −0.30 | −11.57 | −28.28 | −12.61 |
| 1993 | 36.91 | 28.77 | 24.97 | 18.58 | 34.24 | 83.28 |
| 1994 | 6.41 | −5.94 | 9.42 | −2.45 | 4.04 | **52.53** |
| 1995 | 12.42 | −4.40 | 27.40 | 19.02 | 19.35 | 3.96 |
| 1996 | 17.96 | 4.15 | 13.24 | 29.34 | 21.90 | 35.96 |
| 1997 | −9.75 | 2.82 | 14.26 | 13.38 | 35.56 | 17.79 |
| 1998 | 7.08 | 0.49 | 67.74 | −5.40 | 9.48 | **121.12** |

*Note:* Best-performing country in bold.

| France | Germany | Hong Kong | Ireland | Italy | Japan | Netherlands | New Zealand |
|---|---|---|---|---|---|---|---|
| −4.52 | −22.97 | **44.94** | | −17.25 | −11.34 | −5.85 | |
| 0.88 | 24.41 | **75.76** | | −12.19 | 53.89 | 1.04 | |
| 25.39 | 18.46 | **163.34** | | 14.75 | 126.26 | 29.78 | |
| 7.60 | −4.49 | −39.35 | | 11.44 | −20.03 | −4.79 | |
| −25.30 | **17.16** | −56.95 | | −34.20 | −15.72 | −16.00 | |
| 44.71 | 30.14 | 112.66 | | −8.66 | 19.98 | 50.65 | |
| −20.03 | 6.65 | **40.58** | | −26.57 | 25.86 | 17.12 | |
| 5.87 | 25.95 | −11.25 | | −18.77 | 15.89 | 16.05 | |
| **73.17** | 24.68 | 18.39 | | 46.40 | 53.26 | 21.27 | |
| 29.22 | −4.17 | 83.04 | | 17.54 | −11.84 | 19.25 | |
| −1.58 | −10.10 | 73.28 | | **80.43** | 30.71 | 13.83 | |
| −29.38 | −10.74 | −15.85 | | −10.10 | 15.53 | −14.00 | |
| −3.25 | 10.92 | −44.53 | | −18.86 | −0.55 | 17.32 | |
| 32.57 | 23.89 | −2.62 | | 3.80 | 24.63 | 37.76 | |
| 5.58 | −5.16 | **46.94** | | 9.26 | 17.48 | 11.84 | |
| 82.17 | 136.37 | 51.63 | | 134.50 | 43.54 | 61.19 | |
| 78.92 | 35.99 | 56.18 | | 108.12 | 100.35 | 42.40 | |
| −12.54 | −23.84 | −3.95 | | −19.63 | **43.02** | 9.14 | |
| 37.69 | 20.61 | 27.88 | 24.06 | 11.66 | 35.20 | 14.39 | −12.13 |
| 36.94 | 47.22 | 8.45 | 41.10 | 20.35 | 1.78 | 37.78 | 12.72 |
| −13.23 | −8.73 | 9.19 | −16.41 | −18.26 | −36.01 | −1.85 | −36.38 |
| 18.68 | 8.89 | **49.63** | 12.49 | −0.50 | 9.11 | 19.36 | 20.67 |
| 3.04 | −10.08 | **32.15** | −21.53 | −21.70 | −21.39 | 3.01 | 0.38 |
| 21.49 | 36.32 | **116.84** | 42.35 | 29.43 | 25.73 | 36.50 | 69.93 |
| −4.67 | 5.13 | −28.94 | 14.58 | 12.20 | 21.83 | 12.63 | 10.19 |
| 14.48 | 16.56 | 22.54 | 22.13 | 1.56 | 0.42 | 28.52 | 22.30 |
| 22.38 | 14.62 | 33.12 | 29.48 | 13.73 | −14.99 | 28.08 | 18.86 |
| 12.26 | 24.96 | −23.30 | 18.25 | 36.16 | −24.01 | 25.36 | −12.71 |
| 41.70 | 29.65 | −2.90 | 35.02 | 52.91 | 5.08 | 23.63 | −21.79 |

*(Continued)*

| | Norway | Singapore | Spain | Sweden | Switzerland | United Kingdom |
|---|---|---|---|---|---|---|
| **TABLE A.1** | | | **(Continued)** | | | |
| 1970 | 34.40 | | −3.23 | −19.00 | −13.16 | -6.04 |
| 1971 | 18.47 | | 25.62 | 36.54 | 27.40 | 48.57 |
| 1972 | 9.14 | | 41.07 | 16.51 | 28.47 | 3.99 |
| 1973 | **128.78** | | 26.00 | 2.65 | −2.96 | −26.05 |
| 1974 | −39.96 | | −8.94 | 12.05 | −12.62 | −50.64 |
| 1975 | −15.13 | | 0.09 | 21.66 | 41.39 | **116.04** |
| 1976 | 14.66 | | −36.17 | 5.90 | 10.45 | −12.53 |
| 1977 | −22.90 | | −34.22 | −21.35 | 29.07 | **58.48** |
| 1978 | 6.18 | | 7.96 | 23.76 | 21.78 | 14.55 |
| 1979 | **184.94** | | 5.00 | 2.82 | 13.13 | 21.93 |
| 1980 | −18.74 | | 4.35 | 22.93 | −7.83 | 41.44 |
| 1981 | −15.89 | | 12.04 | **37.37** | −10.00 | −10.00 |
| 1982 | −28.19 | | −29.35 | **25.43** | 3.51 | 8.90 |
| 1983 | **81.97** | | −5.23 | 50.30 | 19.26 | 17.46 |
| 1984 | 1.04 | | 41.73 | −21.35 | −10.75 | 5.13 |
| 1985 | 70.14 | | 56.55 | 58.05 | 106.13 | 53.64 |
| 1986 | −1.71 | | **122.98** | 66.91 | 35.00 | 26.91 |
| 1987 | 6.55 | | 39.68 | 3.64 | −8.41 | 35.08 |
| 1988 | 43.26 | | 13.11 | 48.48 | 6.53 | 5.96 |
| 1989 | 46.08 | | 10.63 | 32.26 | 27.02 | 21.92 |
| 1990 | 1.17 | | −12.67 | −20.20 | −5.00 | **10.30** |
| 1991 | −14.99 | | 17.10 | 15.62 | 16.90 | 16.08 |
| 1992 | −22.05 | | −21.10 | −13.87 | 17.71 | −3.82 |
| 1993 | 42.64 | | 31.51 | 37.97 | 46.59 | 24.48 |
| 1994 | 24.07 | 6.25 | −3.97 | 18.75 | 4.21 | −1.60 |
| 1995 | 6.36 | 6.58 | 30.70 | 32.83 | **44.64** | 21.27 |
| 1996 | 28.20 | −7.02 | **42.17** | 38.01 | 3.35 | 27.48 |
| 1997 | 7.85 | −29.91 | 25.90 | 14.44 | **44.22** | 22.93 |
| 1998 | −29.79 | −13.10 | 50.20 | 14.56 | 24.37 | 17.11 |

| S&P 500 | EAFE | MSCI World | Average 21 Developed Countries |
|---|---|---|---|
| 4.01 | −10.51 | −1.98 | −0.73 |
| 14.31 | 31.21 | 19.56 | 21.61 |
| 18.98 | 37.60 | 23.55 | 43.29 |
| −14.66 | −14.17 | −14.51 | 5.38 |
| −26.47 | −22.15 | −24.48 | −19.25 |
| 37.20 | 37.10 | 34.50 | 32.51 |
| 23.84 | 3.74 | 14.71 | 4.63 |
| −7.18 | 19.42 | 2.00 | 3.67 |
| 6.56 | 34.30 | 18.22 | 24.54 |
| 18.44 | 6.18 | 12.67 | 30.09 |
| 32.42 | 24.43 | 27.72 | 18.99 |
| −4.91 | −1.03 | −3.30 | −5.51 |
| 21.41 | −0.86 | 11.27 | −3.57 |
| 22.51 | 24.61 | 23.28 | 28.65 |
| 6.27 | 7.86 | 5.77 | 3.60 |
| 32.16 | 56.72 | 41.77 | 72.92 |
| 18.47 | 69.94 | 42.80 | 50.90 |
| 5.23 | 24.93 | 16.76 | 7.86 |
| 16.81 | 28.59 | 23.95 | 23.06 |
| 31.49 | 10.80 | 17.19 | 28.53 |
| −3.17 | −23.19 | −16.52 | −10.70 |
| 30.55 | 12.49 | 18.98 | 13.52 |
| 7.67 | −11.85 | −4.66 | −7.24 |
| 9.99 | 32.94 | 23.13 | 41.44 |
| 1.31 | 8.06 | 5.58 | 7.43 |
| 37.43 | 11.55 | 21.32 | 18.38 |
| 23.07 | 6.36 | 14.00 | 20.15 |
| 33.36 | 2.06 | 16.23 | 11.90 |
| 28.58 | 20.33 | 24.80 | 21.70 |

*(Continued)*

| TABLE A.1 (Continued) | | | | | |
| --- | --- | --- | --- | --- | --- |
| | *Australia* | *Austria* | *Belgium* | *Canada* | *Denmark* | *Finland* |
| 1970–1998 | | | | | | |
| Geometric mean | 8.48 | 10.76 | 16.97 | 9.57 | 14.63 | 16.38 |
| Arithmetic mean | 11.39 | 14.95 | 19.17 | 10.82 | 17.93 | 23.49 |
| 1989–1998 | | | | | | |
| Geometric mean | 7.82 | 7.94 | 16.59 | 7.61 | 13.83 | 16.60 |
| Arithmetic mean | 9.16 | 11.51 | 18.06 | 8.60 | 15.78 | 24.43 |
| 1970–1998 | | | | | | |
| Standard deviation | 25.75 | 38.89 | 24.42 | 16.74 | 29.66 | 46.51 |
| Positive periods | 18 | 19 | 24 | 20 | 23 | 7 |
| Negative periods | 11 | 10 | 5 | 9 | 6 | 4 |
| 1989–1998 | | | | | | |
| Standard deviation | 18.03 | 34.82 | 20.64 | 15.30 | 21.07 | 48.91 |
| Positive periods | 7 | 6 | 8 | 6 | 8 | 6 |
| Negative periods | 3 | 4 | 2 | 4 | 2 | 4 |
| Number of years best-performing | 0 | 2 | 0 | 0 | 1 | 2 |

| France | Germany | Hong Kong | Ireland | Italy | Japan | Netherlands | New Zealand |
|--------|---------|-----------|---------|-------|-------|-------------|-------------|
| 13.25 | 12.87 | 18.82 | 16.41 | 8.28 | 13.05 | 17.07 | 3.23 |
| 16.56 | 15.80 | 28.86 | 18.32 | 13.71 | 17.71 | 18.46 | 6.55 |
| | | | | | | | |
| 14.13 | 15.10 | 15.93 | 15.67 | 10.35 | −5.25 | 20.62 | 4.90 |
| 15.31 | 16.45 | 21.68 | 17.75 | 12.59 | −3.25 | 21.30 | 8.42 |
| | | | | | | | |
| 29.01 | 29.54 | 51.24 | 20.95 | 39.63 | 35.75 | 18.37 | 28.41 |
| 20 | 20 | 19 | 9 | 17 | 20 | 24 | 7 |
| 9 | 9 | 10 | 2 | 12 | 9 | 5 | 4 |
| | | | | | | | |
| 17.12 | 18.60 | 41.63 | 21.99 | 23.45 | 20.28 | 13.22 | 29.23 |
| 8 | 8 | 7 | 8 | 7 | 6 | 9 | 7 |
| 2 | 2 | 3 | 2 | 3 | 4 | 1 | 3 |
| 1 | 1 | 8 | 0 | 1 | 1 | 0 | 0 |

(Continued)

| | Norway | Singapore | Spain | Sweden | Switzerland | United Kingdom |
|---|---|---|---|---|---|---|
| **1970–1998** | | | | | | |
| Geometric mean | 11.31 | –8.50 | 11.37 | 16.33 | 14.92 | 13.88 |
| Arithmetic mean | 18.85 | –7.44 | 15.50 | 18.75 | 17.25 | 17.55 |
| **1989–1998** | | | | | | |
| Geometric mean | 5.99 | –8.50 | 14.76 | 15.26 | 21.13 | 15.13 |
| Arithmetic mean | 8.95 | –7.44 | 17.05 | 17.04 | 22.40 | 15.62 |
| **1970–1998** | | | | | | |
| Standard deviation | 48.80 | 15.18 | 32.46 | 23.79 | 25.31 | 29.90 |
| Positive periods | 19 | 2 | 20 | 24 | 21 | 22 |
| Negative periods | 10 | 3 | 9 | 5 | 8 | 7 |
| **1989–1998** | | | | | | |
| Standard deviation | 26.28 | 15.18 | 23.63 | 20.33 | 18.49 | 10.80 |
| Positive periods | 7 | 2 | 7 | 8 | 9 | 8 |
| Negative periods | 3 | 3 | 3 | 2 | 1 | 2 |
| Number of years best-performing | 3 | 0 | 2 | 2 | 2 | 3 |

**TABLE A.1 (Continued)**

Source: Morgan Stanley Capital International.

| S&P 500 | EAFE | MSCI World | Average 21 Developed Countries |
|---------|------|------------|--------------------------------|
| 13.48 | 12.75 | 12.41 | 15.23 |
| 14.68 | 14.74 | 13.60 | 16.82 |
| | | | |
| 19.19 | 5.85 | 11.21 | 13.53 |
| 20.03 | 6.96 | 12.00 | 14.51 |
| | | | |
| 16.21 | 21.86 | 16.09 | 19.97 |
| 24 | 22 | 23 | 23 |
| 5 | 7 | 6 | 6 |
| | | | |
| 14.71 | 15.67 | 13.35 | 15.59 |
| 9 | 8 | 8 | 8 |
| 1 | 2 | 2 | 2 |
| | | | |
| 0 | | | |

### TABLE A.2   Total Returns of the World's 21 Developed Markets from 1970 to 1998, Expressed in Local Currencies

|      | Australia | Austria | Belgium | Canada | Denmark | Finland |
|------|-----------|---------|---------|--------|---------|---------|
| 1970 | −19.19    | 11.46   | 7.18    | 8.27   | −6.53   |         |
| 1971 | −7.49     | −1.03   | 9.64    | 12.97  | 3.82    |         |
| 1972 | 15.38     | 34.44   | 30.72   | 32.51  | 105.88  |         |
| 1973 | −26.27    | 6.94    | 6.75    | −2.62  | −3.19   |         |
| 1974 | −24.03    | −0.69   | −25.10  | −27.36 | −20.16  |         |
| 1975 | 57.22     | 5.03    | 27.05   | 18.25  | 36.03   |         |
| 1976 | 3.77      | 4.60    | −2.95   | 9.18   | 0.42    |         |
| 1977 | 6.73      | −5.29   | 0.13    | 6.20   | 2.16    |         |
| 1978 | 21.03     | 2.84    | 14.26   | 30.65  | −3.46   |         |
| 1979 | 49.47     | 11.23   | 15.78   | 50.64  | 2.50    |         |
| 1980 | 44.98     | −1.97   | −11.47  | 24.03  | 32.90   |         |
| 1981 | −20.17    | −10.13  | 13.17   | −10.68 | 52.43   |         |
| 1982 | −10.74    | −4.11   | 24.79   | 6.36   | 17.65   |         |
| 1983 | 70.11     | 13.53   | 47.77   | 33.82  | **99.59** |       |
| 1984 | −4.80     | 9.98    | 26.84   | −1.37  | −26.34  |         |
| 1985 | 46.54     | **117.00** | 42.65 | 22.94  | 28.39   |         |
| 1986 | 47.72     | 6.73    | 46.86   | 9.41   | −16.35  |         |
| 1987 | 1.55      | −16.43  | −11.49  | 8.11   | −5.47   |         |
| 1988 | 16.82     | 13.61   | **74.89** | 8.15 | 73.11   | 20.68   |
| 1989 | 19.91     | **95.10** | 12.86 | 21.59  | 38.77   | −11.77  |
| 1990 | −14.09    | −5.58   | −21.59  | −12.04 | −12.53  | −38.22  |
| 1991 | 37.80     | −10.52  | 16.63   | 11.59  | 19.72   | −5.78   |
| 1992 | −0.52     | −4.60   | 5.95    | −2.70  | −23.57  | 10.71   |
| 1993 | 38.66     | 38.04   | 35.91   | 23.46  | 44.68   | 102.81  |
| 1994 | −6.82     | −15.95  | −3.66   | 3.37   | −6.64   | **24.78** |
| 1995 | 17.27     | −11.76  | 17.72   | 15.77  | 8.75    | -3.84   |
| 1996 | 10.36     | 12.88   | 22.11   | 29.92  | 30.26   | 43.00   |
| 1997 | 10.30     | 19.00   | 33.52   | 18.33  | 56.72   | 39.17   |
| 1998 | 13.73     | −6.66   | 56.45   | 1.22   | 1.66    | **107.01** |

*Note:* Best-performing country in bold.

| France | Germany | Hong Kong | Ireland | Italy | Japan | Netherlands | New Zealand |
|---|---|---|---|---|---|---|---|
| −5.17 | −23.84 | **45.36** | | −17.58 | −11.38 | −6.55 | |
| −4.53 | 11.46 | **64.82** | | −16.27 | 35.45 | −8.48 | |
| 22.91 | 16.03 | **164.32** | | 12.53 | 117.06 | 28.52 | |
| −1.07 | −19.36 | −45.78 | | 16.30 | −25.85 | −16.66 | |
| −29.49 | **4.44** | −58.47 | | −29.70 | −9.41 | −25.46 | |
| 46.04 | 41.63 | 117.99 | | −3.86 | 21.65 | 61.59 | |
| −11.40 | −3.91 | **30.53** | | −6.00 | 20.77 | 7.03 | |
| 0.24 | 12.22 | −12.35 | | -19.09 | −5.01 | 7.69 | |
| **53.84** | 8.27 | 23.21 | | 39.38 | 24.27 | 4.73 | |
| 24.27 | −9.23 | 88.56 | | 13.89 | 8.59 | 15.41 | |
| 10.56 | 1.71 | 79.66 | | **108.81** | 10.70 | 27.21 | |
| −10.11 | 2.74 | −6.90 | | 15.94 | 25.15 | −0.32 | |
| 13.20 | 16.91 | −36.52 | | −7.37 | 6.28 | 24.73 | |
| 64.56 | 42.00 | 16.65 | | 25.74 | 23.14 | 60.85 | |
| 21.32 | 9.61 | 47.75 | | 27.45 | 27.05 | 29.54 | |
| 43.60 | 84.81 | 51.40 | | 103.32 | 14.62 | 25.88 | |
| 52.75 | 7.23 | 55.86 | | 68.40 | 58.98 | 12.61 | |
| −27.99 | −38.41 | −4.50 | | −31.54 | 8.77 | −12.14 | |
| 56.97 | 36.30 | 28.91 | 38.36 | 26.09 | 39.66 | 30.15 | −7.88 |
| 30.53 | 40.23 | 8.35 | 36.57 | 16.64 | 17.07 | 30.94 | 19.45 |
| −23.53 | −19.26 | **9.10** | −27.14 | −27.25 | −39.55 | −13.27 | −35.73 |
| 20.78 | 10.38 | **49.22** | 14.30 | 1.31 | 0.27 | 20.84 | 31.40 |
| 9.87 | −3.90 | **31.56** | −15.34 | 0.86 | −21.38 | 9.78 | 5.35 |
| 29.97 | 46.21 | **116.30** | 64.13 | 50.00 | 12.42 | 45.77 | 56.19 |
| −13.86 | −6.18 | −28.81 | 4.48 | 6.25 | 8.72 | 0.65 | −3.65 |
| 5.17 | 8.04 | 22.49 | 17.92 | −0.58 | 4.28 | 19.05 | 19.86 |
| 29.49 | 22.87 | 33.12 | 25.00 | 8.72 | −4.79 | 38.68 | 9.87 |
| 30.08 | 45.90 | −23.15 | 37.56 | **58.59** | −14.36 | 45.91 | 5.85 |
| 31.91 | 20.32 | −2.93 | 29.36 | 42.88 | −8.70 | 14.73 | −13.69 |

*(Continued)*

## TABLE A.2   (Continued)

| | Norway | Singapore | Spain | Sweden | Switzerland | United Kingdom |
|------|--------|-----------|--------|--------|-------------|----------------|
| 1970 | 34.22 | | -3.70 | -19.00 | -13.20 | -5.77 |
| 1971 | 11.34 | | 18.96 | 28.49 | 15.57 | 39.33 |
| 1972 | 8.01 | | 35.84 | 13.59 | 23.85 | 13.05 |
| 1973 | **97.34** | | 12.88 | -0.71 | -16.59 | -25.26 |
| 1974 | -45.44 | | -10.28 | -0.33 | -31.58 | -51.17 |
| 1975 | -8.94 | | 6.62 | 30.76 | 45.84 | **150.74** |
| 1976 | 6.45 | | -27.08 | -0.36 | 3.26 | 3.97 |
| 1977 | -23.58 | | -22.06 | -11.00 | 5.39 | **41.55** |
| 1978 | 3.76 | | -6.45 | 13.85 | -1.36 | 7.31 |
| 1979 | **179.47** | | -0.93 | -0.75 | 10.34 | 11.54 |
| 1980 | -14.55 | | 25.01 | 29.64 | 2.87 | 31.89 |
| 1981 | -5.70 | | 37.77 | **75.01** | -8.22 | 12.50 |
| 1982 | -12.78 | | -8.94 | **64.24** | 14.79 | 28.69 |
| 1983 | 99.21 | | 18.24 | 64.85 | 30.32 | 30.73 |
| 1984 | 18.89 | | **56.83** | -11.64 | 5.85 | 31.86 |
| 1985 | 41.97 | | 39.17 | 33.89 | 65.59 | 23.01 |
| 1986 | -4.07 | | **91.51** | 49.46 | 5.55 | 24.33 |
| 1987 | -10.29 | | **12.89** | -12.46 | -28.41 | 6.42 |
| 1988 | 50.69 | | 19.77 | 57.76 | 26.05 | 9.65 |
| 1989 | 46.90 | | 6.86 | 34.15 | 30.44 | 36.60 |
| 1990 | -9.68 | | -23.77 | -27.57 | -21.48 | -7.75 |
| 1991 | -13.78 | | 18.39 | 13.59 | 24.42 | 19.84 |
| 1992 | -9.43 | | -6.19 | 10.08 | 27.18 | 18.73 |
| 1993 | 54.68 | | 63.59 | 62.46 | 48.52 | 27.42 |
| 1994 | 11.58 | -3.33 | -11.52 | 5.95 | -8.19 | -6.97 |
| 1995 | -0.51 | 3.28 | 20.88 | 19.53 | 27.52 | 22.20 |
| 1996 | 30.63 | -7.90 | **51.47** | 42.17 | 20.01 | 15.60 |
| 1997 | 23.24 | -15.74 | 47.87 | 31.87 | 57.34 | 27.54 |
| 1998 | -27.31 | -14.69 | 39.99 | 17.01 | 16.81 | 16.50 |

| S&P 500 | EAFE | MSCI World | Average 21 Developed Countries |
|---|---|---|---|
| 4.01 | −10.51 | −1.98 | −1.26 |
| 14.31 | 31.21 | 19.56 | 13.43 |
| 18.98 | 37.60 | 23.55 | 40.80 |
| −14.66 | −14.17 | −14.51 | −3.40 |
| −26.47 | −22.15 | −24.48 | −24.16 |
| 37.20 | 37.10 | 34.50 | 40.64 |
| 23.84 | 3.74 | 14.71 | 3.65 |
| −7.18 | 19.42 | 2.00 | −1.37 |
| 6.56 | 34.30 | 18.22 | 14.28 |
| 18.44 | 6.18 | 12.67 | 28.78 |
| 32.42 | 24.43 | 27.72 | 25.55 |
| −4.91 | −1.03 | −3.30 | 9.27 |
| 21.41 | −0.86 | 11.27 | 9.33 |
| 22.51 | 24.61 | 23.28 | 44.92 |
| 6.27 | 7.86 | 5.77 | 16.18 |
| 32.16 | 56.72 | 41.77 | 48.05 |
| 18.47 | 69.94 | 42.80 | 31.50 |
| 5.23 | 24.93 | 16.76 | −9.19 |
| 16.81 | 28.59 | 23.95 | 31.83 |
| 31.49 | 10.80 | 17.19 | 28.13 |
| −3.17 | −23.19 | −16.52 | −18.71 |
| 30.55 | 12.49 | 18.98 | 15.55 |
| 7.67 | −11.85 | −4.66 | 2.51 |
| 9.99 | 32.94 | 23.13 | 49.23 |
| 1.31 | 8.06 | 5.58 | −2.31 |
| **37.43** | 11.55 | 21.32 | 12.88 |
| 23.07 | 6.36 | 14.00 | 23.17 |
| 33.36 | 2.06 | 16.23 | 27.09 |
| 28.58 | 20.33 | 24.80 | 17.34 |

*(Continued)*

| TABLE A.2 (Continued) | | | | | |
| --- | --- | --- | --- | --- | --- |
| | Australia | Austria | Belgium | Canada | Denmark | Finland |
| **1970–1998** | | | | | | |
| Geometric mean | 10.76 | 7.78 | 15.52 | 10.92 | 13.98 | 19.17 |
| Arithmetic mean | 13.63 | 10.61 | 17.70 | 12.07 | 18.32 | 26.23 |
| **1989–1998** | | | | | | |
| Geometric mean | 11.47 | 7.28 | 15.70 | 10.32 | 12.97 | 19.01 |
| Arithmetic mean | 12.66 | 11.00 | 17.59 | 11.05 | 15.78 | 26.79 |
| **1970–1998** | | | | | | |
| Standard deviation | 26.22 | 29.60 | 23.07 | 16.04 | 34.50 | 45.43 |
| Positive periods | 19 | 16 | 23 | 23 | 19 | 7 |
| Negative periods | 10 | 13 | 6 | 6 | 10 | 4 |
| **1989–1998** | | | | | | |
| Standard deviation | 17.20 | 34.01 | 21.77 | 13.23 | 26.60 | 47.85 |
| Positive periods | 7 | 4 | 8 | 8 | 7 | 6 |
| Negative periods | 3 | 6 | 2 | 2 | 3 | 4 |
| Number of years best-performing | 0 | 2 | 1 | 0 | 1 | 2 |

| France | Germany | Hong Kong | Ireland | Italy | Japan | Netherlands | New Zealand |
|--------|---------|-----------|---------|-------|-------|-------------|-------------|
| 13.27 | 9.82 | 19.85 | 17.68 | 11.96 | 8.66 | 14.46 | 5.34 |
| 16.24 | 12.59 | 29.85 | 20.47 | 16.69 | 11.88 | 16.53 | 7.91 |
| | | | | | | | |
| 13.23 | 14.40 | 15.83 | 15.79 | 12.97 | −6.16 | 19.84 | 6.76 |
| 15.04 | 16.46 | 21.53 | 18.68 | 15.74 | −4.60 | 21.31 | 9.49 |
| | | | | | | | |
| 26.17 | 25.63 | 51.16 | 25.94 | 35.59 | 29.03 | 22.24 | 24.35 |
| 20 | 21 | 20 | 9 | 19 | 20 | 22 | 7 |
| 9 | 8 | 9 | 2 | 10 | 9 | 7 | 4 |
| | | | | | | | |
| 20.17 | 22.81 | 41.42 | 26.61 | 26.73 | 17.17 | 19.44 | 25.06 |
| 8 | 7 | 7 | 8 | 8 | 5 | 9 | 7 |
| 2 | 3 | 3 | 2 | 2 | 5 | 1 | 3 |
| | | | | | | | |
| 1 | 1 | 8 | 0 | 2 | 0 | 0 | 0 |

(Continued)

**TABLE A.2 (Continued)**

|  | Norway | Singapore | Spain | Sweden | Switzerland | United Kingdom |
|---|---|---|---|---|---|---|
| **1970–1998** | | | | | | |
| Geometric mean | 11.55 | −7.95 | 14.12 | 18.15 | 10.47 | 15.34 |
| Arithmetic mean | 18.36 | −7.67 | 17.37 | 21.19 | 13.05 | 19.11 |
| **1989–1998** | | | | | | |
| Geometric mean | 7.61 | −7.95 | 17.37 | 18.55 | 20.05 | 16.13 |
| Arithmetic mean | 10.63 | −7.67 | 20.76 | 20.92 | 22.26 | 16.97 |
| **1970–1998** | | | | | | |
| Standard deviation | 45.91 | 7.95 | 28.53 | 27.56 | 24.28 | 32.18 |
| Positive periods | 16 | 1 | 19 | 20 | 21 | 24 |
| Negative periods | 13 | 4 | 10 | 9 | 8 | 5 |
| **1989–1998** | | | | | | |
| Standard deviation | 27.47 | 7.95 | 29.50 | 24.12 | 23.38 | 14.27 |
| Positive periods | 5 | 1 | 7 | 9 | 8 | 8 |
| Negative periods | 5 | 4 | 3 | 1 | 2 | 2 |
| Number of years best-performing | 2 | 0 | 4 | 2 | 0 | 2 |

Source: Morgan Stanley Capital International.

| S&P 500 | EAFE | MSCI World | Average 21 Developed Countries | |
|---|---|---|---|---|
| 13.48 | 12.41 | 15.23 | 14.72 | |
| 14.68 | 13.60 | 16.82 | 16.34 | |
| | | | | |
| 19.19 | 5.85 | 11.21 | 14.07 | |
| 20.03 | 6.96 | 12.00 | 15.49 | |
| | | | | |
| 16.21 | 16.09 | 19.97 | 19.33 | |
| 24 | 23 | 23 | 22 | |
| 5 | 6 | 6 | 7 | |
| | | | | |
| 14.71 | 15.67 | 13.35 | 18.73 | |
| 9 | 8 | 8 | 8 | |
| 1 | 2 | 2 | 2 | |
| | | | | |
| 1 | | | | |

**TABLE A.3  Ten-Year Rolling Returns of the World's 21 Developed Markets from 1970 to 1998, Expressed in U.S. Dollars**

|           | Australia | Austria | Belgium | Canada | Denmark | Finland |
|-----------|-----------|---------|---------|--------|---------|---------|
| 1970–1979 | 4.17      | 14.59   | 13.51   | 11.01  | 11.53   |         |
| 1971–1980 | 11.20     | 11.94   | 10.07   | 11.61  | 14.21   |         |
| 1972–1981 | 8.36      | 8.37    | 7.13    | 9.00   | 15.68   |         |
| 1973–1982 | 3.44      | 4.00    | 4.37    | 6.18   | 7.59    |         |
| 1974–1983 | 9.81      | 1.53    | 5.32    | 9.48   | 12.82   |         |
| 1975–1984 | 12.64     | –0.25   | 8.16    | 12.15  | 9.27    |         |
| 1976–1985 | 10.28     | 10.76   | 12.93   | 12.24  | 12.14   |         |
| 1977–1986 | 15.65     | 12.46   | 19.20   | 12.32  | 11.61   |         |
| 1978–1987 | 15.46     | 12.36   | 19.89   | 14.12  | 12.88   |         |
| 1979–1988 | 16.90     | 10.69   | 21.11   | 13.86  | 16.70   |         |
| 1980–1989 | 13.92     | 16.82   | 21.07   | 11.61  | 21.42   |         |
| 1981–1990 | 7.16      | 19.06   | 22.73   | 8.06   | 19.33   |         |
| 1982–1991 | 13.51     | 20.50   | **25.41** | 10.46 | 18.55   |         |
| 1983–1992 | 15.21     | 20.26   | 25.09   | 8.83   | 14.36   |         |
| 1984–1993 | 13.68     | 23.59   | 25.13   | 7.65   | 11.72   |         |
| 1985–1994 | 15.94     | 23.28   | 24.85   | 8.18   | 17.18   |         |
| 1986–1995 | 15.14     | 10.84   | 20.70   | 8.44   | 13.71   |         |
| 1987–1996 | 12.85     | 8.04    | 15.04   | 10.13  | 15.73   |         |
| 1988–1997 | 10.60     | 7.92    | 14.88   | 9.99   | 17.68   | 9.14    |
| 1989–1998 | 7.82      | 7.94    | 16.59   | 7.61   | 13.83   | 16.60   |

*Note:* Best-performing country in bold.

| France | Germany | Hong Kong | Ireland | Italy | Japan | Netherlands | New Zealand |
|--------|---------|-----------|---------|-------|-------|-------------|-------------|
| 10.28 | 10.25 | **25.98** | | −5.41 | 17.27 | 11.32 | |
| 10.62 | 11.97 | **28.25** | | 2.26 | 21.91 | 13.46 | |
| 6.74 | 8.31 | **19.15** | | 2.50 | 18.47 | 11.64 | |
| 4.01 | 7.60 | 1.96 | | −0.99 | 9.12 | 10.52 | |
| 6.20 | 10.44 | 6.91 | | −1.69 | 14.07 | 14.68 | |
| 9.94 | 8.13 | 20.87 | | 3.42 | 17.92 | 18.01 | |
| 12.50 | 14.78 | 16.85 | | 13.64 | **20.06** | 18.81 | |
| 21.94 | 17.60 | 18.08 | | **26.12** | 25.77 | 21.16 | |
| 19.63 | 11.83 | 19.02 | | 25.99 | **28.44** | 20.42 | |
| 16.92 | 11.46 | 19.94 | | 22.62 | **26.84** | 19.72 | |
| 17.60 | 16.35 | 13.83 | | 22.91 | 28.68 | 21.46 | |
| 16.13 | 16.53 | 8.69 | | 13.55 | 19.81 | 19.67 | |
| 22.32 | 18.87 | 15.13 | | 14.71 | 19.13 | 23.66 | |
| 23.09 | 16.40 | **25.57** | | 14.30 | 16.36 | 22.06 | |
| 22.02 | 17.51 | **36.04** | | 16.85 | 16.46 | 21.95 | |
| 20.78 | 18.73 | **26.50** | | 17.16 | 16.88 | 22.04 | |
| 15.30 | 10.63 | **23.84** | | 7.76 | 12.78 | 19.30 | |
| 11.00 | 8.75 | **21.87** | | 1.44 | 3.51 | 18.04 | |
| 13.81 | 14.27 | 19.16 | 14.70 | 6.93 | −2.83 | **19.69** | 6.13 |
| 14.13 | 15.10 | 15.93 | 15.67 | 10.35 | −5.25 | 20.62 | 4.90 |

*(Continued)*

**TABLE A.3  (Continued)**

| | Norway | Singapore | Spain | Sweden | Switzerland | United Kingdom |
|---|---|---|---|---|---|---|
| 1970–1979 | 18.41 | | –0.65 | 6.69 | 12.84 | 8.28 |
| 1971–1980 | 12.60 | | 0.11 | 11.24 | 13.51 | 12.80 |
| 1972–1981 | 8.81 | | –1.03 | 11.30 | 9.64 | 7.29 |
| 1973–1982 | 4.35 | | –7.65 | **12.13** | 7.29 | 7.79 |
| 1974–1983 | 1.98 | | –10.24 | **16.49** | 9.53 | 12.89 |
| 1975–1984 | 7.43 | | –6.18 | 12.44 | 9.76 | **21.76** |
| 1976–1985 | 15.17 | | –1.89 | 15.42 | 13.98 | 17.68 |
| 1977–1986 | 13.41 | | 11.19 | 20.79 | 16.29 | 22.14 |
| 1978–1987 | 17.14 | | 19.88 | 24.17 | 12.37 | 20.20 |
| 1979–1988 | 20.70 | | 20.44 | 26.45 | 10.87 | 19.27 |
| 1980–1989 | 12.90 | | 21.07 | **29.67** | 12.16 | 19.27 |
| 1981–1990 | 15.40 | | 18.94 | **24.19** | 12.50 | 16.34 |
| 1982–1991 | 15.53 | | 19.46 | 22.07 | 15.48 | 19.34 |
| 1983–1992 | 16.48 | | 20.79 | 17.56 | 16.98 | 17.87 |
| 1984–1993 | 13.67 | | 24.81 | 16.56 | 19.42 | 18.55 |
| 1985–1994 | 16.03 | | 20.05 | 21.46 | 21.28 | 17.77 |
| 1986–1995 | 10.71 | | 17.90 | 19.37 | 17.06 | 15.02 |
| 1987–1996 | 13.69 | | 12.71 | 17.12 | 13.97 | 15.07 |
| 1988–1997 | 13.83 | | 11.55 | 18.29 | 19.27 | 13.99 |
| 1989–1998 | 5.99 | | 14.76 | 15.26 | **21.13** | 15.13 |

*Source:* Morgan Stanley Capital International.

| S&P 500 | EAFE | MSCI World | Average 21 Developed Countries |
|---|---|---|---|
| 5.86 | 10.09 | 6.96 | 13.11 |
| 8.44 | 13.78 | 9.83 | 15.18 |
| 6.47 | 10.62 | 7.52 | **12.31** |
| 6.68 | 7.05 | 6.40 | 7.95 |
| 10.61 | 11.11 | 10.37 | 10.12 |
| 14.76 | 14.80 | 14.15 | 12.90 |
| 14.33 | 16.34 | 14.75 | 15.95 |
| 13.82 | 22.23 | 17.29 | 20.27 |
| 15.26 | 22.78 | 18.89 | 20.75 |
| 16.33 | 22.25 | 19.45 | 20.60 |
| 17.55 | 22.77 | 19.92 | 20.46 |
| 13.93 | 16.99 | 14.93 | 17.05 |
| 17.59 | 18.50 | 17.34 | 19.22 |
| 16.19 | 17.11 | 15.54 | 18.76 |
| 14.94 | 17.87 | 15.53 | 19.89 |
| 14.40 | 17.89 | 15.50 | 20.32 |
| 14.84 | 13.95 | 13.72 | 15.85 |
| 15.28 | 8.74 | 11.19 | 13.24 |
| 18.05 | 6.56 | 11.13 | 13.66 |
| 19.19 | 5.85 | 11.21 | 13.53 |

**TABLE A.4  Ten-Year Rolling Returns of the World's 21 Developed Markets from 1970 to 1998, Expressed in Local Currencies**

|            | Australia | Austria | Belgium | Canada | Denmark | Finland |
|------------|-----------|---------|---------|--------|---------|---------|
| 1970–1979  | 4.29      | 6.49    | 7.21    | 11.96  | 7.87    |         |
| 1971–1980  | 10.57     | 5.13    | 5.18    | 13.49  | 11.73   |         |
| 1972–1981  | 8.95      | 4.12    | 5.51    | 10.85  | 16.11   |         |
| 1973–1982  | 6.19      | 0.66    | 5.02    | 8.44   | 9.79    |         |
| 1974–1983  | 15.45     | 1.26    | 8.50    | 11.95  | 18.02   |         |
| 1975–1984  | 18.08     | 2.30    | 14.36   | 15.42  | 17.08   |         |
| 1976–1985  | 17.25     | 10.00   | 15.70   | 15.87  | 16.40   |         |
| 1977–1986  | 21.47     | 10.22   | 20.59   | 15.90  | 14.29   |         |
| 1978–1987  | 20.87     | 8.85    | 19.11   | 16.10  | 13.41   |         |
| 1979–1988  | 20.44     | 9.94    | 24.29   | 13.93  | 20.23   |         |
| 1980–1989  | 17.81     | 16.29   | 23.98   | 11.51  | 23.93   |         |
| 1981–1990  | 11.81     | 15.86   | 22.48   | 7.75   | 18.85   |         |
| 1982–1991  | 18.08     | 15.81   | 22.85   | 10.17  | 16.01   |         |
| 1983–1992  | 19.37     | 15.75   | 20.85   | 9.20   | 11.12   |         |
| 1984–1993  | 16.95     | 18.04   | 19.85   | 8.32   | 7.60    |         |
| 1985–1994  | 16.70     | 14.90   | 16.60   | 8.83   | 10.18   |         |
| 1986–1995  | 14.13     | 5.02    | 14.38   | 8.18   | 8.37    |         |
| 1987–1996  | 10.85     | 5.61    | 12.29   | 10.05  | 13.27   |         |
| 1988–1997  | 11.77     | 9.41    | 17.00   | 11.05  | 19.15   | 12.76   |
| 1989–1998  | 11.47     | 7.28    | 15.70   | 10.32  | 12.97   | 19.01   |

| France | Germany | Hong Kong | Ireland | Italy | Japan | Netherlands | New Zealand |
|--------|---------|-----------|---------|-------|-------|-------------|-------------|
| 6.77 | 2.22 | 23.51 | | −3.01 | 12.67 | 4.39 | |
| 8.42 | 5.22 | 26.16 | | 6.44 | 15.20 | 7.66 | |
| 7.77 | 4.36 | 19.15 | | 9.96 | 14.29 | 8.59 | |
| 6.88 | 4.44 | 3.31 | | 7.85 | 6.42 | 8.26 | |
| 12.46 | 10.52 | 11.54 | | 8.69 | 11.95 | 15.62 | |
| 18.73 | 11.06 | 26.63 | | 15.35 | 15.81 | 22.19 | |
| 18.53 | 14.05 | 22.10 | | 24.32 | 15.12 | 19.18 | |
| 25.17 | 15.31 | 24.28 | | 31.79 | 18.33 | 19.78 | |
| 21.10 | 8.60 | 25.35 | | 29.61 | 19.94 | 17.37 | |
| 21.34 | 11.12 | 25.92 | | 28.31 | 21.35 | 19.95 | |
| 21.94 | 16.06 | 19.13 | | 28.62 | 22.26 | 21.47 | |
| 17.53 | 13.41 | 13.34 | | 15.75 | 15.09 | 16.91 | |
| 21.05 | 14.23 | 18.81 | | 14.20 | 12.56 | 19.18 | |
| 20.69 | 12.01 | 27.80 | | 15.17 | 9.22 | 17.67 | |
| 17.87 | 12.34 | 35.94 | | 17.22 | 8.23 | 16.51 | |
| 13.91 | 10.61 | 26.36 | | 15.11 | 6.56 | 13.61 | |
| 10.41 | 4.83 | 23.71 | | 7.16 | 5.56 | 12.98 | |
| 8.60 | 6.26 | 21.78 | | 2.57 | 0.28 | 15.36 | |
| 15.22 | 15.84 | 19.16 | 16.57 | 11.56 | −2.09 | 21.36 | 7.46 |
| 13.23 | 14.40 | 15.83 | 15.79 | 12.97 | −6.16 | 19.84 | 6.76 |

*(Continued)*

| | Norway | Singapore | Spain | Sweden | Switzerland | United Kingdom |
|---|---|---|---|---|---|---|
| **TABLE A.4** | | **(Continued)** | | | | |
| 1970–1979 | 14.08 | | −1.21 | 4.36 | 2.05 | 9.11 |
| 1971–1980 | 9.04 | | 1.40 | 9.39 | 3.80 | 12.85 |
| 1972–1981 | 7.25 | | 2.90 | 12.82 | 1.43 | 10.46 |
| 1973–1982 | 4.98 | | −1.14 | 17.06 | 0.66 | 11.90 |
| 1974–1983 | 5.08 | | −0.68 | 23.15 | 5.26 | 18.33 |
| 1975–1984 | 13.59 | | 5.03 | 21.68 | 9.95 | 30.69 |
| 1976–1985 | 18.75 | | 7.86 | 21.96 | 11.36 | 21.71 |
| 1977–1986 | 17.52 | | 18.80 | 27.01 | 11.60 | 23.91 |
| 1978–1987 | 19.42 | | 23.28 | 26.80 | 7.37 | 20.42 |
| 1979–1988 | 23.96 | | 26.36 | 31.00 | 10.03 | 20.68 |
| 1980–1989 | 16.24 | | 27.33 | 35.01 | 11.89 | 23.15 |
| 1981–1990 | 16.88 | | 21.18 | 27.38 | 8.91 | 18.83 |
| 1982–1991 | 15.84 | | 19.36 | 21.99 | 12.27 | 19.58 |
| 1983–1992 | 16.28 | | 19.71 | 17.20 | 13.43 | 18.62 |
| 1984–1993 | 13.37 | | 23.66 | 17.03 | 14.92 | 18.32 |
| 1985–1994 | 12.65 | | 16.78 | 19.18 | 13.30 | 14.26 |
| 1986–1995 | 8.72 | | 15.15 | 17.83 | 10.38 | 14.19 |
| 1987–1996 | 12.13 | | 12.48 | 17.24 | 11.80 | 13.36 |
| 1988–1997 | 15.75 | | 15.56 | 22.15 | 20.96 | 15.43 |
| 1989–1998 | 7.61 | | 17.37 | 18.55 | 20.05 | 16.13 |

*Source:* Morgan Stanley Capital International.

| S&P 500 | EAFE | MSCI World | Average 21 Developed Countries |
|---------|------|------------|-------------------------------|
| 5.86 | 5.56 | 6.57 | 9.35 |
| 8.44 | 9.73 | 8.24 | 12.01 |
| 6.47 | 8.94 | 6.84 | 11.59 |
| 6.68 | 6.53 | 6.32 | 8.80 |
| 10.61 | 12.11 | 10.94 | 13.31 |
| 14.76 | 17.43 | 15.51 | 18.25 |
| 14.33 | 15.94 | 14.79 | 18.85 |
| 13.82 | 19.53 | 16.22 | 21.72 |
| 15.26 | 18.64 | 16.59 | 20.71 |
| 16.33 | 20.38 | 18.16 | 22.45 |
| 17.55 | 21.49 | 19.13 | 22.39 |
| 13.93 | 15.19 | 13.74 | 17.18 |
| 17.59 | 14.86 | 15.24 | 17.84 |
| 16.19 | 13.08 | 13.32 | 17.08 |
| 14.94 | 12.82 | 12.88 | 17.43 |
| 14.40 | 10.43 | 11.59 | 15.41 |
| 14.84 | 8.72 | 10.74 | 12.32 |
| 15.28 | 6.07 | 9.54 | 11.59 |
| 18.05 | 7.67 | 11.76 | 15.40 |
| 19.19 | 5.82 | 11.24 | 14.07 |

| Fund Name | Address | Web Site |
|---|---|---|
| **TABLE A.5  Global Funds in Existence for 10 Years or More—Contact Information** | | |
| Alliance Global Sm Cap A | Alliance Capital Funds 135 Avenue of the Americas New York, NY 10105 | www.alliancecapital.com |
| Dreyfus Global Growth | Dreyfus Group One Exchange Place Boston, MA 02109 | www.dreyfus.com |
| Elfun Global | Elfun Mutual Funds GE Mutual Funds c/o NFDS P.O. Box 219631 Kansas City, MO 64121 | www.ge.com/mutualfunds |
| Evergreen Global Opport A | Evergreen Funds 200 Berkeley Street Boston, MA 02116 | www.evergreen-funds.com |
| First Invest Global A | First Investors Group 581 Main Street Woodbridge, NJ 07095 | www.firstinvestors.com |
| Founders Worldwide Growth | Founders Fund P.O. Box 173655 Denver, CO 80217 | www.founders.com |
| GAM Global A | GAM Funds 135 East 57th Street, 25th Floor New York, NY 10022 | www.gam.com |
| Hancock Global B | John Hancock Funds 1 John Hancock Way Suite 1000 Boston, MA 02217 | www.jhancock.com |
| Lexington Global Corp Lead | Lexington Group Park 80 West, Plaza 2 Saddle Brook, NJ 07663 | www.lexingtonfunds.com |
| Lord Abbett Global Equity A | Lord Abbett Family 767 Fifth Avenue New York, NY 10153 | www.lordabbett.com |
| Merrill Lynch Global Holdg A | Merrill Lynch Group Financial Data Services 4800 Deer Lake Drive East Jacksonville, FL 32246 | www.ml.com |
| Merrill Lynch Global Holdg B | Merrill Lynch Group Financial Data Services 4800 Deer Lake Drive East Jacksonville, FL 32246 | www.ml.com |

| TABLE A.5 (Continued) | | |
| --- | --- | --- |
| *Fund Name* | *Address* | *Web Site* |
| MFS Global Equity B | MFS Family of Funds 500 Boylston Street Boston, MA 02116 | www.mfs.com |
| Midas U.S. & Overseas | Bull & Bear Group Midas U.S./Overseas Fund 11 Hanover Square New York, NY 10005 | www.midasfunds.com |
| New Perspective | American Funds Group 333 South Hope Street Los Angeles, CA 90071 | www.americanfunds.com |
| Oppenheimer Global A | Oppenheimer Funds P.O. Box 5270 Denver, CO 80217 | www.oppenheimerfunds.com |
| Phoenix-Aberdeen Wldwde OppA | Phoenix Funds 100 Bright Meadow Blvd. P.O. Box 2200 Enfield, CT 06083 | www.phoenixinvestments.com |
| Prudential Global Genesis B | Prudential Mutual Funds P.O. Box 15,000 New Brunswick, NJ 08906 | www.prudential.com |
| Prudential World Global B | Prudential Mutual Funds P.O. Box 15,000 New Brunswick, NJ 08906 | www.prudential.com |
| Putnam Global Growth A | Putnam Funds One Post Office Square Boston, MA 02109 | www.putnaminv.com |
| Scudder Global | Scudder Funds Two International Place Boston, MA 02110 | www.scudder.com |
| Templeton Global Small Co A | Templeton Group 777 Mariners Island Blvd. San Mateo, CA 94404 | www.franklin-templeton.com |
| Templeton Growth A | Templeton Group 777 Mariners Island Blvd. San Mateo, CA 94404 | www.franklin-templeton.com |
| Templeton World A | Templeton Group 777 Mariners Island Blvd. San Mateo, CA 94404 | www.franklin-templeton.com |

*Source:* Morningstar, Inc. www.morningstar.com or 800-735-0700.

# Glossary

**accounting standards** the way companies are required to report their finances. The standards may vary from one country to another.

**allocation** the process of dividing a portfolio's total assets among several different subsets such as mutual funds, geographic markets, stock sectors, or other subsets selected by the investor.

**alpha** a factor that measures fund performance on a risk-adjusted basis; an alpha of 1.0 means that a fund manager's performance on a risk-adjusted basis matches the market while alphas above or below 1.0 mean that the manager is doing better or worse than the market, respectively. *See also* **beta**.

**American Depositary Receipt (ADR)** a certificate of receipt tradable in the United States indicating ownership in a foreign company stock that is being held by a U.S. trust company or bank.

**annual report** a report provided by a mutual fund company summarizing its activities for the prior fiscal year; frequently an excellent source of data about the mutual fund.

**annual return** the return of portfolio or mutual fund when adjusted to annual basis, typically calculated as a geometric return. The actual calculation can be very complicated particularly if there have been cash contributions or disbursements. The calculation assumes that the returns for all years are the same. *See* **arithmetic rate of return; geometric rate of return**.

**arithmetic rate of return** the average (mean) of the annual returns. For example, to determine the arithmetric return over a 10-year period, add the annual return for each of the 10 years and divide by 10. Unless the returns for each year are exactly the same (they usually are not), the arithmetic return will always exceed the geometric return. *See also* **geometric rate of return**.

**asset allocation** distribution of investment funds among asset types such as stocks, bonds, or cash, among stocks themselves, among sectors, among markets, or among any other subsector chosen by the investor.

**asset class** a group of similar investments having similar characteristics—for example, cash, bonds, stocks, or real estate. Foreign stocks and U.S. stocks are frequently thought of as separate asset classes.

**back-end load** a sales charge paid when an investor sells mutual fund shares.

**basis point** a hundredth of 1%; 100 basis points equals 1%. Used in calculating investment fees or bond yields.

**bell curve** symmetrical curve of a normal distribution.

**benchmark** a base against which the performance of a fund or portfolio can be compared. Island investors frequently use the World Index or the average of other global funds as a benchmark.

**beta** a factor that shows a fund's sensitivity to market movements. A beta of 1.0 means its volatility is the same as the market. A beta in excess of 1.0 means the fund is more volatile than the market. A beta less than 1.0 means the fund is less volatile than the market. *See also* **alpha**.

**blue chip stock** a traditional term describing the stock of a highquality company.

**bond** a long-term debt security issued by a government or corporation that typically pays interest to its owner.

**buying power risk** the uncertainty that individuals face because they do not know the purchasing power of their dollars in the future.

**capital** a person's investable assets.

**capital gain** the gain in value of a stock or mutual fund when it is sold versus what an investor paid for it including the cost of subsequent investments or reinvestments of dividends or other distributions; taxed by the federal government at a lower rate than ordinary income, typically 20%.

**capitalization** the total value of a company, a market, or an index. *See* **index capitalization; market capitalization**.

**correlation** a description of how the prices of two investments, indexes, or markets move in relationship to the other.

**correlation coefficient** a mathematical measurement showing how closely the prices of two different investments track one another. A correlation coefficient of 1.0 means that the movement of one investment is fully explained by the movement of another; a correlation coefficient of zero means the movements of the two investments are independent of each other; a correlation coefficient of –1.0 means that the investments move in opposition to one another.

**country fund** a mutual fund that invests in stocks in only one country.

**currency devaluation** when a government lets the value of its currency drop (or encourages it to drop) versus other currencies. Usually done to increase competitiveness of the country's products in world markets, it reduces the buying power of the country's own citizens when they buy foreign goods and services.

**currency exposure** the currencies that a fund's assets are held in. A high exposure in foreign currencies increases the volatility of the portfolio but, over the long term, hedges the portfolio's buying power.

**currency fluctuation** a change in the value of the currency of one country versus that of another. Like stock prices, most currency prices are changing all the time.

**currency hedging** a transaction that offsets the changes in foreign currency values so changes do not affect the value of non-U.S. stock holdings in a portfolio.

**currency risk** the additional risk added to a portfolio because a portion of it is denominated in non-U.S. currencies and is, therefore, subject to the effects of currency fluctuations.

**developed markets** those 21 markets around the world with a proven history of relatively strict regulator climates.

**developing markets** those markets around the world that are growing and progressing but that do not yet have a proven regulatory climate.

**diversification** owning a variety of different types of investments to reduce risk in the portfolio.

**dollar valuation** the value of a stock or mutual fund or market measured in U.S. dollars instead of foreign currencies.

**Dow Jones Industrial Average** a weighted index of U.S. blue chip stocks. Historically, a very popular measure of the U.S. stock market.

**EAFE®** an abbreviation for the Morgan Stanley Capital International Europe, Australia, and Far East Index.

**efficient frontier** a computer-modeled curve charting the optimum return for two or more investments for any given level of risk.

**efficient market** the concept that investors have full knowledge of information in the market, which is then reflected in their actions. Since no single investor can benefit because he or she has better information than anyone else, all securities are therefore fairly priced. The market for large company stocks in the United States is an example of an efficient market.

**emerging markets** developing markets.

**exchange rate** the price at which two currencies are traded for one another. In an open market this rate is continually changing.

**expected return** the amount an investor hopes to earn on the capital used to purchase a particular investment, usually expressed as a percentage of that capital.

**Federal Reserve Board** the board that oversees the operations of the Federal Reserve System; important for its role in setting the interest rates at which banks can borrow from the Federal Reserve System.

**forecasting risk** the risk that the future will not be a simple linear projection of historical trends and events.

**foreign** term used within the financial community to indicate investment opportunites around the world excluding the United States; everywhere except the United States.

**foreign fund** a mutual fund that can invest in the stocks of countries around the world except the United States; the same as an international fund.

**foreign investing** investing in non-U.S. stocks; used interchangeably with the term "international investing" within the financial community; sometimes mistakenly equated with global investing.

**401(k) program** a popular retirement program sponsored by many companies in which income taxes are deferred.

**front-end load** a sales charge levied when mutual fund shares are purchased; typically calculated as a percentage of the value of the shares purchased.

**fund family** a company that manages a group of mutual funds.

**geometric rate of return** rate of return at which an investment compounds over a period of years; compounded rate of return. *See also* **arithmetic rate of return**.

**global** term used within the financial community to identify investment opportunities in markets throughout the world including the United States (the term "foreign" excludes the United States).

**global company** a company that has operations in many parts of the world; a multinational company.

**global fund** a mutual fund with holdings throughout the world including the United States; a world fund.

**global investing** investing anywhere throughout the world without specifically excluding any particular geographic market.

**growth style** an investment style under which managers primarily buy stocks with a pattern of consistently growing earnings or sales. *See also* **value style**.

**highly correlated** a relationship where two investments move closely together or exactly alike. *See* **correlation**.

**Ibbotson Associates, Inc.** a consulting firm located in Chicago, Illinois, that collects and distributes comprehensive historical stock market data and provides consulting services to investment professionals and institutional clients.

**index** a composite of individual stocks that is designed to represent the movement of a particular market or segment of a market. *See also* **Dow Jones Industrial Average**; **EAFE**; **World Index**.

**index capitalization** the total value of all of the stocks in an index, calculated by taking the market price of each stock in the index times the number of shares, and then adding them all together.

**index fund** a mutual fund that has a portfolio designed to simulate the movement of a particular market index.

**individual retirement account (IRA)** a popular retirement program authorized by the federal tax code. There are two types: regular IRAs and Roth IRAs.

**insider trading** using information from company sources that is not available to the general public when buying or selling stocks; generally an illegal activity in highly regulated markets.

**internal management costs** a mutual fund's costs to operate the fund including overhead, salaries, and other business expenses. By tradition, does not include the commissions paid when funds buy and sell securities. *See* **load**.

**international fund** a mutual fund that owns securities throughout the world except in the United States; the same as a foreign fund or non-U.S. fund.

**international investing** investing in countries throughout the world excluding the United States; used interchangeably with the term "foreign investing" within the financial community; sometimes mistakenly equated with global investing.

**investment strategy** a comprehensive plan for achieving one's investment goals and objectives.

**investment style** the overall style a manager uses in managing a portfolio such as value, growth, large company, or small company.

**island investor** an investor who follows the concepts of The Island Principle.

**Island Principle** *see* **The Island Principle**.

**large cap** short for large capitalization stocks; a style of portfolio management that emphasizes stocks of larger companies.

**load** a sales charge levied either when an investor buys a mutual fund or when the investor sells it, based on a percentage of the investor's purchase.

**load fund** a fund that requires that investors pay a sales charge or load when they either buy (a front-end load) or sell (a back-end load) the fund.

**local currency** the currency in which a stock is traded in its home market.

**long term** a period of more than several years. Typically, an investor should not own stocks unless he or she intends to be in the market for five years or more; therefore, the long term would be five, ten, or more years.

**long-term risk** the possibility that investors may not achieve their objectives over long periods of time—a very different type of risk from the short-term volatility that most investors equate with risk.

**low correlation** a relationship where the movement of one investment does not appear to be greatly affected by the change in price of another investment. *See* **correlation**.

**management fee** an amount charged by a mutual fund company to manage a fund; excludes loads and the commission charges when the fund buys and sells securities.

**management style** a term describing whether a mutual fund manager buys small company stocks, large company stocks, value stocks, or growth stocks.

**market allocation** distribution of assets to various geographic markets.

**market bubble** a situation where stock prices increase way beyond rational valuations because of investor enthusiasm. Then, when investor enthusiasm peaks and wanes, stock prices collapse and the market crashes. Because it is difficult to determine when investor enthusiasm will falter, the timing of a bubble's crash is impossible to predict reliably.

**market capitalization** the value of all stocks in a particular market, determined by taking each stock's market price times the number of shares and adding them all together.

**market correction** term used for a drop in stock prices after an advance, which assumes that the market advance got ahead of itself and which implies that the drop is temporary rather than a prolonged drop that could signal a bear market.

**market crash** a sudden drop in the market in a relatively short period of time, typically in excess of 30%.

**market efficiency** a measure of how well market prices reflect information. In an efficient market, all investors gain access to information simultaneously and act on it instantaneously, so new information is reflected in immediate price movements. In an inefficient market, investors gain information access at different times so prices move more slowly. The first investors to gain access to information have a competitive advantage.

**market risk** the risk inherent in a market that affects all of the stocks in it. *See* **systematic risk**.

**market selection risk** the risk of choosing the wrong market or markets to invest in.

**market volatility** the normal up-and-down movement of stock prices. Stock prices are continuously changing as investors receive new information and change their desire to own stocks.

**Markowitz, Harry** Nobel prizewinning economist who did work in 1952 to define and calculate the efficient frontier. *See* **efficient frontier**.

**mean** the average value of a given set of numbers.

**mid-cap** shorthand for medium capitalization stocks. A style of portfolio management that emphasizes medium-sized companies.

**Modern Portfolio Theory** a group of investment theories that have been developed by economists starting in the 1950s with a groundbreaking dissertation by Harry Markowitz. *See* **portfolio theory**.

**Morgan Stanley Capital International Europe, Australia, and Far East Index** a stock index that includes all of the 19 developed markets in Europe, Australia, and Asia but excludes the United States and Canada; abbreviated EAFE.

**Morgan Stanley Capital International World Index** a stock index that includes all the world's 21 developed markets (including the United States and Canada) as well as many of the world's developing markets; referred to as the World Index.

**Morningstar** a reporting service based in Chicago, Illinois, that specializes in collecting and distributing information on mutual funds.

**MSCI** an abbreviation for Morgan Stanley Capital International, a company that provides benchmark products and services to the investment community.

**mutual fund** an entity meeting a specific set of federal rules and regulations that owns and manages a portfolio consisting of securities including bonds, stocks, or cash for its shareholders.

**National Association of Securities Dealers (NASD)** an organization established by securities dealers to regulate the actions of their member firms and brokers as they buy and sell stocks, bonds, mutual funds, and other securities for their customers.

**New York Stock Exchange** a major stock exchange based in New York City; one of several marketplaces for the trading of U.S. stocks.

**New York Stock Exchange Board** the organization that predated the New York Stock Exchange.

**no-load fund** a mutual fund that does not charge a commission to buy or sell shares.

**nonsystematic risk** risk that is unique to individual stocks that can be eliminated by buying multiple stocks. *See* **single-market risk**; **systematic risk**.

**non-U.S. investing** investing in securities of companies that are based outside the United States; used with the same meaning as foreign or international investing within the investment community.

**normal distribution** a statistical term that shows how data tends to fall within a bell-shaped curve.

**normal range of outcomes** a term used in this book to mean the range of events that an investor expects to happen, recognizing that there is uncertainty in the future and the expected outcome is a range of expected events, not a single point.

**normal range of outcomes risk** a term used in this book to mean the amount of risk investors face given normal market volatility and expected long-term rates of return.

**offshore investing** a term sometimes used to describe investing in non-U.S. stocks but more frequently used to mean investing in a way to avoid U.S. government regulations—a practice not described in this book.

**Pacific Rim** that area of the world including the countries of Hong Kong, South Korea, Singapore, Taiwan, China, Malaysia, Indonesia, the Philippines, New Zealand, and Australia. Because of its size and influence, Japan is frequently treated as a region separate from the Pacific Rim.

**performance** how the price of a stock or market has done over a period of time; typically measured as a rate of return.

**political risk** risk investors face because governments may change their laws, regulations, and other policies.

**portfolio** an investor's overall holdings of mutual funds, individual stocks, and bonds, viewed as a whole.

**portfolio manager** the individual who decides which stocks to own in a mutual fund.

**portfolio snapshot** what Morningstar calls its portfolio summaries.

**portfolio summary** an analysis of all of the holdings within a portfolio.

**portfolio theory** the body of economic theory used by investment analysts to develop investment portfolios. *See* **Modern Portfolio Theory**.

**portfolio volatility** the volatility of a portfolio as a whole, in contrast to the volatility of any single investment within the portfolio, and of greater importance to investors than the volatility of any single investment.

**predictable risk** a term used in this book to mean an event that is within the range of outcomes that an investor expects. *See also* **unpredictable risk**.

**price/book ratio** the ratio that shows the price per share divided by the book value, a factor useful in determining how fairly a stock is priced.

**price/cash flow ratio** the ratio that shows the price per share divided by cash flow, a factor useful in determining how fairly a stock is priced.

**price/earnings ratio** the ratio that shows the price per share divided by the earnings per share, a factor useful in determining how fairly a stock is priced.

**price ratios** comparisons of a company's price to other economic factors; used by investors to assess the company's value. *See* **price/book ratio**; **price/cash flow ratio**; **price/earnings ratio**.

**Principia Pro** premium reporting service from Morningstar available to individual investors through subscribing investment analysts; it is capable of summarizing a portfolio containing multiple mutual funds. *See* **Morningstar**.

**private portfolio manager** an investment specialist who manages a portfolio (not a mutual fund) for a fee.

**prospectus** a legal document describing the goals, investment criteria, management criteria, costs, and past performance of a mutual fund, which must be offered to anyone seeking to invest in that fund. Historically these have been filled with legalese and have been difficult to read; regulators are encouraging mutual fund companies to make them more consumer friendly.

**quarterly report** a document prepared by the mutual fund company for shareholders describing the activities of the fund over the prior three months.

**range of expected outcomes** a term used in this book for the range of likely outcomes that an investor expects to achieve; not just a single point. *See* **predictable risk**; **unpredictable risk**.

**regional exposure** amount of fund invested in a particular geographic region.

**regional fund** a mutual fund that invests in stocks in only one region of the world.

**regulatory system** the rules and regulations that cover the buying and selling of securities.

**reverting to the mean** a concept that there is a historical trend line that stock prices eventually return to after they have been considerably above it or below it.

**risk** a term used with many different meanings related to unpredictability; the chance that an investor will not achieve the expected outcome. *See* **alpha**; **beta**; **standard deviation**; **volatility**; *see also specific types of risk*.

**risk-adjusted basis** a method of evaluating a mutual fund manager's performance that combines the amount of risk he or she took on to achieve a certain level of returns with that level of returns. *See* **alpha**; **Sharpe ratio**.

**risk aversion** the tendency for investors to avoid risk of loss of capital.

**S&P 500** abbreviation for the Standard & Poor's 500 Index.

**sector** a term used to group industries; examples include financials, energy, and technology.

**sector weighting** amount of a mutual fund or a portfolio that is allocated to various market sectors.

**semilog scale** a graphing scale that makes all of the numbers proportional to one another; one axis uses a logarithmic scale, while the other uses a normal scale.

**share classes** separate classes of the same mutual fund which have different sales loads and expenses.

**Sharpe ratio** a formula developed by Nobel prizewinning economist William Sharpe to show risk-adjusted performance.

**short term** a length of time that deals from an hour to a day to as much as a year, or perhaps longer.

**short-term risk** the volatility normally seen in the market on an hourly or a daily basis, or even as long as a year or more.

**single-market risk** the risk inherent in being in a single market, a risk which an investor cannot escape as long as he or she invests only in that market. *See* **systematic risk**.

**small cap** short for small capitalization stocks; a style of portfolio management that emphasizes stocks of smaller companies.

**Standard & Poor's Depositary Receipt (SPDR or "spider")** a tradable security that simulates the Standard & Poor's 500 Index.

**Standard & Poor's 500 Index** a broad market index that includes stocks of 500 of the largest companies in the United States; commonly referred to as the S&P 500.

**standard deviation** a statistical measure of the volatility or up-and-down changes of the value of a mutual fund or a market around its mean, used as an indicator of risk. Standard deviation may be expressed as a raw number or a percent; in other words, a standard deviation of 0.25 may also be referred to as 25% standard deviation or 25% risk.

**stock** a negotiable security indicating ownership of a company.

**style** the bias of a mutual fund, its manager, or of an individual investor to hold stocks of a certain type such as those of large companies, midsize companies, small companies, companies that appear to be good values based on their price ratios, or companies that appear to be candidates for strong future growth.

**survivor bias** the tendency of long-term performance records for mutual funds or stock indexes to be biased upward because funds or stocks in an index that have failed or merged with others are no longer included. Performance data and records for global indexes also may be biased because they include only data from successful countries and exclude data from countries viewed as less successful.

**systematic risk** the risk that is inherent in the market (or the system). Systematic risk cannot be eliminated through additional diversification in that market (by buying additional stocks). *See* **nonsystematic risk**; **single-market risk**.

**tax liability** income taxes individual investors must pay when mutual fund managers sell stocks and which reduce the investor's net returns.

**The Island Principle™** a long-term global investment strategy using diversification into multiple markets around the world chosen by multiple global mutual fund managers in order to reduce portfolio risk, increase portfolio returns, or do both simultaneously.

**trading costs** the cost of buying and selling a stock, typically commissions.

**transparency** the ability for investors to see information about a company's finances and plans. U.S. security rules require a great deal of disclosure for companies whose stocks are publicly traded. Investors in other geographic markets frequently do not have access to this level of information, although investors are beginning to require it of companies seeking financing from global sources.

**true global investing** treating all of the world's available markets as potential opportunities without restricting choices by geographic location.

**trumpet chart** a chart that looks like a trumpet or horn, which shows that the range of expected returns narrows over time.

**12b-1 fee** a fee mutual fund companies pay to brokers for servicing an account (advertising, marketing, and distribution). A typical 12b-1 fee for a stock fund is 0.25%.

**unhedged** not hedged against currency fluctuations. *See* **currency hedging**.

**unpredictable risk** a term used in this book to refer to an event that is outside the range of outcomes that an investor expects. *See also* **predictable risk**.

**unweighted average** an average that ignores capitalization (most indexes are weighted by market capitalization).

**value style** a style of investing that chooses undervalued stocks. Value is frequently measured using ratios such as price to earnings, price to book value, and price to sales. *See also* **growth style**.

**volatility** the up-and-down movement of the price of an investment or a market, often equated with risk and used interchangeably with that term.

**Wall Street** colloquial term used to refer to the U.S. stock market and all the surrounding institutions; street in New York City where the New York Stock Exchange is located.

*Wall Street Journal* financial paper published by Dow Jones Publishing Company throughout the United States that emphasizes investment-related news.

**World Equity Benchmark Shares (WEBS)** a tradable security that simulates a market index, available for 17 foreign country markets.

**world fund** a mutual fund with holdings throughout the world including the United States; the same as a global fund.

**World Index** shorthand for Morgan Stanley Capital International World Index.

**yen** currency used in Japan.

# *Bibliography*

Association for Investment Management & Research (AIMR). *Developments in Global Portfolio Management*. Charlottesville: Association for Investment Management & Research, 1997.

Bernstein, Peter L. *Against the Gods: The Remarkable Story of Risk*. New York: John Wiley & Sons, Inc., 1996.

Chase Investment Performance Digest. *Investment Performance and Volatility Ranking Tables*. Concord, MA: Chase Global Data & Research, 1995.

Derosa, David F. *Managing Foreign Exchange Risk: Advanced Strategies for Global Investors, Corporations, and Financial Institutions*. Chicago: Irwin Professional Publishing, 1996.

Gibson, Roger C. *Asset Allocation: Balancing Financial Risk*. New York: McGraw-Hill Companies, Inc., 1996.

Gorman, Stephen A. *The International Equity Commitment*. U.S.A.: The Research Foundation of the Institute of Chartered Financial Analysts, 1998.

Grubel, Herbert G. "Internationally Diversified Portfolios: Welfare Gains & Capital Flows." *American Economic Review*. (December 1968): 1299–1314.

Ibbotson, Roger G., and Brinson, Gary P. *Global Investing: The Professional's Guide to the World's Capital Markets*. New York: McGraw-Hill Companies, Inc., 1993.

Lederman, Jess, and Klein, Robert A. *Global Asset Allocation: Techniques for Optimizing Portfolio Management*. New York: John Wiley & Sons, Inc., 1994.

Rouwenhorst, K. Geert. *European Equity Markets & EMU: Are the Differences between Countries Slowly Disappearing?* New Haven: Yale University School of Management, 1998.

Vivanti, Alberto, and Kaufman, Perry. *Global Equity Investing*. New York: McGraw-Hill Companies, Inc., 1997.

Wang, Charles Hongxin. "Essays in International Market Correlations." Ph.D. diss., Yale University, New Haven, 1999.

# Index

Accounting standards, 20, 22, 223
Accounting systems, 22–23
Active trading, 87
Aggressive growth investors, 49–51, 81–83
Alliance Global Sm Cap A, 220
Allocation, 44–45, 223
Alpha, 143, 223
American Depositary Receipts (ADRs), 122–123, 223
American Funds, 149, 220
Analysis, in Morningstar report, 154
Annual rate of return, 31, 35
Annual reports, 60, 223
Annual return, 81
Arithmetic rate of return, 110, 112–113, 223
Asset allocation, *see* Diversification
  benefits of, 107–108
  defined, 61, 223
  fund management and, 192
  in Island Principle, 85, 106, 127
Asset classes:
  defined, 224
  distribution among, 171, 173, 176
  market selection risk and, 44
  multiple, 60–65, 106, 171, 173, 176
  types of, generally, 15
Asset mix, 51
Asset protection, 127
Association for Investment Management and Research, 21
Average return, 10

Back-end load, 145, 224
*Barron's*, 141
Basis point, 147, 224
Bear markets, 73, 144
Beebower, Gilbert, 62
Bell curve, 29, 34, 224. *See also* Normal distribution
Benchmarks:
  allocation analysis, 177–178
  defined, 224
  implications of, 11, 55
  Island Principle, 106–108
  management selection and, 141–142
Beta, 143, 224
Blue chip stocks, 10, 224
Bond market, 15, 61, 63–65, 78, 81, 224. *See also* Asset allocation
Brinson, Gary, 62
Brokerage houses, 146, 148
Bull and Bear Group, 220
Bull markets, 8, 12, 71, 73
Buy-and-hold strategy, 31–32, 36
Buying power risk, 25, 88, 102–103, 116, 224

Capital, defined, 17, 224
Capital gains, 124, 224
Capitalization, defined, 224. *See also* Market capitalization
Capital preservation goals, 75–76
Capital World Growth and Income fund, 181–182
Cash investment, 61

CDA Wiesenberger, 136, 146
Certificates of deposit, 28, 50, 75
Charles Schwab, 146
Compounding, 113–114
Conservative investors, 143
Conservative stocks, 49–50
Correlation, defined, 224. *See also
specific types of correlations*
Correlation coefficients, 7, 53–56, 62,
166, 181, 224
Country exposure, in Morningstar
report, 159–160
Country fund, 132, 225
Currency, generally:
devaluations, 102, 225
exposure, 147–148, 161, 225
fluctuations, 20–21, 23–25, 147–148,
225
hedging, 25, 225
risk, 23, 225
Current investment style, in
Morningstar report, 158–159
Cyclical markets, 11–12

Data interpretation, 26–28
Day trading, 70
Decision-making, 88. *See also* Market
selection risk
Deflation, 39
Devaluation, 83, 97
Developed markets:
defined, 4–6, 18–19, 225
efficient market and, 90–93
market diversification and, 90–93
returns in, 9–12, 126, 196–219
risk in, 26
Developing markets, 18–19, 179, 225
Diversification, generally:
currency and, 24–25
defined, 15, 21–22, 225
importance of, 1–2
key to, 53–57

market, 89–93
multiple asset classes, 60–65
multiple markets, 65–67, 96–103,
105, 125
multiple sectors, 58–60
multiple stocks, 57–58
political risk and, 21–22
returns and, 52
as risk reduction strategy, 51–53
understanding, 57–67
Dividends, 78, 81
Dollar valuation, 42–43, 225
Dow Jones Industrial Average, 88, 106,
115, 225
Dreyfus Global Growth, 220

EAFE, *see* Morgan Stanley Capital
International (MSCI), Europe,
Australia, and Far East Index
(EAFE)
Efficient frontier, 61, 63–66, 89–92,
117, 225
Efficient market, 9, 14, 27–28, 225
Elfun Global, 220
Emerging markets, 18–19, 226
Evergreen Global Opport A, 220
Exchange rates, 23–24, 43, 226
Expected returns, 7, 55–56, 63, 97–99,
226
Expenses, mutual funds, 145–147

Federal Reserve Board, 41, 226
Fidelity Funds, 149
Financial press, as information
resource, 134, 148
*Financial Analysts Journal*, 62
First Invest Global A, 220
Fixed income investors, 76–78
Forecasting risk, 38–40, 226
Forecasts, inaccurate, 99–101
Foreign, defined, 5, 18–19, 226
Foreign fund, 121, 226

Foreign investing, 3–4, 17, 226
Founders Worldwide Growth, 220
401(k) program, 48, 124, 226
Front-end load, 145, 226
Frontier markets, 5
Fund family, 134, 168, 226
Fund management:
  allocation analysis, 170–181
  correlations and, 165–168
  investment style, 145, 176–177
  number of managers, 164
  portfolio assembly and, 168
  portfolio revisions, 181–188
  risk tolerance, 145
  style, 140, 165–168
Fund managers, role of, 44, 119. *See
  also* Fund management
Fund research:
  benchmarks, 141–142, 144
  hard data, example of, 150–161
  information resources, generally,
    134–136
  management, identification of,
    143–144
  questions to ask, 137–148
  shortcuts, 136–137
  soft data, examples of, 148–150

GAM Global A, 181–182, 220
Geographic allocation, 133
Geometric rate of return, 110–113,
  226
Global, defined, 7, 226
Global companies, 13, 226
Global fund manager, functions of,
  44
Global funds, generally:
  defined, 22, 226
  regional funds *vs.*, 130–133
  research strategies, 133–148
Global investing, defined, 227
Global markets, defined, 19

Global mutual funds, *see* Global
    funds
  defined, 44
  number of, 120
Global portfolio, shift to,
    125–127
Goals:
  aggressive growth, 81–83
  fixed income, 76–78
  growing income, 78–80
  importance of, 70
  investing for sport, 71–72
  long-term, 69–70
  matching the market, 72–75
  preserving capital, 75–76
  realistic returns, 108–114
  total returns, 80–81
Gorman, Stephen A., 107–108
Growth stock, 158, 176
Growth style, 159, 227
Grubel, Herbert G., 66

Hancock Global B, 220
Hedging strategies, 57
High correlations, implications of,
    53
Highly correlated, defined, 59,
    227
Histograms, 29
Historical data, 117–118
Historical profile, in Morningstar
    report, 155
Historical returns, 122
History, in Morningstar report, 157
Holowesko, Mark, xi
Hood, Randolph, 62
Hyperinflation, 39

Ibbotson, Roger G., 42, 62, 133
Ibbotson Associates, 10, 75, 108, 136,
    227
Income growth investors, 78–80

Index(es), generally:
  capitalization, 73, 227
  defined, 2, 227
  market matchers and, 72–75
Index fund, 74, 227
Individual investors, 44, 69, 118, 120
Individual retirement account (IRA),
  48, 124, 227
Inflation, implications of, 42–43, 77,
  80, 83, 102
Insider trading, 26, 227
Internal management costs, 146–147,
  227
International fund, 119, 227
International investing, 3, 6, 227
International Society of Financial
  Analysts, 21
Internet:
  impact of, 2–3, 27
  trading, 71. See also Day trading
Investment horizon, 11, 39, 75
Investment philosophy, 138, 140
Investment strategy, 2, 228
Investment style:
  defined, 228
  in Morningstar report, 156
  types of, 145, 176–177
Investment value, political instability
  and, 21–22
Investor psychology, 28–32, 96–97
Investors, types of, 69–80
IRS forms:
  Form 1099-DIV, 125
  Form 1116, 125
Island investors:
  characteristics of, 2–3, 8, 83–84
  defined, 228
  investment guidelines, generally, 126
  profile of, 86–89
Island Principle, overview:
  asset allocation, 85–86
  benchmarks, 106–108

benefits of, generally, 193–194
defined, xvii, 3, 234
development of, xii–xiii
goal-setting, 108–114
as investment strategy, 2, 20
market diversification, 89–93
mutual funds, 117–125
returns, impact on, 104–106
risk level objectives, 114–117
risk management and, 69, 76–78, 87
risk reduction strategies, 93–104
strategy of, 83–84
volatility, control of, 76

Japanese market, 9, 12, 37–39, 74. See
  also Market bubble; Yen

Kaplan, Paul, 62, 133

Large cap, 75, 158, 228
Leveraging, 50
Lexington Global Corp Lead, 220
Load, defined, 146, 228
Load fund, 150, 228
Local currency, 23, 228
Long term, defined, 24, 228
Long-term risk:
  buying power, 41–43, 116
  defined, 228
  forecasting, 38–40
  market selection, 44–45
  normal range of outcomes, 33–38
  single-market, 40–41, 45, 101–102
Lord Abbett Global Equity A, 220
Low correlations:
  defined, 53, 228
  implications of, 53–57, 59, 62–64,
  89, 92, 103, 126, 165

Management, generally:
  fees, 122, 228
  of funds, see Fund management

money, *see* Money managers
style, 125, 130, 140, 165–166, 228
Market allocation, 44, 132, 228
Market bubble, 37–39, 228–229
Market capitalization, 5–7, 9, 11, 183, 229
Market corrections, 191, 229
Market crash, 38–39, 229
Market diversification, 89–93
Market efficiency, 9, 229. *See also* Efficient market
Market indexes, 6
Market matchers, 72–75
Market risk, 229
Market sectors, 15, 58–60
Market selection risk, 44, 88, 103–104
Market volatility, *see* Volatility
defined, 17, 229
impact of, generally, 7
investor psychology and, 28–32, 96
normal, 37
risk and, 29
short-term, 30, 33–38
Markowitz, Harry, 61, 63, 66, 229
Matching the market goals, 72–75
Mature emerging markets, 5
Mean, defined, 54–55, 229
Median capitalization, 179
Merrill Lynch Global Holdg A/B, 220
MFS Global Equity B, 221
Mid-cap, 159, 229
Midas U.S. & Overseas, 221
Modern Portfolio Theory (MPT), 61–64, 101, 143, 229
Money managers:
functions of, 23, 44, 118
international, 131
performance of, 107
selection of, 103–104
Money market accounts, 50, 76

Morgan Stanley Capital International (MSCI):
Europe, Australia, and Far East Index (EAFE), 6, 9–11, 13, 65, 74, 115, 141, 178, 188, 225, 229
World Index, 6, 14, 106, 109, 113, 123, 126, 190, 230, 235
Morningstar:
category, 156
defined, 230
as information resource, 115, 122, 132, 136–137, 142, 146, 150–152
portfolio snapshots, 170
Principia Pro, 120, 136, 166–167, 170, 178, 180, 182, 232
MSCI, *see* Morgan Stanley Capital International (MSCI)
Multinational companies, 13–14
Mutual funds:
allocation analysis, 170–181
basic philosophy of, 138, 140
benefits of, 14, 104, 120–123
costs/expenses, 145–147
course corrections, impact of, 189–193
currency fluctuations, impact on, 147–148
defined, 230
distributions, 124
diversification and, 121
fees, 122
global funds, list, 220
global funds *vs.* regional funds, 130–133
global portfolio, shift to, 125–127
hard data, 150–161
historical returns, 122
management, *see* Fund management; Fund managers
minimum investment, 121–122
non-U.S. stocks, access to, 122–123

Mutual funds (*Continued*)
  performance, 140–143, 180
  portfolio revisions, 181–188
  portfolio summary, 169–170
  professional management, 120–121.
    *See also* Fund management
  reporting services, 135, 143, 148
  research, *see* Fund research
  soft data, 134–135, 137, 148–150, 154
  standard deviation and, 115
  taxation, 123–125, 192–193
  types of, 119

National Association of Securities
    Dealers (NASD), 19–20, 135, 230
New Perspective Fund, 150, 152–161,
    164, 183, 221
New York Stock Exchange, 5, 11, 230
New York Stock Exchange Board, 5, 10,
    230
Newly emerging markets, 5
Newsletters, as information resource,
    135
No-load fund, 146, 230
Non-U.S. investing, 3, 6, 19, 230
Nonsystematic risk, 41, 58, 60, 101, 230
Normal distribution, 29, 38, 230
Normal range of outcomes risk, 33–38,
    230

Offshore investing, 19, 231
OneSource (Charles Schwab), 146
Oppeneheimer Global A, 221
Other developed markets, 5
Other measures, in Morningstar report,
    158

Pacific Rim, xi, 19, 132, 164, 176, 192,
    231
Performance:
  defined, 231
  in Morningstar report, 153–154

quartile, in Morningstar report, 157
significance of, 8, 13, 140–143,
    183
Phoenix-Aberdeen Wldwde OppA,
    221
Political risk, 21, 231
Portfolio, generally:
  analysis, in Morningstar report, 158
  defined, 2, 231
  diversification, *see* Diversification
  mix, 55, 140
  movement, 62
  snapshot, 170, 231
  summary, 169, 231
  theory, 7, 15, 85, 110, 231. *See also*
    Modern Portfolio Theory (MPT)
  volatility, 15, 24, 231
Portfolio managers:
  conservative, 49–50
  defined, 231
  in Morningstar report, 152–153
  private, 122, 232
  role of, generally, 3
Predictable risk, 30, 231
Price/book ratio, 159–160, 231
Price/cash flow ratio, 159–160, 231
Price/earnings ratio, 159–160, 180,
    231
Price ratios, 159, 231
Principia Pro, 120, 136, 166–167, 170,
    178, 180, 182, 231–232
Private portfolio manager, 122, 232
*Professional's Guide to the World's
    Capital Markets, The* (Ibbotson),
    42
Prospectus:
  defined, 21, 232
  objective, in Morningstar report,
    152
Prudential Global Genesis B, 221
Prudential World Global B, 221
Putnam Global Growth A, 221

Quarterly reports, 135, 232

Range of expected outcomes, 31, 232
Rate of return, 9. *See also specific types of returns*
Real estate investments, 61
Regional exposure:
  defined, 161, 232
  in Morningstar report, 160, 176, 183
Regional fund, 119, 130–133, 232
Regulatory systems, 25–26, 232
Reinvestment, 80
Retirement planning, 109
Returns:
  diversification and, 51–52
  historical, 122
  low volatility and, 49
  potential, 104–105
  significance of, 8–12
Reverting to the mean, 232
Risk(s):
  accounting systems, 22–23
  buying power, 41–44, 116
  currency fluctuations, 23–25
  data interpretation, 26–28
  defined, 8, 232
  forecasting, 38–40
  in foreign markets, generally, 19–21
  foreign phobia, 18–19
  hedges, 20, 42–43, 57, 96
  long-term, 29, 32
  market selection, 44–45
  normal range of outcomes, 33–38
  political instability, 21–22
  predictable, 30
  regulatory systems, 25–26
  returns and, 8–12, 15, 28
  short-term, 29, 32
  single-market, 40–41, 101–102

systematic, 33
  unpredictable, 30–31
Risk-adjusted basis, 142, 232
Risk analysis, in Morningstar report, 157–158, 180, 188
Risk aversion, 29–30, 49–51, 232
Risk level objectives, 114–117
Risk management, overview, 47–48
Risk reduction strategies, 93–95
Risk tolerance, 63, 70

Sales fees, in Morningstar report, 54
S&P 500, defined, 12, 232
Savings accounts, 28, 75–76
Scudder Global, 221
Sector, defined, 15, 232. *See also* Market sectors
Sector weightings:
  defined, 233
  Morningstar report, 160–161
  significance of, 135, 146, 178
Semilog scale, 37, 233
Share classes, 146, 233
Sharpe, William, 61, 143
Sharpe ratio, 143–144, 233
Short term, defined, 24, 233
Short-term risk, 29, 233
Short-term volatility, 31, 48, 87, 98
Singer, Brian, 62
Single-market risk, 40–41, 45, 83, 101–102, 233
Small cap, 158, 233
Smallcap World growth fund, 181–182
Software programs, fund research, 136, 170. *See also* Principia Pro
SPDR, 123
Spider, 123
Sport investors, 71–72

Standard & Poor's 500 Index (S&P 500), 6, 11–13, 55, 65, 73, 88, 91, 106, 115, 188
Standard & Poor's Depositary Receipt (SPDR/"spider"), 123, 233
Standard deviation:
  defined, 233
  implications of, 7, 54–55, 63, 89, 142, 190
  risk level and, 115–116
Statement of Additional Information (SAI), 135
Stock(s):
  adjusting the amount in, 50–51
  blue chip, 10, 224
  defined, 1, 233
  growth, 158, 176
  large cap, 75
  multiple, 57–58
  portfolio diversification strategies, 105–106
  value, 176
Style:
  defined, 103, 233
  growth, 159, 227
  investment, 145, 156, 176–177, 228
  management, 125, 130, 140, 165–168, 228
  value, 158
Survivor bias, 114, 233–234
Systematic risk, 33, 41, 59, 61, 101, 234

Taxation, mutual fund investments, 123–125, 192–193
Tax liability, 124, 234
Technology sector, 73–74
Templeton Funds, xi–xii, 149–150
Templeton Global Small Co A, 181–182, 221
Templeton Growth A, 221

Templeton World A, 221
The Island Principle, see Island Principle
Tobin, James, 61, 66
Total return goals, 80–81
Trading costs, 71, 234
Traditional investors, 80
Trailing returns, in Morningstar report, 178–179
Transparency, 26–27, 234
Treasury bills, 28, 50–51, 61, 75
True global investing, 3, 7, 234
Trumpet chart, 34–35, 234
12b-1 fees, 154, 234

Unhedged, 25, 234
U.S. dollar, 2. See also Dollar valuation
U.S. stock market:
  current value of, 7
  historical performance, 9–10
Unpredictable risk, 30–31, 234
Unweighted average return, 10, 234

Valuation multiple, in Morningstar report, 180, 188
Value stocks, 176
Value style, 158, 234
Venture capital, 82
Volatility:
  benchmarks, 142
  defined, 15, 235
  jitters, management of, 96–97
  psychological impact of, 70–72
  risk reduction strategies, 47–68
  risk tolerance and, 114–117
  short-term, 31, 48, 87, 98

Wall Street, 1, 8, 14, 235
Wall Street Journal, 4, 7, 141, 235

Wang, Charles, 92
Wealth creation, 42
Weighted average, 56
Wilson Associates, 136
World Equity Benchmark Shares
    (WEBS), 122–123, 235
World fund, 119, 235

World Index, *see* Morgan Stanley
    Capital International (MSCI),
    World Index
World markets, characteristics of, 4–6

Yen, 23, 43, 235

Zonis, Marvin, 21